TABLE OF CONTENTS

HOW TO USE THIS GUIDE

Sam Fisher wants revenge. Revenge against the organization—Third Echelon—that has taken too much from him. Revenge against the man who forced him to kill his best friend. Revenge against the wheelman who ran down his daughter. And with your help, Fisher will lay his vengeance upon all who have wronged him.

Use this guide to get the drop on every enemy, master all weapons and gadgets, and complete every single mission in both Fisher's main mission and the co-op campaign. With our full walkthroughs, you will survive every trial and come out not just alive, but laden with special points (earned through in-game challenges) that can be traded to upgrade guns and gear. You will be unstoppable. You will be as feared as Fisher himself.

The Fisher Files: *Just who is Sam Fisher? This dossier details Fisher's previous missions so you know what drives Fisher and what is at stake in his latest mission.*

INTRODUCTION

Training: *You need Third Echelon–quality training to keep up with Sam Fisher. This chapter explains all of Fisher's stealth techniques so you can slip into the shadows and dispense justice unseen. It also covers interrogating suspects for intel and a complete rundown on all of Fisher's gadgets—including the new sonar goggles. Fisher's new Mark and Execute skill is also detailed, which lets you select targets and take them out before they even know what hit them. All enemy intel, such as the weapons each enemy carries in the different missions (both single-player and co-op), is also detailed in this chapter.*

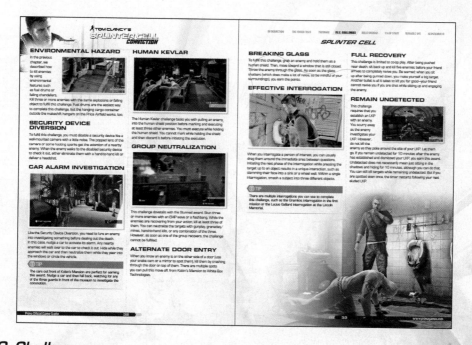

P.E.C. Challenges: *Completing P.E.C. Challenge objectives within the mission results in points that you trade for upgraded weapons and gear. Every challenge is listed here, plus tactics for completing each objective. You'll have a killer arsenal in no time!*

TOM CLANCY'S SPLINTER CELL CONVICTION

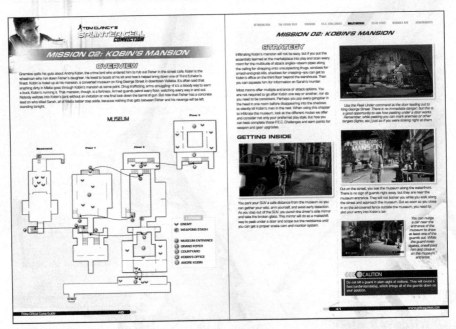

Walkthrough: *Fisher's quest to seek revenge for his daughter's death takes some astonishing twists and turns. Our walkthrough guides you through all 11 missions, offering both stealth and guns-blazing tactics for many situations. Full maps of every area reveal enemy locations, armories, and important objectives.*

Co-op Story: *Grab a friend and play through a special co-op "prequel" that sets the stage for Fisher's mission. This walkthrough is loaded with tips and tricks for fighting off mercenaries and soldiers, and the comprehensive maps detail enemy locations.*

INTRODUCTION

Deniable Ops: In addition to Fisher's mission, agents can participate in a series of single-player operations to clear out enemy strongholds or defend EMP technology from advancing threats. Our maps and tips will make you a super-agent.

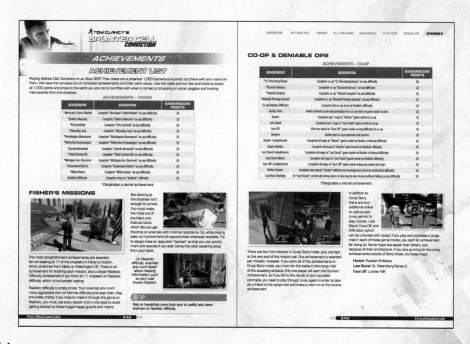

Achievements: Playing Tom Clancy's Splinter Cell Conviction™ on an Xbox 360? Complete every achievement and bolster your Gamerscore with tips for every single objective.

THE FISHER FILES

The information you are about to read has been deemed "top secret" by the National Security Agency (NSA). The classified personnel files and mission reports of former Third Echelon agent Sam Fisher must never leave the confines of the NSA. This information is to remain "eyes-only" because if a hard copy of Fisher's operations fell into the wrong hands, it could compromise national security and cause great harm to our allies. Any suspicion of leaks could result in the loss of security clearances and possible prosecution.

INTEL

SAMUEL "SAM" FISHER

Birthdate: 1957

Place of Birth: Classified

Last Rank: NOC (non-official cover operative)

Former Agencies: USN (Navy), CIA, JSOC, NSA, Third Echelon

Combat Specialities: Krav Maga, demolitions, standard military issue weaponry and ordnance

Fisher is a former agent of the top secret Third Echelon division of the NSA. He was the very first recruit for field agent status with the new Third Echelon, promoted by Col. Irving Lambert (Ret). Prior to his NSA career, Fisher was a Navy SEAL, a CIA operative within the Special Activities Division, and active with the Joint Special Forces Command. Over the course of his career, Fisher has served in hot spots such as Iraq (Operation Desert Storm) and Afghanistan as well as taking special assignments in North Korea, Russia, Panama, the former East Germany, and Georgia.

Fisher's personal life is marked with tragedy from the 1989 death of his wife (from ovarian cancer) to the 2007 drunk driving accident that killed his daughter, Sarah. These events, coupled with Fisher's training and combat experience, have made him a highly effective agent, able to see the world for what it is, not what Fisher wishes it to be. Fisher values loyalty and honor above all. He is ruthless but not cruel, understanding when situations can be talked down versus those that require extreme violence. However, his grief over Sarah's death has led many within Third Echelon to question Fisher's ability to pull himself back from the edge.

Victor Coste, known associate

TOM CLANCY'S SPLINTER CELL®

Operation: Stop Georgian President Nikoladze from taking over Azerbaijan and launching a nuclear attack on America

Year: 2004

Location(s): Former Soviet Republic of Georgia, Caspian Sea, USA, Myanmar, Russia

Allies: Col. Lambert, Anna Grimsdottir, Vernon Wilkes, Jr., Frances Cohen, Doctor John Baxter

Mission Status: Complete

This operation represents Fisher's first mission with Third Echelon. The investigation of two kidnapped CIA agents in Georgia resulted in the discovery of a plot by Georgian President Kombayn Nikoladze to assume control of Azerbaijan's petroleum supplies and an alliance with a rogue Chinese general. Attempts to stop Nikoladze's operation resulted in the deployment of cyber warfare tactics against the United States. Energy infrastructure was temporarily disabled by using virulent software created by Canadian hacker Phillip Masse. The mission culminated in the discovery of a suitcase-sized nuclear weapon planned for detonation on US soil. Fisher neutralized Nikoladze, stabilized US-Chinese relations, and prevented the detonation of the nuclear bomb.

Anna Grimsdottir, Third Echelon

TOM CLANCY'S SPLINTER CELL PANDORA TOMORROW™

Operation: Prevent terrorists from releasing biological weapons inside America

Year: 2006

Location(s): Indonesia, USA, Jerusalem, France, East Timor

Allies: Col. Lambert, Anna Grimsdottir, Douglas Shetland

Mission Status: Complete

American military assets were training East Timor's army to combat militants. The primary terrorist faction was Darah Dan Doa (Blood and Prayer), led by CIA-trained guerilla Suhadi Sadono. Following a Darah Dan Doa suicide bombing on an American embassy, Fisher was deployed to gather intel on the militant group and Sadono. Fisher uncovered a plot—codenamed Pandora Tomorrow—to release a weaponized smallpox virus on American soil. After disrupting Pandora Tomorrow and apprehending Sadono, Fisher tracked rogue CIA agent Norman Soth, who had intercepted a smallpox bomb with intention to use it in Los Angeles. Fisher neutralized Soth and recovered the weaponized smallpox, preventing a deadly outbreak.

TOM CLANCY'S SPLINTER CELL CHAOS THEORY™

Operation: Prevent East Asia destabilization and war between China, Japan, and both Koreas

Year: 2007

Location(s): China, Japan, Korea, Panama, Peru, USA

Allies: Col. Lambert, Anna Grimsdottir, Douglas Shetland, William Redding

Mission Status: Complete

While kidnapped computer specialist Bruce Morgenholt was being tracked down in Peru (Morgenholt was an expert on the Masse code that previously disrupted electrical infrastructure in America), tensions in East Asia are strained to the breaking point by Japan's decision to "re-arm" itself with an Information Self-Defense Force (I-SDF) to combat cyber warfare. The United States Navy sent the USS *Walsh* to the Yellow Sea as a sign of solidarity with Japan against aggressions by China and North Korea. After a North Korean missile sinks the USS *Walsh*, America is drawn into a declaration of war over protests from North Korean government officials that the strike was unintentional. With the recent discovery that the Masse code was in the wild, Fisher was sent to determine whether or not North Korea is telling the truth.

Fisher learned that the Masse code was used by a private military company called Displace International to launch the missile and initiate war for profiteering. After Fisher stopped Displace, I-SDF agents led by Admiral Otomo managed to secure the Masse code and plotted to use it as leverage against the Japanese government. Unless the Japanese government relinquished control to Otomo, I-SDF planned to use the Masse code to launch a North Korean missile at Japan. Fisher prevented Otomo from deploying the missile and captured him so that he could stand trial for his crimes before the United Nations.

TOM CLANCY'S SPLINTER CELL DOUBLE AGENT™

Operation: Infiltrate domestic terrorist organization JBA

Year: 2008

Location(s): US, Russia, Mexico, Iceland, Democratic Republic of Congo

Allies: Col. Lambert, Anna Grimsdottir, John Hodge, Lawrence Williams

Mission Status: Interrupted

Sarah Fisher

Following his daughter's death, Fisher agreed to infiltrate John Brown's Army (JBA), a domestic terror cell. As part of this undercover assignment, Fisher had to engage in criminal activities in order to be sent to the same prison as Jamie Washington, a known JBA operative. Fisher escaped with Washington to further burrow into the cell, going so far as to aid in the seizure of a Russian tanker in the Sea of Okhotsk, which JBA allies wanted to use to deliver a bomb made of an experimental explosive called "red mercury." Fisher's covert work uncovered a larger plot to detonate three red mercury bombs in Los Angeles, New York City, and Mexico City.

Fisher's loyalty to JBA came under question several times during the mission (it was finally put to rest when he shot Lambert in front of JBA loyalists), but his actions led Third Echelon to suspect that Fisher had gone rogue. After stopping the terrorist plot, Fisher disobeyed orders and eluded capture. Fisher was immediately considered AWOL and extremely dangerous.

CAUTION

New intel places Fisher in the Republic of Malta. Fisher is to be taken into custody alive. All agents attempting to apprehend Fisher are encouraged to exercise great caution because he is assumed to be armed and likely unstable. No agent is authorized to reveal the truth about Fisher's daughter.

TRAINING

am Fisher is a splinter cell, a lone wolf operator who was authorized to exercise the so-called fifth freedom. As a splinter cell, he
is off the books and in the shadows, where he could be disavowed if he was ever caught by the enemy. But with Fisher's training
d tactical skills, Third Echelon has not yet had to deny his existence. Fisher's game is to keep his existence a secret until the last
ossible second, stepping out of the darkness to strike and then retreat before anybody knows he was there.

u need this same training if you are to help Fisher complete his most dangerous, and most personal, assignment yet. From a
nverted museum in Malta to a daring mission in Washington DC, Fisher must outsmart and outmaneuver not only a band of
ercenary thugs with military training, but also agents that he himself helped train. Success will require knowledge of every trick in
e book, from giving a glimpse of Fisher's movement to the enemy to establish a possible Last Known Position (LKP) to being an
pert at EMP grenade usage.

THE ESSENTIALS

ur specialty is stealth. Third Echelon agents are trained to be ghosts, undetectable to the average eye. But sometimes a situation
ts out of control and the only way out is shooting everybody is sight while running as fast as possible in an effort to seek a
adow. Once in that shadow, you can disappear again. Learning the balance between direct engagement and stealth is the key to
ctory in this assignment.

When you are injured by a fall or a gunshot wound, the screen
starts to turn red. The redder it turns, the more trouble you
are in. And if it starts pulsing, then you better find cover as
soon as possible to recover. Wait in the shadows or out of
sight until the red dissipates, indicating that you are back to
full health.

 CAUTION

Sam Fisher is a super agent, not superhuman. He cannot
withstand many direct shots.

t before going into detail about different tactics, you must
derstand the essentials of being a Third Echelon agent.
hen you are in a mission, you have a minimal Head's Up
splay (HUD) that only shows your vitals. Instead of worrying
out meters and gauges, survey the scene to uncover the
nartest routes through trouble areas and spot opportunities
r dealing death to your enemies. Here is the main
me screen:

*New objectives are painted on the side of buildings and objects
to help direct you to the next point. You can also call up the
objective at any time after that by pressing the Back button.*

Current weapon: This is your currently selected weapon.
You can carry only two weapons—one sidearm and one
alternate weapon, such as a submachine gun or assault
rifle. Your sidearm has unlimited ammunition, but your
secondary weapon does not. Monitor current ammo stocks
next to the secondary weapon's icon.

Current gear: This is your active gear, such as frag
grenades, remote mines, or portable EMP device. The
number of available uses (when relevant) flanks the gear icon.

Marks for execution: You can mark as many targets as
there are chevrons here. When you have an execution ready
(explained later in this chapter), and targets marked that
are within line of sight and within the precision range of your
weapon, these chevrons turn red and the button prompt for
unleashing the execution turns red.

Target cursor: This is where you are currently aiming
your weapon.

COMBAT

As mentioned, you are almost always better off working from the shadows, employing stealth techniques. But knowing your way around a gun is critical, whether you try to take a room by force or stick to the darkness.

AIMING

Your target cursor appears in the center of the screen. The shape and color of the target cursor indicates the accuracy of your shot, should you pull the trigger. When the cursor is red, you are aiming at a target, either human or environmental, such as a fuel drum or computer terminal, in the precision range of your current weapon. Otherwise the cursor turns white.

> **T TIP**
>
> Always aim for the head. Headshots are instant kills, unless the target is wearing a full-face helmet.

Each weapon has a different accuracy (displayed in the armory). The wider the cursor, the less accurate the weapon. Pistols are highly accurate from stand-still, but lose accuracy quickly. Assault rifles are semi-accurate from stand-still but are more contained as you spray, while shotguns release a blast pattern. (Of course, that blast pattern is quite lethal at close range.) When you are moving and aiming, the cursor widens, no matter which weapon you are holding. When you stop moving, the cursor immediately tightens, which means your accuracy is increasing; the likelihood of hitting your target is much greater. However, to be as accurate as possible, not only should you aim from a complete stop, but also "zoom" in.

Zooming in greatly increases your accuracy, but decreases your peripheral vision, so do not linger in this view unless you are absolutely certain you cannot be flanked.

WEAPONS

As a former Third Echelon agent, you have advanced weapons training. There are dozens of weapons you can use on this assignment, but only after you encounter them in the field or unlock them by completing a mission. You always have a default pistol, the MK .23, which is equipped with a silencer. If you do not have a secondary weapon, you automatically pick up the first additional non-sidearm you run across.

> **T TIP**
>
> When you move across the same type of weapon (G36, MP5-SD3, etc.) you already have, you pick up additional ammunition.

> **N NOTE**
>
> Defeated enemies typically drop their weapons. When you stand near the dropped weapon, a button prompt shows you how to swap to the new weapon. The new weapon comes with two magazines; one loaded and one spare.
>
> All enemies, including their weapons, are detailed at the end of this chapter.

Weapons may be upgraded three times with the addition of larger magazine, scopes, deadlier bullets, and more. Upgrades are purchased with points acquired by completing P.E.C. Challenges, which are in-mission tasks and objectives such as performing a Death from Above attack or a perfect headshot from the shadows. All P.E.C. Challenges and the awarded points are detailed in the following chapter. Upgrades include:

Increased marks: Reflex sight

Increased accuracy: Laser sight, Gun stock

Increased range: 2x/4x scope, match grade ammo

Increased ammo stock: Extended mag

Increased damage: Hollow point ammo

Here is a full list of all weapons you encounter on your assignment, arranged by category. Each weapon is rated by power, range, and accuracy. The number of possible marks (including how many extra you can get through upgrades) and the magazine size is also noted with each entry.

COMBAT

WEAPONS

WEAPON	POWER	RANGE	ACCURACY	1- OR 2-HANDED	FIRE TYPE	CLIP SIZE	MARKS	UPGRADE 1	UPGRADE 2	UPGRADE 3	UNLOCKED VIA
PISTOLS											
MK .23 (silenced)	45	40	30	1-Handed	Single-shot	12	2 (+0)	Extended mag (18-round)	Laser sight	Hollow point ammo	—
MP-446 (silenced)	30	40	40	1-Handed	Single-shot	17	2 (+1)	Reflex sight	Laser sight	Match grade ammo	—
DESERT EAGLE	65	50	25	1-Handed	Single-shot	7	2 (+1)	Reflex sight	Laser sight	Match grade ammo	—
P228	45	30	35	1-Handed	Single-shot	13	3 (+0)	Extended mag (20-round)	Laser sight	Match grade ammo	—
IVE-SEVEN (silenced)	35	35	40	1-Handed	Single-shot	20	3 (+1)	Reflex sight	Laser sight	Match grade ammo	—
USP .45	40	40	35	1-Handed	Single-shot	12	2 (+1)	Reflex sight	Laser sight	Hollow point ammo	—
MACHINE PISTOLS											
SKORPION	40	45	40	1-Handed	Full automatic	20	2 (+1)	Gun stock	Reflex sight	Hollow point ammo	—
SR-2M	45	35	40	1-Handed	Full automatic	30	2 (+1)	Gun stock	Laser sight	Reflex sight	—
SUBMACHINE GUNS											
MP-5N	35	45	75	2-Handed	Full automatic	30	2 (+1)	Laser sight	Reflex sight	Hollow point ammo	—
MP-5SD3 (silenced)	35	45	80	2-Handed	Full automatic	30	2 (+0)	Gun stock	2x scope	Hollow point ammo	—
AKS-74U	60	55	70	2-Handed	Full automatic	30	2 (+1)	Reflex sight	Laser sight	Hollow point ammo	—
UMP .45	40	40	75	2-Handed	Full automatic	30	3 (+0)	Suppressor	Laser sight	Hollow point ammo	—
ASSAULT RIFLE											
AK-47	65	65	75	2-Handed	Full automatic	30	2 (+0)	Extended mag (55-round)	4x scope	Match grade ammo	—
M468	65	60	75	2-Handed	Full automatic	30	2 (+1)	Reflex sight	Suppressor	Hollow point ammo	—
G36C	70	65	70	2-Handed	Full automatic	30	2 (+0)	2x scope	Laser sight	Match grade ammo	—
SC3000	50	70	65	2-Handed	Full automatic	30	2 (+0)	Gun stock	Suppressor	Hollow point ammo	—
SCAR-H	70	60	75	2-Handed	Full automatic	30	2 (+0)	4x scope	Laser sight	Match grade ammo	U-play
SHOTGUN											
M-500	80	30	35	2-Handed	Pump action	8	2 (+1)	Laser sight	Reflex sight	Match grade ammo	—
SPAS-12 (silenced)	75	30	35	2-Handed	Semi-automatic	8	3 (+0)	Gun stock	2x scope	Match grade ammo	Pre-order

Completing missions in both the single-player story and the co-op story unlocks most weapons. (A few weapons are unlocked via downloadable content or pre-order bonuses.) Here is a full list of the weapons you unlock, arranged by mission:

UNLOCKABLE GUNS

MISSION	WEAPON(S) UNLOCKED
SINGLE PLAYER	
Merchant's Street Market	DESERT EAGLE, M-500
Kobin's Mansion	SKORPION, G36C*
Price Airfield	P228, MP-5N
Diwaniya, Iraq	MP-5SD3 (silenced), AK-47 (can be picked up)
Washington Monument	FIVE-SEVEN (silenced)
White Box Laboratories	M468
Lincoln Memorial	USP .45, UMP .45
Third Echelon HQ	SC3000
Michigan Ave. Reservoir	None
Downtown District	None
The White House	G36C
CO-OP	
St. Petersburg Banya	AKS-74U, SR-2M
Russian Embassy	AK-47
Yastreb Complex	None
Mozdok Grounds	None

*Kobin's gun can be picked up if no other secondary weapon was picked up during the entire map

DETECTION

It is extremely important to know when you can and cannot be seen. The easiest way to know if your presence is obscured is to note the colors

on the screen. If the view fades into black-and-white, you are invisible to enemies. When you move back out into the light or an enemy catches a glimpse of you in a flashlight beam or due to an attention-drawing attack, colors return to the scene.

You can also judge whether or not you are about to be spotted by a white arc that appears in the middle of the screen when you are close to

enemies. The apex of the arc points to the enemy who is about to detect you. The appearance of the arc is also accompanied by a flashing "Warning!" and an audio flourish. When you note the white arc, retreat to the shadows if you want to remain undetected. Otherwise, expect to get quite popular.

When an enemy has you dead-to-rights, a red arc appears. The triangle(s) on the arc point toward enemies who are shooting at you.

If you do not retreat from the white Warning soon enough, or you happen to step right into the line of sight of an enemy, a red arc appears around Sam. An arrow on the arc points at the enemy (or enemies, which results in multiple arrows) that has seen you. The word "Detected" flashes above the arc, meaning that the enemy may open fire. Not only does Detected mean the enemy has you dead to rights, but he is also communicating your position to nearby enemies. The longer you remain Detected, the more company you should expect.

To escape being Detected, you must either physically retreat from the scene fast enough to break line of sight as well as put distance between you and your pursuer, or deploy a diversionary measure, such as dropping a flashbang grenade that temporarily blinds your enemies.

COVER

Because you are not bulletproof, use cover whenever possible to keep from getting shot. Duck down and press your body against walls, crates, and whatnot to take cover. You can stay in cover as long as you like, but this will not protect you from enemies trying to flank and attack from a more advantageous angle. While in this position, you can advance to nearby cover and minimize your exposure to prying eyes or the nasty end of a gun.

To determine if you can advance, aim (with your target cursor) at the next piece of cover. If you can move cover to cover, small white arrows appear on the next position. Those arrows point

COMBAT

the direction you will face when you advance. If you decide
move, press the prompted button to advance. You stay low
d rush to the next cover spot and slam flush to it. When
oving, you can be seen or shot, unless the screen is in black-
d-white, which indicates that you are invisible.

ou can also lean
t of cover to fire
n enemies, but
his exposes you.

IAND-TO-HAND KILLS

addition to
ooting them,
u can kill
emies with your
re hands. You
ust be close
ough to an
emy to strike,
ough. When
u are within range, the button prompt for a close kill appears
screen. These kills are unstoppable. Once initiated, your
rget is helpless as you grab their gun and turn it on them
snap their neck with a quick twist of the skull. Hand-to-hand
s are silent, but if you perform one in plain sight, you are
mediately detected by other enemies.

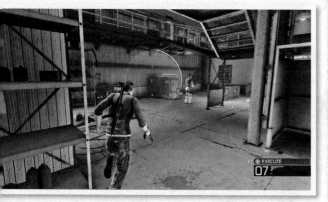

*You can initiate hand-to-hand kills while facing an enemy,
but the safest use of the attack is from the side or behind.
The element of surprise makes submission much easier.*

If you hold the
hand-to-hand kill
button, you do
not immediately
kill your target.
Instead, you pull
him close and use
him as a human
shield. You have
the enemy by his neck, so he does not make any noise. You
can move around the shadows and still not be detected. The
obvious benefit of a human shield is that it absorbs bullets while
you engage the enemy. A human shield can absorb several
bullets from pistols, but gets chewed up by machine guns and
assault rifles. When a human shield is no longer useful, you
automatically discard it.

◀◀◀ Ⓒ CAUTION

You can use only your pistol while holding a human shield.
You cannot use any gear either.

However, pulling an enemy into a human shield and then
dragging him into the shadows lets you decide where exactly
to drop the body. If you want to hide your presence, sneak
up on an enemy and then grab him while nobody is looking.
Retreat into the darkness and then press the same button
to kill him and release the body. Unless an enemy moves into
the shadows with a flashlight and discovers the body, you have
effectively hidden the evidence.

Ⓣ TIP

If you are moving when you kill a human shield, you throw the
body directly ahead of you. This is a good way to "toss" a body
into the shadows when you are in a hurry.

◀◀◀ Ⓒ CAUTION

Be mindful of where you use a hand-to-hand kill. If you snap
the neck of a mercenary while he's standing in a pool of light,
you leave obvious evidence of your presence. Enemies will be
on their toes and have an easier time spotting you.

MARK AND EXECUTE

As a Third Echelon agent, you have an uncanny ability to pick your targets and take them out. *Conviction*, though, takes this to an entirely new level. The mark technique allows you to keep track of multiple targets in your immediate area. When you mark a target, a small chevron appears above it. You can mark human targets as well as environmental features, such as traps and explosives. These chevrons remain constant until you either unmark or eliminate the target.

Marking targets is a great way to keep track of enemies as you survey a scene, moving around to assess the situation before deciding how to act. If you see your enemies splitting into two groups, for example, marking one group allows you to track their positions while you work on the second.

You can also mark targets while peeking under doors, using a piece of broken mirror or your snake cam.

Marked targets can also be dropped in executions— lightning fast attacks that your enemies have no time to respond to due to your

advanced training. Targets within range of execution are noted by red chevrons. Targets can move in and out of range, so keep an eye on the color of those chevrons. A target with a gray chevron will not be killed in an execution. Try to maximize the effectiveness of your executions by making sure all marked targets are within range, because if you leave any survivors following an execution (unmarked targets) within visual range, you are bound to attract some serious attention.

TIP

Different weapons allow for more or fewer marked targets.

You cannot execute marked targets whenever you like. You must first earn an execution. There are a few methods for earning an execution. Hand-to-hand kills (also known as close kills) are the most common. You also earn an execution by dropping on an enemy from a pipe or ledge in a move called Death from Above, which is detailed in the stealth section of this chapter.

You can also execute marked targets while holding a human shield. This is a great way to wade into a dangerous scene and immediately tilt the odds in your favor.

Executions are quiet if you use a silenced weapon. You can execute from the shadows and remain unseen. Shadowy executions are an excellent way to systemically clear a room of bad guys. Mark your targets and execute them with a silenced weapon. Then sneak up behind an unsuspecting enemy and take him down with a hand-to-hand kill. Then find a new vantage point in the scene and mark another batch of enemies for execution.

TIP

Go for close kills whenever possible so you always have an execution "banked."

DOORS

When you approach a door, you have multiple options. You can peek under a door with a piece of mirror or a snake cam to observe what is on the other side. If you want to quietly enter a room, just open the door. You automatically open it with zero fanfare. If somebody has his back to the door, he will not hear you open it. This is a great way to sneak up on an enemy and take him with a hand-to-hand kill, dragging him out of a room without anyone the wiser.

Peeking under a door is not without dangers. Enemies can still open the door and if one does while you are peeking, they discover you looking at the ground. They have the drop and will always get off the first shot. React fast with melee kill.

COMBAT - STEALTH

 TIP

Enemies know which doors should be open or shut. If you leave a door open that was originally closed, the first enemy that discovers it will come looking. This is an excellent lure, actually. The curious enemy gets too close to the door, becoming a prime target for a hand-to-hand kill.

here is a third option: smashing doors. As expected, this makes a lot of noise. But it also surprises everybody on the other side of the door. You have a brief moment to take advantage of that surprise by popping off a few shots, executing marked targets, or grabbing the closest guy and pulling him into a close kill.

ENVIRONMENTAL KILLS

Keep an eye out for things in the environment you can use against your enemies. Shooting fuel drums, for example, results in massive explosions that take out all enemies in the immediate area. But also look for hanging objects that you can drop on enemies. Release chandeliers, cargo containers, and more by shooting the chains holding them up. The falling object instantly kills anybody beneath it. And even if you do not kill anybody with the explosion or falling object, you have still created an effective diversion. Enemies in the area will rush to investigate. This can be used to either bring enemies within range (for an execution, perchance?) or move them to another area so you can easily slip into the darkness.

Fuel drums and hanging objects that can be used to kill enemies still show up in color, even when you are stealthily hidden from view.

STEALTH

The best weapon in your arsenal is stealth. Your ability to slip into a room and remain undetected until you attack and then quickly melt back into the shadows is what makes you such a terror to your enemies. They never know where you are and where you will hit next. And if you are truly a master of the shadows, they will never even know you are there until that first bullet hits them in the neck.

When you are invisible to the enemy, your view turns black-and-white. You can remain in cover like this as long as necessary. Use it to survey each scene and deduce the best path through your resistance, whether that is dropping into full view and opening fire or staying in the shadows as long as possible, eliminating your enemies with kills that do not reveal your position.

You must master several stealth tactics to survive. And you must learn to use them in tandem, as you can actually drop every target without being spotted if you are methodical with your stealth techniques. Use the hint of a Last Known Position to lure an enemy into your firing line, or scurry up a drain pipe to dish out the lethal Death from Above move.

LIGHTS OUT

There are many ways to remain undetected, such as hiding behind a wall or crate. But no cover is more useful than the dark. Seek out the shadows  whenever possible, such as the dark corners of a ballroom or on top of an office. You can also make your own shadows, if necessary. Most lights can be shot out. If the target cursor appears red over a light, pull the trigger to blast it. Shooting out lights can draw attention, though, so be mindful of enemies in the area. They may wonder why a light suddenly went out behind them or be drawn in by the sound of breaking glass.

CAUTION

Some lights cannot be shot out, so if the cursor appears as a white X when you look at a light, find another way to extinguish it (an EMP works) or look for another route. Chemical light sources are not vulnerable to EMP though!

TIP

Some rooms have light switches. Look for these switches near doors. You can even shoot at them to make sure your enemies won't turn them on again.

Shoot out lights to obscure your trail, such as popping headlights to cover an enemy body in shadows.

PIPES AND LEDGES

One of the best places you can hide from detection is on pipes that crisscross ceilings along hallways and over rooms.  Most pipes are accessed by pulling yourself up a vertical length of pipes, usually running up a wall. However, some are low enough that you can jump straight up and grab them. Once on a horizontal pipe, you pull yourself up and swing your legs over it. While shimmying along the pipes, you remain completely out of view—as long as

you don't attract attention. If you open fire with a machine gun from a ceiling pipe, every pair of eyes in the room will look up. Hanging from a pipe with eight guns pointed at you is a terrible, terrible place to be.

However, pipes are excellent vantage points for not only gathering intel on a situation (monitoring enemy patrol routes, spotting environmental  hazards), but also killing your enemies. Arming a silenced weapon and pulling a mark-and-execute from a pipe is a great opening move when facing a room full of enemies. Using a silenced weapon and shooting an enemy by himself while nobody is looking is another good kill that avoids detection.

While hanging from a pipe or ledge, you can use gear, such as throwing a grenade or planting a mine.

Pipes are preferable because your aim is so expansive—you have a 360-degree view of a room. However, ledges are also useful for moving above the average mercenary's line of sight. If you see a ledge along a wall or you are next to a ledge (such as on a balcony), jump up and grab it. You can then shimmy left and right. If you are hanging from a ledge on a wall, you can only aim to each side and behind you.

STEALTH

While hanging from a ledge like a balcony, you can poke your head up and target an enemy. But like peeking out of cover, this exposes you. You might get spotted. But maybe that's your goal. Read the Last Known Position section to see how this is incredibly useful at times.

DEATH FROM ABOVE

While hanging from either a ledge or a pipe, you can perform the Death from Above kill. As an enemy moves beneath you, a button prompt appears onscreen. Initiate the move and you jump down, crashing into them. The takedown is relatively quiet because you muffle their surprised cry as you smash their head into the floor. However, if you do so in an illuminated room or within close earshot of another enemy, you are easily spotted.

 TIP

Performing a Death from Above gives you an execution.

Smash into an enemy in the shadows and then scurry back to the pipe to avoid detection and prep another kill.

WINDOWS

Windows are a devilishly clever tool for dispatching enemies as well as gathering intelligence. Most buildings have windows you can hop through and then hang on the ledge outside. If you have a wall of windows before you, though, you have a virtual shooting gallery. The first thing to be mindful of with windows, though, is whether they are open or shut. To be silent, make sure you slide open a window before attempting to pass through it. If you jump through a closed window, the shattering glass makes enough racket to draw a lot of attention from nearby enemies. Now, that has its uses. The noise from a shattered window will pull enemies to one particular window. You can then scurry to the left or right on the ledge outside and flank the enemies investigating the broken window.

An enemy checking a broken window or a window with your LKP often sticks his head out to look around. He will shoot you if he spots you. But for one moment, all that is exposed is his head. Draw a bead and take him out.

You can also use a bay of windows to flank enemies. Jump out a window and then slide along a corner ledge to peer back in the room and target your enemy's back.

Perhaps the most fun you can have with a window, though, is ambushing an unsuspecting enemy standing next to it. Slip up to an enemy with his back to the window. Then, follow the onscreen prompt to reach in and seize him. You yank him right through the window and throw him to his death. If the window is open and nobody is looking, this is a silent kill. You may need to open the window in some cases. Opening a window can draw attention, so be sure other enemies in a room are looking elsewhere before you lift the glass.

CAUTION

You can pull an enemy through a closed window, but the breaking glass makes a lot of noise.

LAST KNOWN POSITION

Last Known Position is one of the best tricks you have to outsmart your enemies. Using LKP, you can lead enemies around rooms like lemmings, as they desperately try to be the one who takes you down. But the catch is, they are only chasing your ghost. By the time they reach the LKP, you're gone. And that's when they know they're in real trouble.

LKP is represented as a white outline of yourself when you were spotted. If you were leaning out of a door or shimmying along a pipe, your outline is then fixed in that action. Enemies will communicate the LKP to each other and they will focus their attacks on it. Maybe they will shoot at your LKP or attempt to flank it. It doesn't matter. What matters is that you put some distance between you and the LKP and then use it to your advantage.

Sometimes, your LKP is a total accident. An enemy got a peek at your position or you were a half-second too slow jumping out a window. But even if you did not plan your LKP by purposefully leaning into view, you can still make the most of it. The easiest use of the LKP is disappearing. If multiple enemies are converging on you and you spy an escape route, poke your head out of cover to create a LKP and then dart through the shadows. As your enemies focus on your LKP, plan your attack. If multiple targets gather around an LKP, mark them for execution. Circle behind a solo enemy investigating a LKP and hit him with a close kill.

Set traps by getting spotted at a door. As the enemy approaches your LKP, lunge and grab them for a close kill.

If spotted on a pipe, use a countermeasure like a flashbang to divert your enemy's eyes and then move away. When they look back up at your LKP, you are somewhere else—and ready to kill them.

STEALTH - GEAR

LKP at a window is awesome...awesomely lethal. When the enemy leans out to look for you, reach up and pull them to their death.

You find some gear in the field, such as snatching up some frag grenades off a crate. But spent gear is primarily refreshed at weapons stash crates placed in the field, green boxes that you access not only to pick up fresh gear, but also to change your weapons and upgrade them.

INTERROGATION

When you close in on an enemy who you need to extract information from, you can interrogate them. You can't shoot an interrogation target, but be careful not to kill them with any explosives; you need the information they have. When you get close enough to strike, grab them like you would to initiate a hand-to-hand kill. Instead of snapping their neck, you hold their throat and draw them close so they know you mean business.

Not every interrogation target is loose lipped. Some people need to be prompted to open up. When a subject does not answer your question, you need to convince them to do so by either hitting them or driving their face into a nearby object, such as a toilet, television, or piano. Just drag them so their back faces the object and then press the interrogation button. Each object results in a different attack so no two interrogations are the same.

GEAR

You have access to several pieces of gear beyond your two slotted weapons, such as frag grenades and remote mines. These tools are critical for accomplishing your goals. There is no right or wrong way to use gear, but many pieces of gear have multiple uses for different situations. Effectively deploying gear in the right situation can not only help you eliminate a dangerous target, but also escape without detection.

NOTE

All weapon upgrades are detailed in the next chapter.

FRAG GRENADE

Loud. Messy. Deadly. Frag grenades are blunt instruments. They get the job done but they announce your arrival like the angel's trumpet. However, any enemy caught in the blast radius of a frag grenade is instantly killed, which makes it great for crowd control. To throw a frag, select it from your gear menu and then aim just like you were going to shoot a gun. You throw the frag in the direction of your target cursor, but distance and architecture matter quite a bit. Grenades can be banked off walls or thrown through doorways to surprise enemies that either have not seen you or have retreated. Frag grenades roll along the ground until they explode, but if you throw them over a great distance, they may blow up before reaching your target.

CAUTION

Frags makes noise when they hit the ground. If you toss one next to an enemy, he has a second to react and move away.

FLASHBANG

Flashbangs are excellent escape tools. These grenades let off a bright flash of light and noise that causes anybody in the immediate area to hide their eyes and recoil. If enemies are right next to a popping flashbang, they are temporarily stunned. However, starting off an attack with a flashbang is advisable only if you plan on finishing it soon. After enemies recover from the effects of a flashbang, they start looking around for who threw it.

So, instead of using one at the beginning of an attack, use it midway to distract enemies if you are ever discovered. If you are not only spotted but being fired upon, dropping a flashbang while running gives you a few seconds to seek cover and plot a new course. When the effects of the flashbang subside, your enemies will be focused on your LKP, not your new position.

TIP

Execute marked enemies when everybody is stunned by a flashbang. When the survivors come to their senses, they will have no idea what happened and not be looking for you in the immediate area.

EMP GRENADE/EMP DEVICE

Electro-Magnetic Pulse (EMP) technology factors heavily into the terrorist plot you are attempting to stop. EMPs disable anything that runs on electricity, such as a microwave or a computer. You have two EMP devices to use in order to maintain your invisibility: EMP grenades and a portable EMP generator.

NOTE

You do not receive the EMP generator until you meet up with Vic in the fifth mission.

CAUTION

Your generator has a limited number of pulses. You can refresh it at a weapons stash.

Use EMPs to disable lights and create extra shadows and dark areas. A pulse will extinguish every light in a room, including flashlights,

allowing you to move with almost universal impunity. (Enemies can still see a few feet in front of their faces.) But do not linger when moving through the darkness because it is temporary. The lights will come back on after several seconds and it is possible to be caught right out in the open—total disaster.

There are several differences between the EMP grenade and portable generator. EMP grenades produce smaller effects that last longer than those created by the generator. The generator, on the other hand, affects a much wider area, but for a shorter period of time. This makes the grenade useful when you want to control a room while assaulting it, but makes the generator a much more useful tool when you just need an opening to get out of a tight situation.

CAUTION

Toward the end of your assignment, enemies begin setting up chemical lights that cannot be snuffed out with EMP tech.

REMOTE MINE

Throw remote mines against a surface and they stick, making them perfect trap material. Plus, you control when they blow up. As soon as you plant a

remote mine, the gear button turns into the detonator. Watch the site of the remote mine and set it off when an enemy walks near it.

When you throw a remote mine, the detonator is automatically selected. However, you can still swap back to the remote mines in your gadget inventory and place some more. You can use this to lay some more complex traps, and make sure you take out a lot of enemies in one fell swoop.

TIP

Remote mines also make great distractions. Stick one to a wall and then blow it up to make enemies investigate. While they move toward the remote mine, you can either flank them or sl behind them without being noticed.

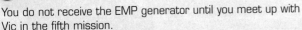

GEAR

STICKY CAMERA

The sticky camera is similar to the snake cam you use to peek under doors. However, this camera has multiple uses beyond surveillance. When you throw it on a surface and access the feed, you can not only look around and mark targets, but the camera can also create a small noise. This noise attracts the attention of nearby enemies, which lures them closer to the camera. Once they're within range, activate a small explosive in the camera to take out nearby enemies.

SONAR GOGGLES

Third Echelon scientist Charles Fryman gives you a pair of sonar goggles that allow you to not only see in the dark, but also peer through walls. When you engage the goggles, a pulse "draws" a diagram of your surroundings. Humans show up as bright white outlines, making them very easy to spot. There is no camouflage from the sonar goggles, so do not worry about somebody hiding from you. You will always see their outline. Environmental hazards you can destroy, such as fuel drums, also appear in white on the sonar goggles.

The farther the pulse travels, though, the weaker it gets. Outlines are fainter. And objects that were spotted closer to you start to fade. Don't worry, another pulse refreshes your view and updates the position of your attackers. You can hunt while looking through the goggles, but it is hard to pull off accurate shots while aiming at human-shaped outlines. It is far better to establish the location of targets and then remove the goggles so you can line up precise shots. Rapid movement makes the signal to noise ratio very high, so you will get the clearest picture of the environment when you are not moving. Also, you can mark enemies while in this view—it's super useful to plan your attacks using the goggles!

◀◀◀ CAUTION

You are not the only person with sonar goggles. You will face down some highly trained agents toward the end of your assignment that also have access to the tech. When you see red lenses on your enemy's face, know that you are never truly hidden.

The sonar goggles also reveal laser tripwires. You will encounter security systems that use laser tripwires in tandem with mounted machine guns that automatically target a broken beam and then unload. Once the gun acquires a target, it does not stop until the clip is empty. You better find cover. So, if you ever spot a mounted gun hanging from the ceiling, activate the goggles and look for "invisible" laser tripwires. Slowly move through the field of lasers by ducking under beams or finding ways over floor lasers via jumping over objects or shimmying along a ledge.

ENEMY INTEL

We have managed to gather intel on the enemies you are likely to face in this assignment. Use these enemy files to know what weapons your enemies are carrying, including the gear and gadgets they may carry.

SINGLE PLAYER ENEMIES

ENEMY	WEAPON(S)	GEAR
MERCHANT'S STREET MARKET		
Thug	DESERT EAGLE, M-500	None
KOBIN'S MANSION		
Thug	DESERT EAGLE, SKORPION, M-500	None
PRICE AIRFIELD		
Black Arrow agent	P228, MP-5N, M-500	Flashbangs
DIWANIYA, IRAQ		
Soldier	AK-47	Frag grenades
WASHINGTON MONUMENT		
Agents disguised as city workers	MP-446 (Silenced)	None
Spotter	None	None
Black Arrow agent	P228, MP-5N, M-500	Flashbangs
WHITE BOX LABORATORIES		
Black Arrow agent	P228, MP-5N, M-500	Flashbangs
Black Arrow elite	P228, MP-5N, M468, M-500	Frag grenades, flares
LINCOLN MEMORIAL		
Suited men	USP .45	Flashbangs
Police	USP .45	None
Third Echelon elites	MP-446 (silenced), UMP .45, M-500	Frag grenades, flashbangs, flares
THIRD ECHELON HQ		
NSA guard	P228, M-500	None
Third Echelon elites	MP-446 (silenced), SC3000	Frag grenades, flashbangs, flares
Splinter Cell	MP-446 (silenced), UMP .45, M568, M-500	Frag grenades, smoke grenades, night vision goggles
MICHIGAN AVE. RESERVOIR		
Black Arrow elites	P228, MP-5N, M468, M-500	Frag grenades, flares
DOWNTOWN DISTRICT		
Black Arrow elites	P228, MP-5N, M468, M-500	Frag grenades, flares
THE WHITE HOUSE		
Third Echelon elites	MP-446 (silenced), UMP .45, M-500	Frag grenades, flashbangs, flares, night vision goggles
Splinter Cell	MP-446 (silenced), UMP .45, M568, M-500	Frag grenades, smoke grenades, night vision goggles

CO-OP ENEMIES

ENEMY	WEAPON(S)
ST. PETERSBURG	
Russian thugs	P228, SR-2M, AKS-74U
Russian SWAT	P228, SR-2M, AKS-74U
RUSSIAN EMBASSY	
Azeri guards	AK-47
Russian security guard	MP-446 (silenced), SR-2M
YASTREB COMPLEX	
Russian security guard	P228
Russian soldier	P228, AK-47, AKS-74U, M-500
Spetznaz	AK-74U, M-500
MOZDOK AIRBASE	
Russian guard	P228, AKS-74U
Russian soldier	P228, AK-47, AKS-74U, M-500
Spetznaz	AK-74U, M-500

P.E.C. CHALLENGES

CHALLENGE AND REWARD

Persistent Elite Creation Challenges are in-game tasks that, when completed, pay out in points that you may use to upgrade your weapons and gear. Upgrades include frag grenades with an expanded blast radius and suppressors that reduce the visual and audio flashes of a weapon. You spend your earned points at the armory in either the single-player or co-op game or at the loadout selection screen when initiating a multiplayer game. (You can spend points on additional uniforms in multiplayer games, for example.) Your points are persistent with your profile, so whether you complete challenges in the main story or in the co-op story, all points go into a central bank.

There are three categories of P.E.C. Challenges: Prepare and Execute, Vanish, and Splinter Cell. Prepare and Execute and Vanish challenges have three tiers. Completing the number of actions required for each tier results in a point payout. The number of actions to fulfill a challenge increases with each tier. Once you have completed the third tier of a challenge, you can no longer earn points for those specific actions, but your successes are still logged.

Here is a complete list of all P.E.C. Challenges, including the number of actions required, the number of points awarded per level for each challenge, and a short description of the challenge. Following the table, you will find additional strategies for fulfilling each challenge.

P.E.C. CHALLENGES

CHALLENGE NAME	CHALLENGE DESCRIPTION	# REQ'D FOR LEVEL 1	LEVEL 1 VALUE	# REQ'D FOR LEVEL 2	LEVEL 2 VALUE	# REQ'D FOR LEVEL 3	LEVEL 3 VALUE
PREPARE AND EXECUTE							
Death from Above	Neutralize an enemy using Death from Above.	5	400	15	450	30	550
Grab from Ledge	Neutralize an enemy by pulling them from a ledge.	5	400	15	450	30	550
5x Predator	Neutralize 5 enemies in a row without being detected.	5	400	10	450	15	550
Stealth Headshot	Neutralize an enemy with a headshot without alerting other enemies (M&E action not allowed).	10	400	20	450	50	550
Mark Proficiency	Neutralize at least 2 enemies in a single mark and execute.	5	400	50	450	100	550
3x Frag Grenade	Neutralize 3 enemies at the same time with a single frag grenade.	10	400	25	450	50	550
Remote Explosion	Neutralize at least 3 enemies by detonating a remote explosion gadget.	10	400	10	450	15	550
Stunned	Neutralize an enemy who is stunned by a flashbang or EMP gadget.	10	400	25	450	50	550
Behind Closed Doors	Use the mirror or snake camera to mark an enemy, then neutralize him.	10	400	25	450	50	550
Sonar Mark	Use the sonar goggles to mark an enemy, then neutralize him.	25	400	50	450	100	550
Shadow Takedown	Perform hand-to-hand takedowns in the shadows without alerting other enemies.	25	400	50	450	100	550
Sticky Camera Whistle	Make noise with the sticky camera to attract an enemy, and neutralize him.	5	400	10	450	15	550
VANISH							
Vanish Silently	Once you are spotted, vanish without neutralizing any enemies.	5	400	10	450	15	550
Cat and Mouse	Perform a hand-to-hand takedown against an enemy who is investigating your last known position.	5	400	10	450	15	550
Last Known Position	Neutralize an enemy while standing at least 10 meters from your last known position.	10	400	25	450	50	550
Portable EMP Escape	Use the portable EMP to vanish. Stun at least 3 enemies while escaping from a combat situation.	10	400	25	450	50	550
Flashbang Escape	Use the flashbang to vanish. Escape from a combat situation.	5	400	10	450	15	550
EMP Grenade Stun	Stun at least 3 enemies with a single EMP grenade.	10	400	25	450	50	550
Choke-Hold Freedom	Free your teammate from a choke hold in any multiplayer game mode.	5	400	10	450	15	550
Reviving Teammates	Revive your teammate in any multiplayer game mode.	5	400	10	450	15	550

CHALLENGE NAME	CHALLENGE DESCRIPTION	VALUE
	SPLINTER CELL	
Mark Mastery	Neutralize 4 enemies with a single mark & execute.	500
Advanced Stealth	Complete a level without getting spotted.	750
Advanced Close Combat	Complete a level without firing a single shot.	750
10x Predator	Neutralize 10 enemies in a row without being detected.	500
Assault Rifle Marksman	Neutralize 15 enemies with a single magazine using an assault rifle without reloading.	500
Pistol Marksman	Neutralize 10 enemies with a single magazine using a pistol without reloading.	500
Collateral Damage	Grab an enemy into human shield, then use him to bash down a door.	500
Human Collision	Knock an enemy down by throwing another enemy onto him.	500
Deadly Fall	Throw an enemy so he falls 10 or more meters.	500
Environmental Hazard	Neutralize 3 enemies using a single trap or explosive.	500
Security Device Diversion	Attract an enemy by disabling a security device, then neutralize him.	500
Car Alarm Investigation	Neutralize an enemy while he is investigating a car alarm.	500
Human Kevlar	Mark & execute 3 enemies while holding a human shield.	500
Group Neutralization	Neutralize 3 enemies who are stunned by a single gadget.	500
Alternate Door Entry	Crush an enemy on the other side of a door by bashing into it or kicking it down.	500
Breaking Glass	Shatter a window by throwing an enemy through it.	500
Effective Interrogation	Use 3 different special moves during a single interrogation.	500
Full Recovery	In any co-op game mode, when you are knocked down, sit up and neutralize 5 enemies before your teammate revives you.	500
Remain Undetected	Remain undetected for 10 minutes after vanishing.	500

PREPARE AND EXECUTE

This category of challenges includes those where you set up situations to take out your enemies through devious means, like yanking them through a window or killing them without anybody else in the room noticing.

DEATH FROM ABOVE

Use the Death from Above technique to take down an enemy while you hang from a ledge or a pipe. Each time you use this move, it is logged toward the next tier of the challenge. Just make sure that no other enemy is looking when initiating the Death from Above, or have everyone else marked so that as soon as you take out the target, you can execute the witnesse

PREPARE AND EXECUTE

GRAB FROM LEDGE

arn this award by pulling enemies over ledges or through
indows (open or shut). Any mission with ledges and windows,
om the interior of White Box Technologies to Kobin's
ansion, offers multiple opportunities to initiate this kill.
very attack counts as one grab kill. The higher the tier in
is challenge, the more grabs you must perform to bank
e points.

 TIP

This challenge dovetails nicely into Vanish Silently or Cat and
Mouse. Pulling an enemy through a window can result in an
LKP if you are spotted making the grab. If you move away,
you can either remain hidden to get the Vanish Silently award
or target the curious enemy investigating the LKP for Cat
and Mouse.

5X PREDATOR

fulfill this
hallenge, you
ust eliminate
e enemies in a
w without being
otted. If you
ave behind an
KP or are shot at
he red arc appears onscreen), the string of kills to earn this
ward is restarted. Completing this challenge requires stealth,
t if you stick to the shadows and target solo enemies or
oups while having an easy escape route, you can notch the
quired series of kills.

 TIP

Kills from any weapon or piece of gear counts toward this
challenge. Rolling a frag into a group of enemies is a good way
to score multiple kills in a single act. Just make sure nobody
sees you doing it!

STEALTH HEADSHOT

You're enveloped
in the shadows.
Nobody sees you.
A lone enemy
moves into view.
You select a
silenced weapon
and target their

head. You pull the trigger when the cursor turns red. The
enemy is cut down by the headshot. As long as nobody hears
the shot or sees the body crumple to the floor, you notch the
Stealth Headshot. However, if somebody was looking while
their ally fell, the headshot does not count, even if no LKP is
established.

 NOTE

A Mark and Execute action cannot be used to complete this
challenge. Also, the shot still counts if the body of the enemy
is found later.

MARK PROFICIENCY

You must mark
and execute
two or more
enemies without
missing a single
target to fulfill
this challenge. It
does not matter
if you are spotted

while performing the execution, but you cannot leave a marked
target alive. The kill count can include a hand-to-hand takedown
initiated at the start of the execution.

 TIP

The kills logged while you are raging from the mention of your
daughter count toward this challenge.

3X FRAG GRENADE

Kill at least three enemies with a single frag grenade. All three
enemies must die in the same blast. To fulfill this challenge, look
for groups of enemies moving together. The smaller the space
the better, because splash damage caused by a frag explosion
in tight corridors is more powerful. The shock wave of an
explosion dissipates faster in a large room.

 TIP

Use sonar goggles to spot a group of enemies coming through
a door or moving through a hallway. These are prime targets
for a 3x Frag Grenade kill.

REMOTE EXPLOSION

Like the 3x Frag grenade challenge, the Remote Explosion challenge is fulfilled when you kill at least three enemies with a single remote mine or sticky camera detonation. Place these devices in doors or near other chokepoints to notch your kills and earn this award.

STUNNED

You can stun enemies with flashbangs or EMP pulses. The reaction is plainly visible. They raise their hands to their faces to shield their eyes or ears and typically buckle at the knees while trying to recover. Dispatch the enemy while they are stunned to notch a kill toward this award. The kill can either be hand-to-hand, headshot, or execution.

BEHIND CLOSED DOORS

While peeking under a door with your snake cam or a mirror, mark a target for execution and then follow through. It doesn't matter if you kick the door down and execute, flank through a different entrance, and scurry up a pipe and deliver the kill shot. You just need to execute the marked target without ever unmarking him before making the kill.

SONAR MARK

This challenge is similar to Behind Closed Doors, but instead of marking and executing with the snake cam, you do so while peering through your sonar goggles. Marking targets behind two walls or just below you counts. You just need to keep the target marked and complete the execution without ever unmarking him. You are not required to stay in the sonar goggles view.

SHADOW TAKEDOWN

The Shadow Takedown shares the same DNA as the Stealth Headshot P.E.C. Challenge. You must eliminate a target with a hand-to-hand kill (either an immediate kill or drag the enemy away as a human shield) without ever being seen or heard. If an LKP is established, the challenge is not fulfilled. However, if other enemies locate the body from the kill later, it does not affect the fulfillment.

STICKY CAMERA WHISTLE

After placing the sticky cam on a surface and using the "make noise" interaction to draw an enemy in to investigate, kill them by detonating the camera, shooting them with a weapon, killing them hand-to-hand, or eliminating them with any other gear (frag grenade, mine, etc.).

Ⓝ NOTE

Killing multiple targets while they investigate the same sticky camera does not result in extra fulfillments. This award is given per sticky camera.

PREPARE AND EXECUTE - VANISH

VANISH

Vanish P.E.C. Challenges are typically related to the establishment of Last Known Positions to lure enemies into bad situations, such as Cat and Mouse where you eliminate an enemy checking out your LKP before he can relay information about it to his comrades.

VANISH SILENTLY

Chances are good you will initiate this challenge multiple times by just playing through the game. When you are spotted and establish an LKP, instead of

killing the enemy who located you to remove the LKP, scurry away and disappear into the shadows again. Allow that enemy to investigate your LKP and discover you are no longer there. This removes the LKP and the enemy goes back on their patrol route or returns to their group. You then bank one instance of this challenge.

CAT AND MOUSE

To earn this award, allow an enemy to spot you and establish a LKP. Instead of moving away like the Vanish Silently challenge, remain close but hidden. When the enemy comes to investigate the LKP, reach out and eliminate him with a hand-to-hand kill before he has a chance to relay your LKP to other enemies.

 TIP

Doorways are a great place to pull off a Cat and Mouse because you can hide just out of view on the other side of a door and then strike when the enemy walks through it.

LAST KNOWN POSITION

Allow an enemy to see you, but then disappear and leave behind an LKP. You must then move at least 10m away from your LKP and then engage any enemies who are focused on it. When the enemy moves in on your LKP, wait until he is close to it, and then kill him. Headshots, remote mines, frag grenades—it does not matter how you eliminate the enemy.

 TIP

One of the easiest ways to fulfill this challenge is to establish a LKP in a room with a pipe along the ceiling or a window. Establish the LKP and then disappear. Because the window or pipe lets you survey the scene, you can wait until the enemy is just within range to dismiss your LKP and then take them out.

PORTABLE EMP ESCAPE

When at least three enemies are acting on your LKP or are actively targeting you (you got spotted), use the portable EMP generator to trigger a pulse. The range of pulse requires you be close to your enemies for them to be effectively stunned by the generator. While the enemies are stunned, escape out of sight by melting into the shadows or leaving the room. You will not get this award if you initiate combat while the enemies are recovering from the stun.

FLASHBANG ESCAPE

This award is similar to the Portable EMP Escape. Instead of releasing a pulse via the EMP generator, drop a flashbang amid three or more enemies who are actively targeting you or closing in on your LKP. While they are stunned from the flash, escape and do not engage.

TIP

Easy way to notch a Flashbang or Portable EMP Escape? Trigger the pulse or flash when near an open window or pipe. As soon as your enemies recoil, run to the escape route.

EMP GRENADE STUN

EMP grenades stun enemies when dropped next to them. To earn this award, you must stun at least three of them with a single EMP grenade. Try rolling an EMP grenade into a group of enemies coming through a door or dropping one on a patrol while you are hanging from a pipe. If the enemies do not spread out when hearing the bounce of the grenade, you will earn the award.

CHOKE-HOLD FREEDOM

While playing a co-op game with a friend, free them from a choke hold. You can either rush the enemy holding your friend and take them out with a hand-to-hand kill or ask your friend to dodge. While your friend ducks, pick off the enemy with a headshot.

REVIVING TEAMMATES

In a co-op game, revive a fallen friend by clearing out any immediate threats and then initiating the cardiac revival. You must complete the revival before an enemy attacks.

 TIP

If any enemies are still around, tell your friend not to sit up and draw attention to themselves. If they are shot while sitting up, the mission ends in failure.

SPLINTER CELL

This category of P.E.C. Challenges is different from the other two. There is a single award for each challenge. These challenges are not tiered with multiple requirements and point payouts. Your fulfillment of the challenge requirements are constantly logged and displayed, but only that initial fulfillment results in a point payout.

MARK MASTERY

This challenge is fulfilled by marking and executing four or more targets at the same time. It is much easier to fulfill this challenge while in rage mode after hearing  something about your daughter, such as in the Third Echelon mission.

ADVANCED STEALTH

To earn this difficult challenge, you must make it through an entire mission without your enemies ever engaging in combat. They may never see you either. They only detection allowed is an LKP through noise.

 TIP

Try to pull off this challenge on shorter missions, such as Washington Monument.

VANISH - SPLINTER CELL

ADVANCED CLOSE COMBAT

omplete a
ission without
ring a single
hot—not even
shot to make
oise and
stablish a LKP for
ur enemies to
nase down. You

ust kill every enemy with a hand-to-hand takedown or a melee-
riented attack, such as pulling them through an open window.

NOTE

When Sam has a weapon in his hand, he will often use it
during melee attacks. Make sure you holster your weapon
(by holding DOWN on the d-pad) to make sure you don't fire a
shot while attempting this challenge.

CAUTION

Mark and executes count against you in this challenge,
including those used while enraged.

0X PREDATOR

his is an advanced version of the 5x Predator challenge. You
ust eliminate 10 enemies in a row without being spotted or
ngaged in combat. You can use hand-to-hand kills, guns, or
ear to notch your kills.

ASSAULT RIFLE MARKSMAN

sing a single magazine, you must eliminate 15 enemies. You
ay not reload or else the count starts over. Any assault rifles
pgrades do not count against you for is challenge. In fact, it
much easier to fulfill this challenge if you upgrade the ammo
pacity or accuracy of a specific assault rife.

ISTOL MARKSMAN

ke the Assault
fle Marksman
hallenge, you
ust take down
enemies
thout reloading.
s best to
ttempt this
hallenge as

oon as you reload your weapon. Use an upgraded pistol with
etter accuracy and damage to maximize the effectiveness of
ch bullet.

TIP

Stealth headshots count toward this challenge, so stick to the
shadows and make clean headshots to notch your 10 kills.

COLLATERAL DAMAGE

To complete this challenge, pull an enemy into the human
shield position and then start looking for a closed door. Move
toward the door and then kill the enemy, which throws their
body through the door. Naturally, this will make some noise, so
be ready for other enemies in the area to investigate the sound
of a splintering door.

HUMAN COLLISION

Human Collision is similar in nature to Collateral Damage.
While holding an enemy as a human shield, close in on another
target. Move toward the target and then throw the enemy into
them so they both crash to the ground.

DEADLY FALL

Deadly Fall is accomplished by grabbing an enemy from a
ledge and pulling them to their death or holding an enemy as a
human shield and then throwing them over a ledge. As long as
the fall is greater than 10 meters, you fulfill this challenge.

TIP

There are ample opportunities to complete this challenge in the
labs of White Box Technologies.

ENVIRONMENTAL HAZARD

In the previous chapter, we described how to kill enemies by using environmental features such as fuel drums or falling chandeliers. Kill three or more enemies with the same explosions or falling object to fulfill this challenge. Fuel drums are the easiest way to complete this challenge, but the hanging cargo container outside the makeshift hangars on the Price Airfield works, too.

SECURITY DEVICE DIVERSION

To fulfill this challenge, you must disable a security device like a wall-mounted camera with a little noise. The popped lens of the camera or some hooting sparks get the attention of a nearby enemy. When the enemy walks to the disabled security device to check it out, either eliminate them with a hand-to-hand kill or deliver a headshot.

CAR ALARM INVESTIGATION

Like the Security Device Diversion, you need to lure an enemy into investigating something before dealing out the death. In this case, nudge a car to activate its alarm. Any nearby enemies will walk over to the car to check it out. Hide while they approach the car and then neutralize them while they peer into the windows or circle the vehicle.

 TIP

The cars out front of Kobin's Mansion are perfect for earning this award. Nudge a car and then fall back, watching for any of the three guards in front of the museum to investigate the commotion.

HUMAN KEVLAR

The Human Kevlar challenge tasks you with pulling an enemy into the human shield position before marking and executing at least three other enemies. You must execute while holding the human shield. You cannot mark while holding the shield and then discard it before initiating the execution.

GROUP NEUTRALIZATION

This challenge dovetails with the Stunned award. Stun three or more enemies with an EMP wave or a flashbang, While the enemies are recovering from your action, kill at least three of them. You can neutralize the targets with gunplay, grenades/mines, hand-to-hand kills, or any combination of the three. However, as soon as one of the group recovers, the challenge cannot be fulfilled.

ALTERNATE DOOR ENTRY

When you know an enemy is on the other side of a door (use your snake cam or a mirror to spot them), kill them by crashing through the door on top of them. There are multiple spots you can pull this move off, from Kobin's Mansion to White Box Technologies.

SPLINTER CELL

BREAKING GLASS

To fulfill this challenge, grab an enemy and hold them as a human shield. Then, move toward a window that is still closed. Throw the enemy through the glass. As soon as the glass shatters (which does make a lot of noise, so be mindful of your surroundings), you earn the points.

EFFECTIVE INTERROGATION

When you interrogate a person of interest, you can usually drag them around the immediate area between questions. Initiating the next phase of the interrogation while pressing the target up to an object results in a unique interaction, such as jamming their face into a sink or a wheel well. Within a single interrogation, smash a subject into three different objects.

(T) TIP

There are multiple interrogations you can use to complete this challenge, such as the Gramkos interrogation in the first mission or the Lucius Galliard interrogation at the Lincoln Memorial.

FULL RECOVERY

This challenge is limited to co-op play. After being pushed near death, sit back up and kill five enemies before your friend arrives to completely revive you. Be warned: when you sit up after being gunned down, you make yourself a big target. Another bullet is all it takes to kill you for good—your friend cannot revive you if you are shot while sitting up and engaging the enemy.

REMAIN UNDETECTED

This challenge requires that you establish an LKP with an enemy. You scurry away as the enemy investigates your LKP. However, do not kill the enemy as they poke around the site of your LKP. Let them go. If you remain undetected for 10 minutes after the enemy has established and dismissed your LKP, you earn this award. Undetected does not necessarily mean just sitting in the shadows and hiding for 10 minutes, although you can do that. You can still kill targets while remaining undetected. But if you are spotted even once, the timer restarts following your next eluded LKP.

P.E.C. CHALLENGE REWARDS

Don't hoard those points earned by completing P.E.C. Challenges. Use them to upgrade weapons and gear to help Fisher in the single-player game and the spies in Co-op Story and Deniable Ops. Spend the points on new uniforms for multiplayer (and great upgrades for those new duds) as well as three upgrades for every single weapon discovered while playing both single-player and Co-op Story. Use this table to track your purchases and determine what's next on your shopping list.

WEAPON UPGRADES

WEAPON	UPGRADE 1	UPGRADE 1 COST	UPGRADE 2	UPGRADE 2 COST	UPGRADE 3	UPGRADE 3 COST
FIVE-SEVEN (silenced)	Reflex sight	400	Laser sight	250	Match grade ammo	250
USP .45	Reflex sight	400	Laser sight	250	Hollow point ammo	250
P228	Extended mag (20-round)	300	Laser sight	250	Match grade ammo	250
MK .23 (silenced)	Extended mag (24-round)	300	Laser sight	250	Hollow point ammo	250
DESERT EAGLE	Reflex sight	400	Laser sight	250	Match grade ammo	250
MP-446 (silenced)	Reflex sight	400	Laser sight	250	Match grade ammo	250
SKORPION	Gun stock	500	Reflex sight	400	Hollow point ammo	250
SR-2M	Gun stock	500	Laser sight	250	Reflex sight	400
MP-5N	Laser sight	250	Reflex sight	400	Hollow point ammo	250
UMP .45	Suppressor	650	Laser sight	250	Hollow point ammo	250
MP-5SD3 (silenced)	Gun stock	500	2x scope	300	Hollow point ammo	250
AKS-74U	Reflex sight	400	Laser sight	250	Hollow point ammo	250
SC3000	Gun stock	500	Suppressor	650	Hollow point ammo	250
G36C	2x scope	300	Laser sight	250	Match grade ammo	250
M468	Reflex sight	400	Suppressor	650	Hollow point ammo	250
AK-47	Extended mag (55-round)	300	4x scope	300	Match grade ammo	250
SCAR-H	4x scope	300	Laser sight	250	Match grade ammo	250
M-500	Laser sight	250	Reflex sight	400	Match grade ammo	250
SPAS-12 (silenced)	Gun stock	500	2x scope	300	Match grade ammo	250

UNIFORMS

UNIFORM	COST
VR Vympel	750
VR Mozdok Telecom	750
3E Black Arrow	750
3E Urban Tracker	750
Classified	750

UNIFORM UPGRADES

UPGRADE	COST
Armor	200
Ammo	200
Gadget	200

MISSION 01: MARKETPLACE

OVERVIEW

When Sam Fisher doesn't want to be found, you don't find him. Not unless your name is Anna "Grim" Grimsdottir, one of the smartest intelligence agents at Third Echelon. Using state-of-the-art eye-in-the-sky technology and a good ol' fashioned hunch, Grim tracked Fisher down in Valletta, the capital of Malta. Apparently, Fisher had picked up a whisper that somebody in the Mediterranean metropolis knew his daughter's death wasn't really an accident. It was an assassination designed to cause maximum damage to Fisher.

Grim has a waiter deliver a mobile phone and earpiece to Fisher as he observes the downtown Valletta scene from a sidewalk cafe. Fisher takes the earpiece and listens to the voice on the other end. He is not amused to hear Grim—he should be harder to find than this. But Grim tells Fisher that she's not the only person who knows his whereabouts. Armed men are en route to the cafe. Grim says she will guide him out of the cafe and through the nearby marketplace. They can talk more about why she found him later. For right now, Fisher just needs to get out of that chair and start moving before a bloodbath occurs in a civilian area.

MARKETPLACE—VALLETTA, MALTA

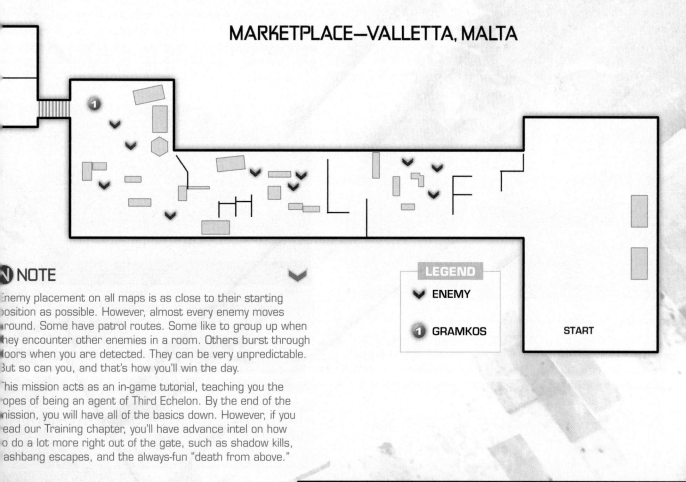

LEGEND	
⌄	ENEMY
①	GRAMKOS
	START

NOTE

Enemy placement on all maps is as close to their starting position as possible. However, almost every enemy moves around. Some have patrol routes. Some like to group up when they encounter other enemies in a room. Others burst through doors when you are detected. They can be very unpredictable. But so can you, and that's how you'll win the day.

This mission acts as an in-game tutorial, teaching you the ropes of being an agent of Third Echelon. By the end of the mission, you will have all of the basics down. However, if you read our Training chapter, you'll have advance intel on how to do a lot more right out of the gate, such as shadow kills, flashbang escapes, and the always-fun "death from above."

STRATEGY

Do not hesitate to follow Grim's directions. She will be your inner ear guide for this mission, assisting you with outmaneuvering the thugs swarming on your current position. This is a short mission, but there are plenty of opportunities to end up in the morgue. If you keep your trigger finger frosty and stick to the shadows, you'll soon have vital information about your daughter's "accidental" death.

STREET BAZAAR

Push through the crowd of panicked civilians rushing out of the booths in the alley behind the cafe. You must enter the alley and take out the armed men who spooked the crowd. Of course, walking up to them with a gun outstretched is not an option—nor is it the Third Echelon way. Grim tells you how to advance from cover to cover up the alley, quickly darting from one position to the next. Taking cover is critical for survival. You are not bulletproof. Advance along the cover opportunities until you see the first two armed thugs.

Grim does you a favor by hacking into the city's power grid and causing a surge. Transformers blow, sending a curtain of sparks into the alley. You now have the benefit of darkness, which is as lethal as the gun in your hand. However, the sudden flash of sparks sends your mind careening into a memory of Sarah's childhood.

You remember one night, when Sarah was just a little girl, she called out to you from her room. Sarah was afraid of the dark. You entered her room, turned on the lights, and calmed her down by explaining that the dark isn't as scary as she thought. After all, in the dark, you can see things moving around the shadows that you cannot when standing in the light. You also told Sarah about how the dark can give you an advantage over whatever is scaring you. For example, if a monster were standing under Sarah's mobile, you could sneakily drop it on the monster's head. Sarah was so pleased with your assurances. But then the sound of breaking glass in another room of the house shattered the spell. Sarah was about to learn that monsters were real.

You flash back to the alley in Valletta. Memories of Sarah will have to wait. The armed men are initially surprised by the sudden darkness. But that's your element. You can see the thugs but they do not see you while you are still hiding behind cover. Lean out from the cover and take aim at the men. Go for clean-kill headshots. A single bullet to the brain will take these guys down. But as you shoot, stay hidden. A third gun joins the pair just as they crumple to the ground. Give him the hard goodbye of a bullet, too.

MISSION 01: MARKETPLACE

tting a bullet
o those thugs
shes you
ck to that old
emory of Sarah.

After telling her to stay in her room, you went to investigate the noise. Burglars had entered the

use. They were disappointed with the potential haul, but one
dly said that perhaps they could still get a good score...when
ur wife came home. Before you could attack, a third burglar
mped out of the shadows and lunged for you. He had no idea
at hit him. You ripped the pistol out of his hand and carved
head like a canoe.

tincts took
er. The whole
om slowed as
u scoped out
e remaining
urglars and
arked them for
ath. Once you
ew your sights
ross them, it
s time for the
ecution. They
served nothing
s. Just like the
y who tried to
ap you, neither
these lowlifes
w you coming. Pop. Pop. One bullet apiece.

t that was also the night Sarah found out exactly what daddy
s capable of when pushed. You tried to avert her eyes from
e dead men, but it was too late. She knew. And there was no
ing that back.

Enough of that memory. You need to put it away for now. Grim can see more thugs filling the alley ahead of you. The gang leader is with them. You

can ask him why he and his men are hunting you as soon as you slice through the gang, one bullet at a time. The alley is still in shadows, so you have the advantage. Try to keep it that way as long as you can. Remember that you always have the upper hand in the dark.

T TIP

There's no better time to practice moving from cover to cover. Even if no thugs are in the alley with you right now, you can still dart from booth to booth to get a better handle on how cover works.

The next thug you encounter has his back to you. You can shoot him, but it's much better to sneak up behind him and drop him with a hand-to-hand kill. Next, mark at least two of the next batch of thugs for execution.

P.E.C. CHALLENGE

Sneaking up on this gang member and snapping his neck gives you your first Shadow Takedown. Start earning these right away so you can upgrade weapons and gear ASAP.

T TIP

Always take a hand-to-hand kill opportunity when it is presented. Having a "banked" execution can often save you in tricky situations when you find yourself terribly outnumbered. With the ability to take down at least two enemies per execution, you can "thin the herd" before moving closer to danger spots on the map.

MARKING FOR DEATH

A little farther up the alley, you discover two more thugs. You must again use your Mark and Execute ability to take them both out. Follow the on-screen prompts.

P.E.C. CHALLENGE

Can you mark for execution right now? If you mark and kill your targets five times without any complications, you score your first Mark Proficiency. You fulfill this P.E.C. Challenge every time you mark all available execution targets and then take them out with a single series of shots.

As you slink up through the stalls, Grim tells you the gang leader's name is Gramkos. He is surrounded by his men in the intersection ahead. Inch up to the table next to the intersection. One of the thugs will break from the pack to check the alley. Let him come to you. When you get the cue that he is within range (the button assigned to hand-to-hand kills pops up), strike.

Take the thug's weapon, but instead of killing him right away, draw him close to use as a human shield. Now you can execute two of the thugs and not worry about incoming fire for a few seconds.

CAUTION

Do not get too greedy with human shields. A human torso can only withstand a few basic pistol shots before it is ripped meat that bullets pass through. A human shield withstands even less abuse from an automatic weapon, like an AK-47.

Execute the two closest gang members. While holding you shield, advance into the intersection and drop the rest of th crew. Headshots make for the quickest kills.

Gramkos breaks from the shootout and ducks into the Sema Bar. As the tip painted on the side of the building say "Follow him."

Inside the bar, Gramkos locks himself in the men's room. Approach the door. It's locked. Smash through the door to se Gramkos reeling backward. He's dazed but not out. He raises his gun, but he's too slow. You snatch his pistol and eject the clip, tossing it aside. No guns. This needs to be messy. It's tim to interrogate Gramkos and find out why he and his thugs we trying to kill you.

MISSION 01: MARKETPLACE

RAMKOS'S INTERROGATION

amkos's interrogation starts out exactly as you might expect. Even though your hand is wrapped around his neck, Gramkos uses to cooperate. Drag Gramkos around the bathroom between each question. You can mash his head into a urinal or a sink, even toss him through the door to one of the stalls, freaking out a bar patron inside. Each time you rough Gramkos up, his lips sen. He was sent by Andriy Kobin to kill you. Who's Kobin? Besides being a gangster, gunrunner, and smuggler, Kobin was also ind the wheel of the car that killed Sarah.

NOTE

ach time you play the game, experiment with interrogations. ressing your quarry against different objects—or just holding em in the middle of a room—causes different actions with ach new round of questioning.

P.E.C. CHALLENGE

am Gramko into three different objects during the interrogation to omplete the Effective Interrogation challenge and earn 500 points!

KNOWN INTEL

Eluding police and the NSA after foiling the red mercury plot, Fisher dropped completely off the grid. How did Grim find Fisher all the way in Malta—and why now? Surely it is for a reason other than just missing his gruff mug around the office. Fisher also now has a lead on who killed his daughter: Andriy Kobin. However, there has to be a heavier client behind Kobin. Smugglers don't randomly take out the family members of Third Echelon agents. Fisher needs to go to Kobin's converted museum and question him to find the next person up the ladder. After all, there is always a bigger fish.

e last memory jog for Gramkos gives you a lead on Kobin. 's holed up at the old museum in Valletta, on King George eet. It's his joint now. You crush Gramkos's windpipe. body crumples to the sticky floor. If you want any more swers, you must go to the museum and beat them out of in. Maybe he'll give them up easier than Gramkos. Hopefully, ugh, he won't.

MISSION 02: KOBIN'S MANSION

OVERVIEW

Gramkos spills his guts about Andriy Kobin, the crime lord who ordered him to rub out Fisher in the street cafe. Kobin is the wheelman who ran down Fisher's daughter. He loved to boast of his kill and how it helped bring down one of Third Echelon's finest. Kobin is holed up at his mansion, a converted museum on King George Street in downtown Valletta. It's often said that anything dirty in Malta goes through Kobin's mansion at some point. Drug trafficking, arms smuggling—if it's a bloody way to earn a buck, Kobin's running it. That mansion, though, is a fortress. Armed guards patrol every floor, watching every way in and out. Nobody waltzes into Kobin's joint without an invitation or one final look down the barrel of gun. But now that Fisher has a concrete lead on who killed Sarah, all of Malta better step aside, because nothing that gets between Fisher and his revenge will be left standing tonight.

MUSEUM

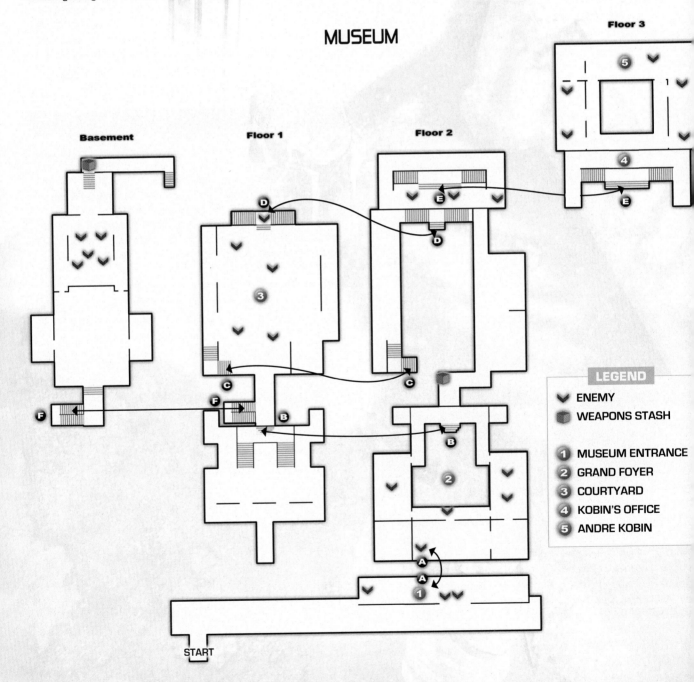

MISSION 02: KOBIN'S MANSION

STRATEGY

...iltrating Kobin's mansion will not be easy, but if you put the ...sentials learned at the marketplace into play and scan every ...om for the multitude of attack angles—steam pipes along ...e ceiling for dropping onto unsuspecting thugs, windows for ...ash-and-grab kills, shadows for creeping—you can get to ...bin's office on the third floor beyond the warehouse. Then ...u can squeeze him for information on Sarah's murder.

...ost rooms offer multiple entrance or attack options. You ...e not required to go after Kobin one way or another, nor do ...u need to be consistent. Perhaps you pop every gangster in ...e head in one room before disappearing into the shadows ...silently kill Kobin's men in the next. When using this chapter ...infiltrate the museum, look at the different routes we offer ...d consider not only your preferred play style, but how you ...n best complete those P.E.C. Challenges and earn points for ...eapon and gear upgrades.

GETTING INSIDE

...u park your SUV a safe distance from the museum so you ...n gather your wits, arm yourself, and avoid early detection. ...s you step out of the SUV, you punch the driver's side mirror ...d take the broken glass. This mirror will do as a makeshift ...ay to peek under a door and scope out the resistance until ...u can get a proper snake cam and monitor system.

Use the Peek Under command at the door leading out to King George Street. There is no immediate danger, but this is a good opportunity to see how peeking under a door works. Remember, while peeking you can mark enemies or other targets (lights, etc.) just as if you were looking right at them.

Out on the street, you see the museum along the waterfront. There is no sign of guards right away, but they are near the museum entrance. They will not bother you while you walk along the street and approach the museum. But as soon as you close in on the ad-covered fence outside the museum, you need to plot your entry into Kobin's lair.

You can nudge a car near the entrance of the museum to draw at least one of the guards out. While the guard investigates, sneak past him and close in on the museum entrance.

 **CAUTION**

Do not kill a guard in plain sight of civilians. They will cause a fuss (understandably), which brings all of the guards down on your position.

Gathering intel is always your best first step. Use the mirror to peek under the door of the museum fence along the street to spot a single guard lingering. There are two guards near the front door of the museum. As you see, the prime entrance to the museum is via one of the open

windows on the second floor. If you scramble up to a ledge on the front of the museum, you can hoist yourself inside the building.

If you want to go in shooting, creep up to the front entrance and lean out to pop the guards in the head. This causes a scene and the remaining two guards draw their weapons and shoot.

Using a car alarm near the small door presents a stealth entrance opportunity. Elbow a car close to the fence. The

closest guard steps through the door to check it out. If you duck down and wait for the guard to open up, you can surprise him with a hand-to-hand kill. Because this pushes the guard back inside the fence, no civilians react. Take the guard hostage as a human shield and then either gun down the front door guards or toss the body into the shadows and make a beeline for the drainpipe running up the face of the building.

P.E.C. CHALLENGE

Using one of the guards as a human shield during a shootout notches one for the Human Kevlar P.E.C. Challenge.

P.E.C. CHALLENGE

Climb up the pipe to the left side of the entrance to the mansion and shimmy over to the window. Pull the guard with his back to the window out to start earning your way to the first level of the Grab from Ledge challenge.

The window grants access to the building. You're in. The coast is clear in a small hallway. But you can already hear noises coming from the grand foyer beyond the hall. How will you handle the multiple threats? Guns blazing or stealth?

There are multiple targets inside the foyer and a smaller patrol in the back of the L-shaped hallway that surrounds the second floor of the foyer. Slip through the window at the corner of the building and slink around the ledge to the right. You spot a handful of unwitting thugs inside. Save for the henchman standing near the window next to the drainpipe, none of the thugs in the L-shaped hallway surrounding are close enough to yank out of the window—although you can fix that by taking a shot and then darting away, using the Last Known Position (LKP) technique.

⊤ TIP

Turn the lights off in the hallway to obscure your position. Always look for light switches on the walls before shooting out lights.

MISSION 02: KOBIN'S MANSION

ou want to take these guys out in a forward assault, kick down the door leading to the back of the L-shaped hallway. The smashed or surprises them. They hesitate. Draw your weapon and peg the closest guard. Now you have their attention. You can use the or as a funnel to lead the guards toward you, but this leaves your flank exposed. The shots raise an alarm and thugs will stream t of the foyer to attack from behind. After dropping that first guard, though, you can run and bail through a window. (Choose already open window. If you break through glass, you give the guards a noise to follow.) Shoot them from open windows or get hind them and take one hostage.

These guards are armed with ubmachine guns. Their bullets rip through human hields, so do not unt on protection for very long.

making a bunch of noise and alerting the guards in the foyer, too. Instead, stick to the shadows by turning off the hall lights and snatching a guard just inside the foyer. Use your mirror to spot one alone and then slink up and take him into a close kill. Pull the guard out of the foyer and dump his body in a shadowy corner so nobody finds him. You can now execute at least two enemies.

CAUTION

The problem with a guns blazing assault on the museum is that several thugs in the foyer rush into the hall if you raise the alarm by knocking off a guard in plain sight. Once you start this assault, it is very difficult to slow it down. You have to do something drastic, such as leave the building without being spotted and lay low for a few minutes until the heat subsides.

Now, the guard closest to the door you can peek under to monitor the first group occasionally pops out into the main hall to patrol the area. If he finds

nothing, he returns after just a moment. But if you leave the door to the foyer open, you've set a trap—as long as you are ready to spring it. Get into a crouch next to the door and take the patrolling guard hostage. Dump his body in the corner so another strolling guard can't spot the corpse and sound the alarm.

you choose to ke the museum stealth, you ed to peel off e guards one one without tracting y unwanted tention. The ards in the shaped hallway ways start nverged in the ck half of the ea. Shooting e through e window is t stealthy. The others see the dead guard and go berserk,

TIP

Open doors are a great way to trap an enemy. If a door should be shut, seeing it open draws the enemy near. Hide out of sight and when the enemy goes to close the door, lunge and pull them into a close, silent kill.

GRAND FOYER

The museum foyer represents your first major battle. If you entered the museum by dropping several guards in plain sight, the foyer is now half empty and guards are swarming the halls looking for you. You need to either escape the scene and let them return to their normal patrols or nimbly pull them into bad situations and drop them one by one as they attack. Luring them to the windows or into an ambush (taking cover at a wall or behind an art display in the hall), helps you cull their numbers.

Because no windows look into the foyer, stealth players need to stick to the pipes that run above the foyer to take the room by total surprise. Use the pipes to survey the foyer and note the positions and patrol routes of the guards. They walk along the upper floor and the main floor, waving their flashlights around in hopes of spotting an intruder. As long as you stay up on the pipes along the ceiling (there are two of them, too), they will not spot you—until you take a shot. That's when the thugs start looking up.

You can also attempt to slink along the floor, taking refuge behind railings and shooting out lights to create shadows. Popping lights does attract attention, but that attention can be converted into a kill if you seek cover and the guard inspecting the "broken" light fixture gets curious enough to walk past your position.

 NOTE

Want to start the foyer off with a bang? Shoot the golden chandelier when a guard crosses beneath it. The chandelier crushes him.

Death from Above is always tempting. If you use it, you risk being spotted by other guards, though. Make sure your target is alone and in front of a door that you can quickly escape through. The thugs will circle around to the bo to take a peek. If you can wait on the other side of a door and hop out a window and watch the guards, you can actually take out a second or third as they peer down at the body.

P.E.C. CHALLENGE

The foyer is a great location for notching at least two Death from Above kills by hanging from the pipes.

The best reason to take out a guard with a hand-to-hand kill when you first enter the museum? You can execute guards while on their patrols. Whether you do it from the pipes above or while hiding in a corner, executing two of the guards helps clean out the room. However, be mindful of where your targets are in relation to lights. If you execute a guard while he stands in a pool of light, that's where the body lies and it will be spotted.

MISSION 02: KOBIN'S MANSION

Of course, leaving a body in the light can also be used to your advantage. Hide while a guard is checking out a body and then grab him, too. Now you can execute again. Scurry back up a pipe and drop two more guards from the shadows.

After emptying the foyer, slip through the corridor on the room's main door. Stop in at the weapons stash to change your weapon loadout, and upgrade your gear.

ⓃNOTE

This is the first mission with a weapons stash, so you can spend P.E.C. Challenge points on upgraded clips, bullet damage, and more.

COURTYARD

Upon entering the courtyard, you discover that you are behind bulletproof glass. The lounge on the landing overlooking the courtyard is empty, but still full of light. Shoot out some of the lights so you can pass through the bar overlooking the courtyard without being spotted. The only way into the courtyard is via a steam pipe that runs up the wall on the far end of the bar and passes over a set of locked doors. (You cannot unlock these doors.)

The steam pipe does not extend very far into the courtyard and there is no way to shimmy down. You must drop off the pipe to access the courtyard. Several guards are in the courtyard, all armed to the teeth. One is directly below the pipe. Before performing a Death from Above, though, you should distract the other guards to take their attention away from the guard below you. What better way to do this than staging an "accident" with that giant sculpture hanging from the ceiling of the courtyard?

Shoot the chain holding up the sculpture to drop it on the guards and kill at least one of them. Every guard in the room is now focused on the fallen sculpture.

While everybody is looking away, you can either shoot a guard from the pipe or drop down on the one still standing beneath you. This kill may get their attention, but you have time to move back into the shadows before the guards notice your LKP.

The stairs beneath the pipe are an excellent chokepoint. The guards will come in to inspect the body and your LKP.

You can either use execute to take them out as they approach or wait in the shadows and grab one as

he comes near. Ripping the thugs out of the light and into the shadows creates a new LKP, but you can use this as a trap to keep luring them into your line of fire.

If you want to take these guards head-on, use a human shield whenever possible to absorb bullets as you go on the attack.

If you prefer stealth and the scene gets too hot, dive through a window on the landing opposite the lounge and wait until the guards lose their edge.

Most of the guards remain on the main floor of the courtyard. If you keep their eyes trained on the steps under the pipe via your LKP, you can pick them off by slipping along the landing on the left side of the room (if you are facing the hanging sculpture) and dropping down behind them. Flanking an enemy focused on another target, such as your LKP, is a key tactic to minimizing your exposure—and maximizing your lethality.

The last courtyard guard is in the narrow corridor on the room's far side. His corridor is lit by both a small chandelier and a floodlight. Shooting out both lights casts the corridor in darkness, allowing you to advance to the crates in the hall without being spotted. It's much easier to drop the guard halfway down the hallway with a headshot.

RECEPTION ROOM

As you exit through the rear of the storage area, stop at the weapons stash to change out gear or upgrade and look for three EMP Grenades on a crate along the left wall. These EMP grenades temporarily disable the lights (as long as they are electrical—later you will encounter enemies smart enough to set up chemical lights unaffected by EMP blasts) as well as stun any enemy near the grenade when it gives off its pulse. These EMP grenades are a huge help when cornering Kobin in the next area. With so much light in the room and several guards willing to take a bullet for their boss, the EMP blasts tilt the odds back in your favor.

The "guns blazing" approach requires you to grab one of the thugs for a human shield. You face too many guns to attack without the protection. Hiding at the bar or behind a pillar allows you to sneak up and snatch one of the guards. Then you can execute two of the remaining thugs as well as target them individually while holding your hostage.

MISSION 02: KOBIN'S MANSION

P.E.C. CHALLENGE

Fulfill the Cat and Mouse requirements by getting spotted in the light and then absconding to the shadows to take out a handful of guards via the pipes or by luring a single guard into a LKP.

The pipes give you a clean look at the entire reception room and the loading area in the rear. Scramble up to the pipes (via the left side of the room) and watch the guards filter out into the reception room. They will not look up unless you take a shot at one of them. Equip EMP grenades so you can use them as distractions for when you do start the attack. Taking shots (with a silenced weapon) will draw their attention, but if you keep one step ahead of your LKP, you can play cat and mouse with the thugs.

P.E.C. CHALLENGE

Use the drainpipes along the ceiling to target henchmen from the shadows and earn Stealth Headshots.

N NOTE

You do not need to eliminate every thug in the reception room. If you shoot out enough lights to create a trail of shadow through the room, you can slip by the majority of the guards undetected (use hand-to-hand kills on any that surprise you) and escape through the rear exit.

If you have created darkness by shooting out lights, purposefully get spotted on the pipes by shooting a thug or dropping a grenade. The guards will look up at your LKP. You can then pop them from the safety of the shadows either elsewhere on the pipes or from the floor if you drop down out of sight.

Two guards remain in the small room at the very back of the loading area. You can plug them both from just outside, however you may wish to rush in and attack with a close kill so you earn an execution. Having an execution at the ready when you enter the next area is exceedingly useful.

The stairs leading up from the small room take you back outside. To re-enter the museum and continue your pursuit of Kobin, use the drainpipe to shimmy up to a window looking in on the second floor. Three guards are around the stairs. One has his back to the window. Yank him

out of the window for a silent kill. Then, if you have an execution ready, you can easily drop the remaining guards at the stairs. Otherwise an EMP gives you the cover you need to slip inside and take them down with gunfire.

P.E.C. CHALLENGE

Yanking a guard through a window awards the Deadly Fall award.

After eliminating the guards, climb the steps. Kobin is just beyond the double-doors on the landing. However, so are his best-trained guards. You can try to go in guns blazing, but you will not get very far. Instead, use a window to climb out on a ledge and slide under the windows that look into Kobin's office. You can still launch a forward assault from here, but at least you won't be cut down by a storm of bullets. The ledge is also the ideal place to stealthily take out Kobin's men before going for the big score, Kobin himself.

KOBIN'S OFFICE

Kobin's office is well lighted with a host of ceiling fixtures, illuminated wall panels, and lamps. An EMP grenade will knock out the lights temporarily. You can also attempt to shoot them out, but remember that every shot-out light draws attention—especially if you blast one of the huge light panels from the windows. Now, drawing attention to the windows is not a bad thing—particularly if you want to take on Kobin's guards in a direct manner.

Shoot lights from each window going down the side of the building. Each popped light raises tensions in the room. By the time you reach the end of the line, several guards are at the windows, looking around. Either sneak into the office via the last window or snatch one of the guards and use him as a shield as you pull yourself into the building. Now you can target the guards looking out of the building via executions or direct fire, preferably right to the face for single-shot kills.

Alternately, you can creep into the office via an open window and use EMP grenades to put out light panels and target the guards in the dark.

After taking out the guards, all that is left in the office is Kobin. Kobin is armed with a machine gun and he has a flashlight for spotting you in the shadows. You must sneak up on him or else expect a face full of lead. An EMP grenade tossed into his office puts out the flashlight and makes Kobin recoil. Use this moment to sneak into the office and get closer to Kobin. Hide behind a chair or bar to avoid detection. Crazed, Kobin spins around looking for you. When his back is turned, rush him and initiate a hand-to-hand kill. This doesn't neutralize Kobin, though. It begins his interrogation.

MISSION 02: KOBIN'S MANSION

...errogate Kobin ...st as you did ...amkos. As you ...k Kobin about ...ur daughter, ...ove around the ...ice. Smash ...obin into the ...ano. The window. ...e bar. Each ...ne you bounce ...obin's head ...f one of these ...jects, he spills a ...le more about ...hy he killed your ...ughter. At first ...e claims he didn't mean anything he said about killing her, but ...ter interrogating him twice, you pick him up from the floor ...d he confesses, saying "they" told him to do it. Kobin cannot ...aborate on "they" much more, saying only that the party is ...gger than you, him, Third Echelon—it's a massive conspiracy. ...d somehow killing your daughter factored into it.

...efore you can get any more information out of Kobin, Third ...chelon agents storm the museum. Crashing through the ...ylights, the agents quickly fan across the room and surround ...u. Grim comes over the earpiece. She needs you to go with ...e agents—she asks for your trust. You reluctantly give it to ...r. A tranquilizer dart—and a boot from Kobin—put you on ...e floor.

KNOWN INTEL

...Fisher now knows that Kobin killed his daughter, but he was acting on orders ...from somebody else or another organization. That puts a new angle into play. ...Why would the death of Fisher's daughter actually matter? Why kill Sarah Fisher? ...And to what end? How does enraging a killing machine like Fisher advance any ...goal—especially a sinister one? Fisher was unable to kill Kobin in revenge, too. ...Grim managed to stop him just in time, which means she overheard enough of ...the conversation to know when to stop it. Fisher is now like a worm on a hook. ...He's bitten down on something and cannot let go. When he wakes up, Grim better ...have a good explanation for why Fisher was supposed to not kill Kobin and allow ...himself to be captured by Third Echelon agents.

MISSION 03: PRICE AIRFIELD

OVERVIEW

Grim told Fisher to allow the agents from Third Echelon to take him at the museum in Malta. But the next thing Fisher knows, he's waking up in restraints on a gurney. His vision is fuzzy as the effects of the tranquilizers wear off and Fisher can see vague outlines of familiar shapes. Men pushing the gurney. The back of an airplane cargo hold opening. The control tower of an airport. A giant hangar. Fisher is definitely no longer in Malta—and he is an unwelcome guest.

While unable to really get a visual on his surroundings, Fisher eavesdrops on his captors. He hears familiar names. Both Kobin and Tom Reed, the acting head of Third Echelon, are mentioned— but in the third-person. How were these two in league with each other? And where are they taking Fisher? If Grim is with these hired guns, she better have some answers.

MISSION 03: PRICE AIRFIELD

PRICE AIRFIELD

EXIT

LEGEND

ᗐ ENEMY

◈ WEAPONS STASH

① C4 STOCKPILE
② HELICOPTER (C4 TARGET)
③ POWER RELAY
④ SATELLITE DISH (C4 TARGET)
⑤ SECURITY CHECKPOINT

START

STRATEGY

The airfield is evenly divided between interiors that you can tackle with stealth and exteriors that require deft maneuvering to avoid detection because attacks could then come from any number of angles. The entire airfield is guarded by armed men, so you must consider every single human being a potential threat—and a definite target.

GRIM INTERROGATION

When you finally come to, you're in a small room on the airfield still strapped to the gurney. Grim is in the room, too, working on a laptop computer. She seems to be purposefully avoiding eye contact. Tom Reed is standing over you, looking at his prize. Certain that you are tied down and not a threat, he turns away from you and addresses two armed men. They are members of some sort of paramilitary force, definitely not American military. They discuss an operation moving into its final phases.

Reed then thanks Grim for wrapping you up nice and tidy in Malta. But now it's time for the dirty stuff. Reed orders Grim to interrogate you by any means necessary to find out what you know about some EMPs. Reed assumes that's why you were after Kobin. This makes no sense. You weren't in Malta looking for weapons—you were looking for your daughter's killer. Something doesn't add up. After Reed and his two cohorts leave, the remaining paramilitary thug approaches you with a syringe and a menacing grin. Grim puts a bullet in his back.

Grim tells you she is working as a mole inside Third Echelon on special request from the president. She says that Reed is the new director of Third Echelon

(replacing Lambert, whom you had to put a bullet in before disappearing underground) and he is working with the private military contractor (PMC) Black Arrow to acquire Russian EMP technology. That's what was being run through Malta. She releases you from the gurney. But should you trust her?

Grim explains that an investigation into Third Echelon has been launched, but Reed is stonewalling the president's efforts. He's backed by

a strong power base somewhere in Washington—somebody who can put a stop to a special investigation authorized by the president. Because she is working inside Third Echelon, she cannot do anything that would jeopardize her cover. However, you can help get to the bottom of Reed's scheme. But to get out of the airfield and maintain Grim's cover, you need to do something horrible—you need to strike her so it looks like you overpowered her and escaped.

Grim cannot convince you to hit her, so she goes below the belt and brings up Sarah. That starts the interrogation.

Grim confirms that Sarah is alive. She says if you help her, you get to see her again. If not, well, that's out of her hands.

Unfortunately, you do what you must do. With a bloodied nose and a fat lip, Grim's cover will be maintained.

MISSION 03: PRICE AIRFIELD

im hands over the keys to a car parked outside the irfield. She stripped the GPS from it so it will not show up on

hird Echelon
omputers. There
e weapons
the trunk.
owever, you
eed one now.
rim gives you
er silenced pistol.
im's last words

advice are to get some C4 just outside the hangar and use to cause enough damage to the airfield that the Black Arrow ugs cannot immediately follow you. Once you have the C4, im will tell you the best places to use it on the airfield.

GET THE C4

ove through the darkness in the hangar beyond the terrogation room. Only a handful of Black Arrow guards are nsite, but all of them are outside the hangar. You only need slow up once you are about to step outside. Two PMCs and guard over a small stack of C4. A third patrols the area etween the hangar and a machine shop nearby.

Wait for the patrolling PMC to walk by and turn his back. Then ump out and take him down with a hand-to-hand kill. Either use im as a human shield to take out the other guards or dispose of his body in the shadows.

Though the kill
gives you an
execution, hold
on to it for now.
You can put that
execution to
better use in the
machine shop
after obtaining the

C4. Instead, shoot the two guards in the head from a distance. They are completely unaware of your presence, so you have a moment after the first kill to take down the other PMC. Once the two guards are on their backs, pick up the C4 and await further instructions from Grim.

P.E.C. CHALLENGE

Hide behind the forklift and shoot the PMC thugs through the cab to pick up a Stealth Headshot. Using Mark and Exceute on batches of guards also adds to your Mark Proficiency count.

MACHINE SHOP

After you pick up
the C4, Grim tells
you that you need
to place a charge
on a chopper
inside the machine
shop. Even though
she has disabled
the GPS, Black

Arrow can still follow the car. You need to destroy the chopper. There are three ways to enter the machine shop. There is a door at the top of some metal stairs. Windows flank the door—both are open and can be accessed by running up the walls and grabbing light fixtures or pipes.

The snake cam reveals a guard on the landing just inside the door. Since his back is to the door, quietly open the door, grab him like a human shield, pull him back through the door, and finish him off outside where no one will see the body.

TOM CLANCY'S
SPLINTER CELL
CONVICTION

CAUTION

Don't linger outside the door. The guard sometimes opens it to peek outside. if you are standing right there, every single PMC thug in the shop goes on high alert.

Another guard stands right in front of the window to the left of the door. If you execute him, his body slumps down behind the metal panel along the railing and is obscured from view.

Creeping through the window to the right puts you in the path of the patrolling guard. Wait for him. When he gets close to the corner next to the  window, pull him close and snap his neck. This drops his body in the dark corner where it will not be easily spotted. Watch out for a second guard who occasionally walks up to these catwalks from the bottom floor. If you spot him coming up, hide and wait for him to close in. Then step out and silently kill him.

A pipe near the right window connects to a network of pipes running along the ceiling. It also offers a Death from Above attack on the PMC just below.

CAUTION

Move slowly along the catwalk. if you run, your footsteps attract attention from the guards. They will investigate.

If you would rather take the room by force, just know that in addition to the duo of guards on the catwalks, four more are on the ground floor. Two of the PMC guards are standing next to the chopper and will hear any alarm raised by the other guards. Even the two guys painting the  chopper with some special anti-EMP coating will pick up guns to attack. Move across the ground floor, using cover to launch attacks on the PMCs.

If you grab a hostage on the bottom floor, dispose of the body inside one of the elevator cars below the catwalk so the body is not found right away, thus raising the alarm.

P.E.C. CHALLENGE

Drag a hostage to one of the elevator cars and then finish him off to earn a Shadow Takedown.

MISSION 03: PRICE AIRFIELD

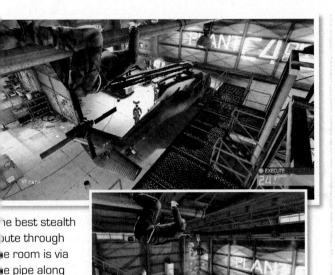

There's a weapons stash just outside the machine shop, through the door marked with your next objective.

he best stealth ute through e room is via e pipe along e ceiling. From is position, u can pull off

ree shots that kill four PMCs. If you still have an execution, ark the two painters. Execute the painters; none of the nearby MCs in the shop spot your position right away, but you need act fast to keep it that way. Now, see that jet engine hanging ove the chopper? The two PMC guards are standing directly elow it. Shoot the pulley holding it up. The engine crashes onto e guards. They will be busy inspecting the dropped engine.

Have good aim? Pop the guards as they inspect the engine wreckage while still hanging from the pipe.

fter eliminating l of the Black rrow thugs from e shop, plant the rst C4 charge n the side of the hopper. You then ecide to move n the airfield's

ectrical grid. If you disable it, the PMCs will have a hard me coordinating an attack. Grim advises you that the most lnerable spot, the power relay, is inside one of the barracks. t to reach the barracks, you need to cross part of the rfield, and several guards patrol between here and there.

Flashbangs not only cause guards to avert their eyes, but they also create distractions. Targets are temporarily blinded while they investigate the source of the flash. If you move during that period of disorientation, you can effectively vanish.

BARRACKS

The barracks are not far from the machine shop. When you exit the machine shop, walk toward the wooden pallets stacked up outside, pausing to stock up at the

weapons stash. A series of small garages and barracks line each side of a small strip of road. The power relay is inside the last barracks on the right side of the road. As you creep up on the pallets, look for one guard under a lamp on the right side of the street. Although he's far away, he has a good view of the entire area. Stay out of his line of sight unless you are going for an assault plan rather than stealth.

Shooting out the light over the guard gets the attention of everybody inside the barracks. The door opens and everybody files out to investigate. This gets the attention

of the guards in the structure across the street, which is right next to the pallets. If you have an execution ready, mark two of the PMCs in the street and then tag them both to start the assault. Fall back and use the cover behind the barracks to funnel the guards into your sights.

Use LKP to draw the guards into the small spaces behind the barracks or among the pallets. From back here, you can leap through windows and use them as cover to shoot the Black Arrows thugs when they investigate and mow down the troopers as they weave through the tight spaces.

 TIP

Frag grenades do extra damage in tighter spaces. If you lure two or three guards into one of the alleys behind or between the barracks, roll a frag at their feet to take everybody down. There are frags in the first barracks. Once you use them up you can always retreat to the weapons stash to refill your supply.

Purposefully use a louder weapon to create a LKP in a spot you can easily cover, such as the last barracks on the left. When the LKP is investigated, you're ready with your gun to mop up the merc.

P.E.C. CHALLENGE

Hiding close to a LKP behind one of the barracks and then killing the approaching enemy earns you the Last Known Position award.

 TIP

If at any time the shootout gets too hairy, drop an EMP grenade to douse the lights. Melt into the shadows to fall back and regroup.

If you want to reach the power relay in a stealthier manner, avoid the road that goes between the two sets of barracks at first. Stick to the fence and slink behind the pallets to completely avoid the PMCs on the street. Pick off the rest of the guards in the barracks farther up the road before dealing with the first merc and the other Black Arrow inside his barracks. Start by taking out the two guards inside the first barracks on the left from the window with a silenced weapon.

Next, sneak up behind the guards patrolling the barracks. Wait for them to go on a walk and then spring out to grab them. Pull them close and then dispose of the bodies behind the barracks so nobody is the wiser.

You need to get rid of that first merc under the lamp without alerting the guards inside the barracks behind him. You should have an execution ready if you killed a patrolling merc behind the barracks with a stealth kill.

MISSION 03: PRICE AIRFIELD

Once you clean out the barracks, enter and throw the relay. When the power goes off, you automatically rip the switch out of the box so the mercs cannot easily get the grid back up. Grim comes back over the air. She tells you that she's discovered a satellite dish on the base that is linked to a private spy drone. You need to plant some of that C4 on the dish so Black Arrow cannot use the satellite to track the car when you speed away from the base. The catch (and there always is one) is that the dish is on the other side of several hangars and the area is heavily guarded.

Move behind the barracks. Open fire on the mercs. They may try to escape through the front door, but they will be back to take you down. Either wait for them to come back through the door and shoot them as they seek you out or jump out a window and circle around the barracks to eliminate them from behind without them even seeing you.

Three guards are stationed inside the barracks with the power relay. They hold their ground if they hear an attack outside, so you can always count on them to protect the relay. Should you still have an execution, you can pop them from the window. Dropping an EMP inside the room distracts all of them for a second, giving you a chance to take at least two of them out before they recover from the blast.

There is a weapons stash just beyond the gate opened by trashing the power relay. Use it to upgrade your gear and replenish spent supplies, such as frags and EMP grenades.

HANGARS

To reach the dish, you need to cross through a series of hangars. When you leave the barracks, the path directs you to two structures with canvas tarps. As you pass the first structure, look inside and pick off the merc standing watch over the trucks. Then, slip through the tarp on the

next structure. Slink up to the guard patrolling the area (he is typically just under the wing of a fighter jet) and take him down with a stealth kill. Now you have an execution ready, which is useful whether you storm the hangars by force or attempt to infiltrate via stealth.

If you cannot eliminate all three PMCs in the room with an execution or silent headshots, establish an LKP at the window and then creep around to the side door. Quietly open the door to eliminate the guard while he is trained on your LKP.

TOM CLANCY'S SPLINTER CELL CONVICTION

Shooting out lights to create shadows is always a solid strategy when dealing with multiple guards. From the dark, you can then safely lean out and score headshots on PMCs, such as the pair moving around the airplane in the hangar with the open canvas flap. Also, use the pipes

in the ceiling of the first hangar to attack the thugs from above. Eliminate any in the hangar with silent headshots or Death from Above. There are several guards outside the hangar, though. Shooting the ground near those guards gets their attention and leads them closer to the hangar. Once within range, take aim and go for stealth headshots to eliminate the batch.

◀◀◀◀ Ⓒ CAUTION

Do not use non-silenced weapons for this trick. The hard "br-r-r-ap" of an SMG clip draws the PMCs' eyes right to the ceiling, whereas the source of bullets from a silenced pistol are much harder to track.

Ⓣ TIP

Alternately, you can shoot the pulley holding up the giant container above the mercs' heads. It drops on the patrol, killing all three. As other guards investigate the "accident," you can use LKP to draw them to the gas canister.

P.E.C. CHALLENGE

Roll an EMP grenade into the trio of PMC guards to earn the EMP Grenade Stun award.

Reload your pistol before taking on the guards at the hangars. If you kill 10 of them (and there are more than 10 guards in this area) without reloading, you nab the Pistol Marksman award.

Opting for a stealth run through the hangars? Use the series of smaller tents to the right of the jet plane to poke out and fire on the guards.

Ducking from one tent to the next keeps you out of sight. Use EMP grenades to put out the lights if the mercs get too close. With the area so open and

mercs able to hear and see each other, using hand-to-hand kills is the best way to go undetected for the majority of the passage. However, killing guards with a silenced weapon but leaving their bodies in a pool of light does create a trap. When a guard investigates, slip out of the shadows and grab him.

The satellite dishes are easy to spot next to the hangars. After dropping the guards, approach the dishes and plant the C4 on the marked location. Grim confirms the proper location of the C4 and then tells you that you need to take out the airfield's security system so you can finally leave. However, as soon as you start walking back across the hangars, all lights in the base flash on and an alarm is sounded. Your escape is broadcast.

A large Black Arrow patrol moves straight down the middle o the hangars and then spreads out. Use an execution to pop a few of the mercs before they fan into the hangars to search for you.

Prima Official Game Guide   58 ⟫⟫⟫

MISSION 03: PRICE AIRFIELD

here are just o many PMCs make a decent ontal assault nd not be cut own. You need employ some ealth tactics. n EMP grenade temporarily sable the ini-Vegas light now is a good st step to gaining the dvantage. Using KP to draw a uard into a bad position (so you can pull them into a human hield) is another strong move. Each execution you earn is asily translated into two more kills.

Do the mercs have you made in one of the hangars? Blast the ights so they cannot see you and then slip through one of the side flaps.

he ceiling pipes the first hangar re an excellent intage point r dealing with e horde. Rush ross the street nd dive into e shadows. Then, make your way up the pipe and use the ame tactic of luring PMCs into the hangar with the noise of unshots bouncing off the walls or striking the ground.

(T) TIP

Remember, the music is a great way to tell if any enemies are left. Once the thumping music subsides, you know you've taken down the last threat...in that specific area.

SECURITY CHECKPOINT

As you approach the checkpoint to disable the airfield's security system, Grim comes over the air. She says she needs to push back the call with your daughter. That doesn't sit well with you. At all. But there's no time to argue; a PMC patrol is heading up the street leading away from the base entrance and they are all aware you are in the vicinity. Take cover behind the truck or planter and immediately start creating shadows by shooting out lights. The darker you make the scene, the greater your chances of survival.

The two trucks at the bend in the street are great cover. Use them to mount your early attacks on the patrol. If you have created enough shadow, you can score silent headshots on the milling guards. If you have an execution ready, peek around the corner and look at the checkpoint. Mark the first three guards you see and take the shot.

Establish LKP at one of the two trucks to lure a guard close. Watch the flashlight beams to tell when the PMC is right at the corner of the truck and then lunge out for the hand-to-hand kill. Use the guard as a human shield and either go for headshots or try another Mark and Execute. Move fast because the Black Arrow thugs have no loyalty to their comrades. They will shoot through the human shield within five to ten seconds (with complete exposure).

Use the route on the right side of the road, behind the half wall, to minimize your exposure and get the best view of the road. Plus, from this angle, you can see inside the security shack at the gate, which also houses at least two Black Arrow guards.

Once inside the shack, turn off the alarms. This raises the ground pillars so you can escape the airfield via the door in the chain link fence outside the checkpoint and take off in Grim's unmarked car without being followed by other vehicles. The drive gives you plenty of time to mull over old memories and see if you can dredge anything out of your past to help explain what is happening with Reed, Third Echelon, and this EMP technology that seems to be at the center of the madness.

⌖ KNOWN INTEL

So, even though it looked like Grim betrayed Fisher in Malta, it turns out she's actually on his side—to a degree. She has been withholding information about Sarah for a very long time and is now using it to get Fisher to help her stave off some sort of plot involving EMP tech and Third Echelon. Though Fisher feels no loyalty to Third Echelon, he is compelled to help Grim if it means finally seeing his little girl again.

As Fisher escapes the airfield, more questions arise as others are answered. Who is helping stop the investigation into Third Echelon? Is Reed at the top of this plot? Is this plot somehow connected to the investigation? And where did Kobin go after he was rescued in Malta?

MISSION 04: DIWANIYA, IRAQ

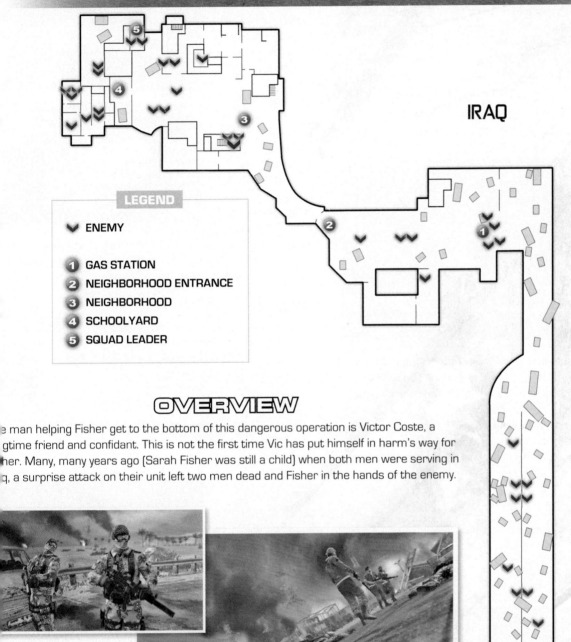

IRAQ

LEGEND

∨ ENEMY

① GAS STATION
② NEIGHBORHOOD ENTRANCE
③ NEIGHBORHOOD
④ SCHOOLYARD
⑤ SQUAD LEADER

OVERVIEW

e man helping Fisher get to the bottom of this dangerous operation is Victor Coste, a
gtime friend and confidant. This is not the first time Vic has put himself in harm's way for
her. Many, many years ago (Sarah Fisher was still a child) when both men were serving in
q, a surprise attack on their unit left two men dead and Fisher in the hands of the enemy.

risked life and limb to fight through enemy resistance and locate Fisher. Using only his
s and the weapon slung over his shoulder, Vic took down dozens of enemy combatants to
scue Fisher from a vicious interrogation. Together, the two then withstood one last push
the enemy until reinforcements could arrive and escort them out of the hot zone.

START

STRATEGY

Because Vic is rescuing Fisher in this mission, you do not have access to most of Fisher's moves and talents. As such, this is not a stealth mission at all. Not that you should just stand and shoot, but there are no executions, no use of stealth-related gear such as EMP grenades or flashbangs. Instead, this mission is about fighting your way from point A on the bombed-out roadside to point B, the school where the nationals are holding Fisher hostage.

THE ROAD

Watching them take Fisher away was not easy, but if you tried to play hero in the attack, you would have ended up as dead as the other two men in your squad. When the coast is clear, though, you stand up, recover your weapon, and survey the scene. Command comes over the radio. They have registered the attack and list Fisher as Killed in Action (KIA). Command tells you to hold your position until evacuation. Naturally, you ignore that order.

Ⓝ NOTE

Vic is armed with a handful of frag grenades and an AK-47. That weapon is not silenced, so any shot you take will potentially alert the enemy to your presence. Pick your targets wisely to minimize attention.

Advance up the street, using the shelled cars and twisted wreckage as cover. There are no enemies in your immediate vicinity, but just walking down the street is ill-advised.

The first enemies you encounter are a pair of soldiers talking next to a burnt-out car. Take cover at the concrete barrier that divides the street and peer through your scope. The soldiers are standing close enough together that you can drop one with a headshot and quickly pivot to the other before he escapes and can dig in to a covered position. Move fast because the first shot you take with that AK eliminates the element of surprise.

Ⓝ NOTE

Though your AK-47 is loud enough to alert nearby enemies, there is enough noise on this road that your shots will not raise the suspicion of patrols farther up the scene.

P.E.C. CHALLENGE

Because this mission does not use Fisher, there are no P.E.C. Challenges.

The next soldier is inspecting the wreckage of a transport. Slow down when you near a burned out van on the right side of the highway and look down your scope at the new target. Although you can only see one soldier, be assured that more are nearby. Several more, in fact. As soon as you take that first shot, the other soldiers start moving toward your van. Make that first shot count and then backtrack to the rear of the van and look to the left. The other soldiers are moving up between the cars. The red car in the middle of the highway is as far as you should let them go. Raise your scope and bring them down quickly before they realize you've moved to the other side of the van.

MISSION 04: DIWANIYA, IRAQ

GAS STATION

Bombs have rendered the highway unusable. Between vehicle wreckage and bomb craters, any soldiers have to detour to the left. This smaller road winds past a gas station and into a neighborhood. Several soldiers are holding a checkpoint at the gas station near the end of the usable highway. They have not heard the shooting on the highway, so unless you strut up toward the checkpoint, cavalierly firing into the gas station, they will not see you coming. Keep low and advance from cover to cover until you reach the covered truck parked in front of the checkpoint.

...ntinue moving ...until you see ...e red car in ...e middle of the ...hway near the ...nt blue signs. ...small patrol is ...oving through ...re. Take cover ...d wait for your targets to be facing away from from you ...fore shooting. Take your easiest shot to start the assault—or ...ve up as close as you can get and roll a frag into the group. ...you get your drop just right, you can eliminate the entire ...trol with a single frag.) As soon as the group is alerted to ...ur presence, dive into new cover and start picking off the ...ops as they move up the highway. The truck is an excellent ...aging point.

You have multiple options at the checkpoint. You can go in, guns blazing, near the gate. The soldiers will be caught off guard and you should be able to drop at least two of them before they dig in behind the concrete blocks.

What the AK ...cks in subtlety, ...it makes up in ...wer. Just two or ...ree shots to the ...est is all it takes ...o drop a target.

...rtunately, the ...low bus and ...er wrecked ...s block most ...the highway ...d the soldiers ...e funneled ...ough a narrow ...ace if they try ...make an aggressive move on you. Mow them down as they ...empt to move down the highway toward you. While you ...y lack Fisher's hand-to-hand skills, you can still do quite a bit ...damage. If you let an enemy come to you and react quick ...ough, they cannot even raise their rifle. Do not move any ...ther up this stretch of highway until you have eliminated the ...tire group of soldiers.

That huge gas tanker makes an appealing target, too. Look for soldiers to walk next to it. Reload and then shoot the tanker until it explodes, killing the nearby soldiers. The explosion distracts the troops at the actual checkpoint. They turn away from you as they inspect the fire. Big mistake. Cut them down when they look away.

As the fire rages, move toward the garage next to the gas station. It makes excellent cover for taking out the incoming patrol coming toward the checkpoint from the opposite direction of the highway.

As you near the gas station structure, be on the lookout for at least one shooter just inside the eastern door.

Use the windows of the garage to pick off the enemy soldiers in the street.

You may not have the stealth tactics and gear Fisher uses to kill enemies from the shadows, but you can still use basic LKP techniques to flank these soldiers. Your enemies here are smart enough to seek cover when they need to reload. Fire on them from one position and then duck down when they shoot back. Then, when they drop

down to reload, move to the left or right and crouch behind an obstacle. The enemy cannot see through concrete and will not notice you have moved. When they stand up to shoot again, they are aiming at a ghost. You, however, are about to turn them into one. The final soldier in the gas station attacks from behind the barriers, but is sitting next to a fuel drum. Pop the drum to neutralize the guard and move up to the next area.

After emptying the checkpoint, continue down the road unt you reach a blue gate. The neighborhood where the enemy holding Fisher is just beyond the gates.

NEIGHBORHOOD

The neighborhood has been severely damaged by bombing raids and firefights. The buildings that remain standing have holes in the walls large

enough to drive a Humvee through. However, this is to your advantage because you can see the troop patrols coalescing in the structures. You must also be mindful of snipers on the rooftops. When you first enter the neighborhood, there is on sniper on the building directly ahead of you. Stay crouched an advance along cover to prevent him from spotting you.

Advance to the right so you can peer inside the closest buildi This may give you away, but if you aim for the fuel drum inside the building, the explosion will take out enough enemy fighters that you can deal with the increased attention, especially because the shockwave from the explosion causes any troop outside the blast radius to shield their eyes or temporarily buckle over.

MISSION 04: DIWANIYA, IRAQ

Never walk up the center of the street. Stick to the bombed-out buildings so you have cover when clearing out the rest of the enemy troops.

The first sign of attack brings reinforcements. You can see ...em moving down the middle of the street. Use cover to keep ...m being shot and return fire when you note even a second of hesitation in your enemy.

...ing the rooftops ...sniping perches ...ot easy ...cause you have ...assault rifle, ...a sniper rifle. ...wever, you can ...e the rooftops ...lure enemies ...o chokepoints. ...mbing the stairs ...the structure ...u blew out with ...e fuel drum ...es you a decent ...w of the street ...nning up the

...nter of the neighborhood. Shooting at the troops from the ...oftop gives away your position, but you can easily cover the ...ly way up and cut down enemies as they attempt to reach ...u. Expect several reinforcements to come up the street as ...on as you start sniping.

 TIP

...he AK makes 'em dance. If you can only see the foot of an ...nemy, pop a toe or two to make the enemy stumble into view.

 **CAUTION**

The building to the right is a good perch because there are no explosive drums on the roof. Two of the buildings directly across from it do have these drums. They are great tools of destruction to take out enemy shooters, but not so hot when you are on the rooftop yourself.

Fisher is being held in the schoolhouse on the far side of the neighborhood, just beyond the blue metal gates. Unless you sniped from the first two rooftops and lured reinforcements into the street, another bombed structure to the right of the gates holds several enemy troopers. Creep up to the building to lure the enemies into showing themselves, then back away and target the two fuel drums in the courtyard. They are close enough together that popping one sets the other off. The powerful explosions shatter the soldiers and clean out the building. You can now safely move up on the school.

TIP

If you can help it, do not blow up the fuel drums near the schoolhouse gates. Saving these for later makes the end of the mission much easier.

SCHOOLHOUSE

The schoolhouse appears empty as you approach, but only the outside perimeter is empty of troop presence. The interior is a different situation. As you approach the schoolhouse, drop to a crouch and cautiously enter the front door. Slow as you weave around the overturned bookcases, though, because the next enemy patrol is in the corridor just beyond.

Use the desks and bookcases as cover to take down the patrol. There are two or three soldiers in the first wave, but stay down. Additional soldiers rush the hallway to take cover behind desks on the far end of the corridor. Trade gunfire, waiting to pop your head out and fire only when you spot a break in the action.

At least three more soldiers lurk in a small room just beyond a white door at the end of the corridor. You can burst through the door to surprise them or flank to the left and cut them off. However, as soon as you start shooting into the room, the survivors flee through the white door in an attempt to flank you.

Keep an eye on the door and when you see the soldiers pile through it, turn around to take them out before they rush you

Continue advancing throu the school to clo in on Fisher's position. Cros the outdoor playground to find the room where the ener is holding your friend.

FISHER

As you cross the playground, you hear shouting. Two men are interrogating Fisher. They grow angry, as he gives them nothing. Wait until the

men have backed away from Fisher before initiating the attac You can shoot from the large bay of windows, smash through the door around the corner to surprise them, or unload a clip through the window to the left of the door.

Reload so you have a full clip to take down Fisher's assailant

After killing the two interrogators, you free Fisher from his bonds. He's understandably happy to see you. You call in for a pick-up from the

schoolhouse, but before you can relay the coordinates, one o the walls explodes. The enemy has you surrounded. You mus hold them off until your ride arrives in just a few minutes.

MISSION 04: DIWANIYA, IRAQ

NOTE

When you rescue Sam, you receive two new frag grenades. These are helpful for holding off the onslaught.

...sher grabs a pistol. You still have your rifle. You both dive ...to cover at the rubble left behind by the explosion. Well ...er a dozen enemy soldiers swarm the street outside of the ...hoolhouse. They do not attempt to enter, but lay down some ...avy fire to keep you pinned. Stay hidden until you spot a break ...the assault and then take your shots where you can.

...aving those fuel ...drums from the ...neighborhood ...sweep gives ...you a series of ...nakeshift bombs ...blast. Use these ...eliminate entire ...aves of enemies.

...atch for snipers ...n the rooftops. ...If you can take ...hem down, you ...ssen the stream ...f incoming fire, ...aking it easier to ...op the troopers ...in the street.

...you need to ...right now ...take out as ...any soldiers ...possible and ...st survive. ...e situation ...oks dire. The

...nboldened enemy draws closer to the schoolhouse. However, ...fore your position is overrun, Allied jets scream through ...e skies above and drop bombs on your enemies. A few giant ...plosions later, you and Fisher are the only things moving in ...e area. A chopper drops to the street to pick you up, ending ...e flashback.

MISSION 05: WASHINGTON MONUMENT

OVERVIEW

Fisher needs to meet with Vic to share information about Black Arrow and the Third Echelon plot. Vic arranges for a rendezvous at the Washington Monument. There is a carnival happening adjacent to the monument that should provide some modicum of cover for the meet—with a lot of civilians on-site, Black Arrow or Third Echelon will be unable to take Fisher or Vic by force. Too much noise with too many witnesses.

Vic is an old hand at this espionage game, though, and has no problem spotting three Black Arrow agents making the round at the fair, seeking out Fisher. Vic says he cannot meet with Fisher until all three agents tailing him are out of commission.

MISSION 05: WASHINGTON MONUMENT

WASHINGTON MONUMENT

LEGEND

- ⌄ ENEMY (AFTER MEETING VIC)
- ① TAIL
- ② TAIL
- ③ TAIL
- ④ WASHINGTON MONUMENT
- ⑤ VIC COSTE

START

TOM CLANCY'S SPLINTER CELL CONVICTION

STRATEGY

Just as the Iraq was primarily an action-oriented mission, this Washington Monument mission requires primarily stealth. If you are spotted by any of the three Black Arrow tails seeking you in the carnival, they raise the alarm and the mission ends in immediate failure. So, you must sneak up on each of the three Black Arrow tails and interrogate them out of sight of civilians. If a civilian spots you grabbing one of the tails by the neck, they freak and the resulting noise grabs the attention of the tails. Wait for the tails to slip into the shadowy passages between the rides, food tents, and midway games. While under the cover of darkness, you can safely interrogate the Black Arrow thugs without any sort of alarm raised.

However, after finally dropping all three tails and meeting up with Vic, getting back out of the fair is a different matter entirely...

THE FAIR

As you approach the fair, slides of the tails are flashed on a white wall near the ticket booth. These slides give you a good idea of what the tails look like, but the more useful indicators are the X markers that hover above each of the three tails. No matter how many walls or booths are between you and the tails, you can use the X's to track their general position.

 NOTE

The X's referenced here are the gray marks that hover above the tails, allowing you to track their movement through the carnival. These are different from the chevrons that appear above enemies marked for execution or the chevrons on our maps.

Moving through the fair is pretty easy. None of the civilians give you a second glance as long as you are just walking. However, if you start ducking down and advancing from cover to cover, using booths and counters, the civilians will make note of you. You will hear things like "What's that guy doing?" If a civilian utters something like that within earshot of one of the tails, there is a strong chance the tail will turn around to see what the civilian is talking about. This is a good way to get spotted.

The first tail is directly ahead of you when you enter the fair. He's bald and dressed in a black suit. He's facing away from you. His appointed rounds take him

away from the fair entrance. Hang back and follow him from a safe distance so that if you see him slow down or start to turn his head, you can step into the crowds or slide behind a booth.

 TIP

If you are in danger of being seen, a white arc appears around you with a small arrow pointing toward the tail. You have may two seconds to make yourself scarce. If the tail makes you, the mission ends in failure.

Watch the Black Arrow thug slip into the dark alley behind the snack bar. As soon as the color starts to drain from the scene, initiate the interrogation. You snatch the tail by the neck and drive him into the shadows.

Interrogate the Black Arrow agent, asking him about Vic. The tail feigns ignorance, which is the wrong answer. You have little patience, though, to yard a

real answer out of him. There are two more agents out there to question. Crush the agent's neck and drop his body in the shadows. Now, you must seek out the remaining two tails. Use the X's as your guide and check the map for the location of a shadowy areas in the fair.

MISSION 05: WASHINGTON MONUMENT

ere are two ways
u can eliminate
e remaining tails:
her follow them
o the shadows
 lead them into
ps. The closest
ent is African-
erican and
ming down the
h between the
dway games to
 left of the snack
r. He makes

eft turn at the
ack bar, heading
o a small food
urt. Get close enough to the agent that he starts to suspect
mebody is behind him. Duck out of the way just as the white
c appears. You have hooked the fish. Now move into the
adowy area where you killed the first tail and hide until the
ent enters the back alley to check the body. Hop out and
ab his throat.

Use the crawl
paces below the
ailers behind the
ooths to follow
e agents around
the fair.

ou just pursue this agent instead of luring him into an
ey, watch for him to veer either to the left or the right after
ssing the lemonade stand. There are dark alleys on either
e. Follow the agent into the alley and then snatch him up by
e throat to get some more answers.

The Black Arrow agent tells you that he was assigned to follow
you and wait until you were spotted talking to Vic. As soon as
the tail had both of you at the same spot, back-up was going
to rush in. So, now you know that reinforcements are waiting
off-site for a signal. Kill the agent to make sure that he cannot
call in the calvary.

Ⓝ NOTE

There is no time limit to this mission. You can take as long as
you want to follow the tail through the fair.

The food court is
a central feature
of the fair. If you
fall back and
wait outside the
food court, the
third agent (he is

Asian) will eventually pass through it. The agent will likely veer to
the dark alley the other agent did not take. (If the second agent
went to the left, this third one will cross to the right.) Track the
agent into the back alley and smash him into a trailer to start
the interrogation. This agent tells you that he was not supposed
to make a move on you, but was supposed to call it in when
you were spotted. He also says that Vic is not the target. He is
auxiliary to the operation. You are the prime target.

The tails can be tackled in any order. You are not required to take them down in this order. You can track them around the fair and watch them move in and out of the crowds, ducking into the dark alleys and waiting until just the right moment to strike.

MEETING VIC

As soon as you kill the third tail in the fairgrounds, Vic comes over the air. He is ready for the meet. He tells you that he is waiting for you in the small administrative building at the base of the Washington Monument. Look for the gleaming white spire poking above the fair and then walk toward it.

ⓣ TIP

Don't worry about being spotted as you cross the open area between the fair and the monument.

Inside the small building, Vic warmly greets you. You know the history between these two men now, so you can imagine how each is willing to stick his neck out for the other even in such dire circumstances as being tracked by a dangerous PMC like Black Arrow. Vic gives you a backpack loaded with weapons and gear, including a portable EMP generator that temporaril[y] knocks out all electrical objects in the immediate radius.

Vic tells you about a research lab called White Box that has a government contract. The link? White Box specializes in EMP technology. And the company recently hired Black Arrow to handle all of its security. Black Arrow has never done corpora[te] security before, so the fact they took on the White Box accou[nt] raises Vic's suspicions.

While you and Vic talk, an announcement goes out over the PA system at the fair. A gas leak has been detected and the evacuation of the fair has been ordered. That's too much of a coincidence for your tastes. It's Black Arrow. Their three missing agents means you are obviously on-site and it's time t[o] call out a full force. The gas leak is just a cover operation. You must now cross back through the fairgrounds and reach your car to escape. The EMP generator is key to getting through th[e] Black Arrow forces. There are just too many of them to take on directly. You need to minimize your exposure to the Black Arrow team so you reach the car in one piece.

ESCAPE

Screaming people flee from the fair. As you run back toward the entrance to the fairgrounds from the base of the monument, you see the first signs of the Black Arrow team. They are disguised as gas company workers but these gas company workers are carrying some heavy-duty firepower: machine guns. With at least five of them milling around the ticket booth, you must deploy the EMP generator to stun them and move into the fairground without being totally ventilated.

MISSION 05: WASHINGTON MONUMENT

Want to take a few Black Arrow mercs down? While the agents reel from the EMP blast, rush up and grab one. Use him as a hostage and execute nearby agents.

Or dive behind the counter of the midway game to the right. As the agents recover and start looking around, shoot one of them. This creates a LKP that then distracts the agents while you escape.

As you near the food court, pump the EMP generator again. The lights pop and flash before going out,

bathing the food court in darkness. Hide behind the counter to the left, marked with all of the kegs. As the patrol recovers from the EMP blast, they start looking around. Wait for the entire patrol to focus their attention away from the beer counter. Leap over the counter and run past the food booths on your way toward the giant pirate sign.

> ## (T)TIP
>
> Gas canisters around the food court show up as red even in the darkness. If the Black Arrow agents cross next to a gas canister, shoot it to not only kill the agents, but create an awesome distraction.

lip under the ailer to the left f the fairgrounds ntrance. The lack Arrow uards will not ee you under the ailer. Duck behind the counter and make sure the agents are oking away before hopping over it and crossing toward the est Your Skill" booth. Duck down and crawl alongside the skee all booth.

Drop down to a crouch and slip into the crawl space under the trailer next to the red truck.

As you exit the crawl space, hit the EMP generator one last time to disorient the Black Arrow patrol at the base of the pirate ship ride. Leap the counter and then run to the right, slipping away from the patrol by running toward the bumper cars. When you spot the large blue arch, you're almost out of the fairgrounds.

Look for your headshot and then take it. Once the Black Arrow agents have been taken down, make a break for the car to end the mission.

KNOWN INTEL

Vic has managed to link Third Echelon, Black Arrow, and White Box, a tech firm that specializes in EMP technology, which dovetails right into the revelation that Kobin was trafficking in stolen EMP technology in Malta. Without a doubt, something very significant is about to go down and it involves Fisher's former employer. Fisher must now infiltrate White Box to discover what Reed is planning to do with the EMP devices the research lab is making.

Dive into the shadowy alley to the left of the blue arch. Hop the small fence at the end of the alley. There are likely a few Black Arrow agents waiting for you near the ticket booth.

Grab one of the Black Arrow guards to use as a human shield. Now, mark as many of the nearby agents as possible. Execute them to clear a path to your car. If any survive, dive behind the nearby planters or trucks for cover.

MISSION 06: WHITE BOX TECHNOLOGIES

OVERVIEW

anks to intel passed along by Vic, Fisher has a new lead on Reed's operation: White Box Technologies. White Box is a leading searcher of EMP technology and was recently bought by another corporation—perhaps the same that owns Black Arrow, the vate military contractor. Whoever bought White Box, they bought it for one reason: to get their hands on the EMP devices that re under construction in the double-walled EMP containment structure. (After all, one cannot work on a device that shuts down y-wide power grids near the national mall without some sort of precaution.) Fisher needs to get inside White Box's windowless lding and find somebody with some answers about why exactly the chatter about EMPs has grown to a fever pitch.

WHITE BOX TECHNOLOGIES

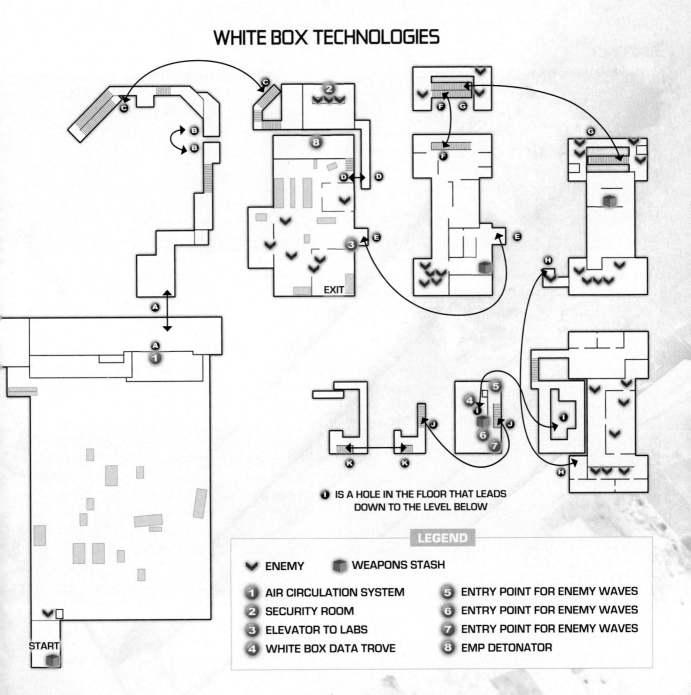

ⓘ IS A HOLE IN THE FLOOR THAT LEADS DOWN TO THE LEVEL BELOW

LEGEND

∨ ENEMY	▦ WEAPONS STASH

① AIR CIRCULATION SYSTEM		⑤ ENTRY POINT FOR ENEMY WAVES
② SECURITY ROOM		⑥ ENTRY POINT FOR ENEMY WAVES
③ ELEVATOR TO LABS		⑦ ENTRY POINT FOR ENEMY WAVES
④ WHITE BOX DATA TROVE		⑧ EMP DETONATOR

STRATEGY

White Box Technologies is a multi-story building with no windows and few doors. You must infiltrate the building by discovering a weakness in its heavy protection. Once inside, prepare yourself for a lengthy engagement with Black Arrow mercs on multiple floors. White Box is essentially a building inside a building, so there are plenty of windows and pipes within the shell to use for stealth tactics. Lab equipment, desks, and walls also make for good cover opportunities if you choose to take White Box by force. However, with the sheer number of mercs inside, even an assault on the building must be tempered with some sneaking (either by using the shadows or tech such as a sticky camera), otherwise you risk getting overwhelmed by numbers.

ENTRY

White Box looks impregnable from the exterior, but Vic has identified a possible entrance: the air circulation system. Look at the front of the building. That vent system on the sixth floor is your ticket inside. However, you need to scale the building to access it. And before that, you must get by the Black Arrow guard at the parking gate in front of the site.

Before moving on White Box, access the weapons stash in the trunk of your car to choose your loadout.

The guard is alone, which makes this an easy task. There are multiple ways to handle this, from sneaking up along the concrete barriers and then dropping the thug with a headshot to putting out the lights with an EMP grenade and then taking him down with a close kill. The close kill is a great move because you're then armed with an execution, and that will give you an advantage when you discover the first patrol of Black Arrow thugs inside the building.

To draw the merc away from the gate, take a shot at him. Th LKP lures him out toward the trees. Now you can sneak behi the target through the tall grass and grab him.

P.E.C. CHALLENGE

Wait in the weeds for the merc to close in on your LKP. When he does not find you and the heat dies down, you get the Vanish Silently award

As you cross the parking lot to move on White Box, Vic tells y that after you breach the industrial air exchanger, you need t locate the security hub to survey the entire site.

MISSION 06: WHITE BOX TECHNOLOGIES

se the shelves leaning against the right side of the loading dock r the pipe on the left side) to start climbing the building exterior.

The orange pipe is your way in. Climb along the pipe and then drop down once you breach the exterior shell. You're now inside White Box. It's time to find the security monitoring system.

Leap over the pipes as you weave through the ventilation system and look for the exterior of the building within the building. You must drop down several floors to find the security room. As you rush down the stairs, observe the White Box scientists at work in the various labs. There is little

ext, scurry up the air conditioners and power boxes to reach the third floor.

sign of Black Arrow, but that's by design—scientists don't do their best work with guns pointed at them. The mercs will show themselves soon enough, though.

limb up the drainpipes to reach the air exchanger. Slide along the face of the building via the fissures in the grating.

Once you reach e air exchanger, climb the pipe near the giant fan and then nove across the ellow scaffolding to locate a tall orange pipe.

Slow down as you close in on the security room. There are two ways into the room: smash through the door to surprise the guards or drop through the hole in the ceiling.

Use your snake cam on the door to spot the three mercs inside. If you have an execution, mark your targets through the snake cam. Smashing

through the door will give you about two seconds of surprise; that's enough time to execute guards. If you don't, you can eliminate one guard in the moment of surprise and then use the door as cover to target the remaining mercs.

P.E.C. CHALLENGE

Marking the mercs through the snake cam here and then executing them via the hole in the ceiling gives you the Behind Closed Doors award.

The pipe next to the monitoring room extends over the hole in the ceiling. As you cross the center of the hole, you can see all three targets. This is a

good place to execute. However, if you don't have an execution, you can use a Death from Above to kill one of the guards, which in turn gives you an execution. If you already marked the mercs, quickly initiate the execution to drop the remaining targets before a single thug knows what happened.

Now, access the security cameras through the terminal on the desk.

Cycle through the cameras until you locate a feed looking down on three scientists working on a device that

looks like a jet engine. It's one of the EMPs. The scientists are surrounded by Black Arrow mercs. And surprise—they do not do their best work with guns to their heads. One of the scientists turns on the Black Arrow thugs and tells them that their boss, Lucius Galliard, will be displeased by their treatment. Just before opening the scientist's chest with a blast of bullets, the merc tells him that he also works for Galliard. The merc then grabs one of the two remaining scientists and drags her away, leaving just one to finish up preparations on the EMP device. You need to question that scientist before he gets killed, too.

Leave the monitoring system via the open door to the left of the control panel and cross the catwalk until you locate a window looking on the loading bay where the scientists were prepping the EMP device.

MISSION 06: WHITE BOX TECHNOLOGIES

OADING BAY

everal mercs are
side the loading
y. The remaining
cientist is working
the EMP device
the center of
e bay. One merc
ways stands over
e scientist while

o other remain in close proximity. The remaining mercs patrol
e bay. One typically moves up and down the right side of the
y, against the wall opposite the window. Another moves along
e wall directly below the window, but never makes it all the
ay up to the window. From time to time, one may come up to
e middle of the bay and then stop at the base of the stairs
ading up to the landing just under the window. There are pipes
ong the ceiling of the bay. This is a great place to observe the
om, but you must first cross to the opposite wall through the
adows to reach the bottom of the pipe.

 **CAUTION**

Do not move fast on the landing. Your footsteps on the metal
grate reverberate through the bay, alerting the mercs that
somebody else is in the room with them.

*An execution will take out at least three of the mercs. If you
need one, or just want to lower the number of mercs in the
room before making a bigger play, drop to the floor and hide
next to one of the consoles. Grab a merc as he walks toward
your half of the bay.*

*Take this merc
close, into a
human shield,
o you can drop
the body in the
shadows and
ower the odds of
etection. Dispose
f the body near
the wall under
the landing.*

*Feeling brave? Use the human shield and then step toward the
rest of the mercs to engage. Act fast, though, because that
merc torso can only absorb about six or so bullets.*

P.E.C. CHALLENGE

If you allow yourself to be spotted, either here or back at the security
room, and then use a flashbang or EMP to cover your tracks, hang
out on the pipe above the bay for 10 minutes to earn the Remain
Undetected award.

Crawl along the
pipe and hang
over the EMP
device. From
here, you can
target three of
the mercs: the
merc standing
over the scientist,

one guarding the elevator, and another standing near a forklift.
However, be warned that executing the merc near the EMP
device drops his body right in a pool of light. The surviving
mercs will see his body and go on full alert.

Performing a
Death from Above
on one of the
mercs opens a
new front. The
other mercs may
hear your landing
and investigate.
There is a lot
of light near the
testing room, too,
so immediately
move away from
your kill. Seek
cover and mark
your targets for
execution, then pull
the trigger to clear out the area.

TOM CLANCY'S
SPLINTER CELL
CONVICTION

Temporarily take out the lights with an EMP grenade. In the darkness, you can perform a Death from Above with near impunity.

Casting the bay in darkness also lets you take advantage of LKP tactics. Shoot one of the mercs from the pipe or from behind an object (console, forklift, crate), and then quickly move once you see that your LKP has been established. As the mercs target your ghost, you can take shots at them or line up a great execution.

Once all of the mercs are down, question the remaining scientist. He tells you that he was working on an EMP countermeasure for the government but ever since new

management moved in, things have changed at White Box. Robertson, the new head of White Box, allowed Black Arrow to put the place on lockdown and has been collecting all data from the scientists and then purging the system to keep each team in the dark about the others. The scientist also says that Galliard is the owner of White Box and the one who hired Black Arrow and Robertson to handle security. The frightened scientist then opens the elevator for you so you can ascend the interior and locate Robertson's office. Hopefully, you can download his data and get it to Grim, painting a better picture of what you are truly up against.

FOURTH FLOOR

When the elevator doors open, you discover a grisly scene. Black Arrow has assassinated several scientists to contain

the spread of data. Use the weapons stash to the left of the elevator to load up on gear and upgrade any weapons. You receive a new gadget when you access this weapons stash: Sticky cams. These little devices are great for causing distractions, surveying foes, setting up traps, and misdirecting your enemies. Once you are happy with your loadout, close the weapons stash and turn your attention to the nearby doors.

ⓣ TIP

There is an M-500 shotgun in the small room behind the desk to the right of the weapons stash.

The snake cam reveals a whole crew of Black Arrow mercs about to murder two scientists. You cannot stop them. Observe the two Black Arrow mercs at the windows, though. Those look like good first targets.

ⓣ TIP

Got an execution ready? Mark targets with the snake cam and then kick down the door. Unleash your shots and then fall back to disappear, leaving the patrol in complete chaos.

MISSION 06: WHITE BOX TECHNOLOGIES

Enter the small room through the single room door near the weapons stash. Open the window and crawl out on the ledge. If you jump through the window, the breaking glass just attracts unwanted attention, taking the mercs away from the other windows.

When you pop up from a window to take a shot, you establish a LKP. The mercs all rush for that window. Move around to the adjacent wall and then look in on the mercs as they investigate your window. Use this system of cat and mouse to empty the room of mercs so you can push deeper into White Box.

Silently open the window behind a merc and then pull him to his death. This makes some noise. You may be spotted., but your LKP [i]s a powerful tool. Slide to one side of the window, wait for another PMC to stick his head out, and either blast him or grab him.

P.E.C. CHALLENGE

[P]ulling a merc through a window satisfies the Grab From Ledge [c]hallenge.

Don't ignore your frag grenades. They are not finesse instruments, but they guarantee kills in close quarters.

[T]oss a sticky [ca]m through one [of] the windows [to] observe the [m]ercs. Mark any [ta]rgets through [th]e sticky cam [m]onitor, but hurry [b]ecause the little

[d]evice does not have unlimited juice. Make a little noise with the [ca]m to draw a merc close and then detonate it. This gets the [m]ercs' attention, but they have no idea where to direct it. Use [th]at confusion to your advantage, targeting the mercs from [ou]tside the windows with an execution or headshots.

Follow the sound of gunfire until you reach the base of stairs marked with "Find Robertson's Office." You must ascend two more stories, but those stairs will lead you directly into two Black Arrow patrols.

Use the pipes next to the stairs to silently survey the mercs on each of the two floors.

From the pipe, you can Mark and Execute enemies with little risk.

Whether you are going for a forward assault or a stealthy approach at the stairs, the portable EMP generator is great for knocking out the lights in this area—and there are a lot of them.

TIP

Place remote mines on the stairs and then lure mercs down to you by getting spotted on the steps. The mercs chase down your LKP and walk right into your trap.

Use the windows and ledges to avoid detection while plotting your next move. These ledges allow you to target mercs for executions, individual shots, or Death from Above. The windows are better suited for yanking guards to their doom because the ledges are not always above empty space. The windows, though, are always on the exterior of the inner structure and offer a long fall.

TIP

The noise emitted by sticky cams is good for luring mercs into disadvantageous positions, such as near windows or explosive canisters.

HERE'S A CLEVER LITTLE TRICK

The sticky cam detonation can kill at close range, but you can effectively triple its power by placing it on one of the gas canisters in the lab. While hanging from a ledge, throw the sticky cam on a canister. Enter the camera controls and make the little noise to attract attention. Now listen. If nobody reacts right away, keep making the noise. Sooner or later, a Black Arrow thug will pick up on it and investigate. He might even bring a friend. When you see their faces appear in the sticky cam monitor, detonate it. This sets off the gas canister, creating a massive explosion and notching a Sticky Cam Whistle PEC for you.

MISSION 06: WHITE BOX TECHNOLOGIES

...ere are explosive ...isters on each ...el. The first ...nister is on the ...ding between ...two stairs.

...der the cover of ...rkness, you can ...close to the ...l overlooking ...nd then pop it ...t as Black Arrow ...rcs move close ...t. The upstairs ...nister is better ...t while hanging ...r the ledge.

...e a LKP to distract the mercs so they are not tracing ...r passage along the ledge, and then open fire as one or ...o mercs move near the canister. The explosions are quite ...werful with an extended blast radius. You can usually catch ...east two mercs in each explosion.

NOTE

...en when you knock the lights out with an EMP, if you are ...lainly spotted, the scene temporarily reverts to color.

...Use LKP on the ...wer floor to lure ...the mercs into ...eaning over the ...ailing, exposing their heads.

...ere is another ...apons stash ...the top floor, ...ectly to the right ...en you reach the ...of the stairs. ...s room doubles ...a good trap. Get ...otted going into ...e room so an ...P is at the door. ...op a remote ...e at the open ...or and then wait ...the mercs to ...e chase. The ...plosion at the

...or is strong enough to bring down at least one curious merc.

TIP

Return to weapons stashes as often as you like to restock on gadgets like mines and grenades. While you can only carry a few of each gadget at a time, the weapons stash is bottomless.

SIXTH FLOOR

As you close in on Robertson's office, Grim comes over the earpiece. She needs you to contact her once you reach Robertson's system. However, you need something from her first—to speak to your daughter. Grim patches her through, but coldly cuts the call short so you can focus on the task at hand.

After Grim hangs up, quietly open the small white door. Slip up to the edge of the shelf and peek out to spy at least one Black Arrow guard standing watch over a dead scientist. Though you cannot see any other mercs right now, he is not alone. While his back is turned, either take the silent headshot or stealthily creep behind him and slip through the window to access the ledge outside the room.

There are four more mercs just a little bit farther down the corridor from the initial thug. Shooting the first merc gets their attention, but if you get through the window without being spotted, lure the other mercs within range via a sticky cam whistle or a stray shot. You want to get them near the windows, because then they are playing to your strengths. You can pop up, nail a merc with a headshot and establish an LKP. When the other mercs investigate the LKP, you can then either yank them through the window or blast them as their heads appear in the frame.

Pulling a merc through the window to his death results in a Mark and Execution, which is perfect for clearing out the remainder of the mercs.

You have so many ways to dispatch the mercs in this area. If you tire of yanking them through windows, get them to cluster in a corner via an LKP and then drop a frag grenade right behind them. Or jump in and immediately take one of the Black Arrow thugs as a human shield. While his friends ventilate his body, you can either perform a Mark and Execute or just go for headshots. Move beyond the door and climb the pipe on the catwalk to move over Robertson's office and access it from the ceiling. You must first drop down into a small office storage room. There are several mercs just beyond the door. Use your snake cam to mark them.

TIP

Before moving on, sweep the room for extra flashbangs and remote mines.

Listen into the mercs. One mentions that the lab is using smart lighting. If sensors in the floor are triggered, lights turn on. When the mercs see light, they will rush the room.

The lab to the right uses the smart lighting. As soon as you step into the lab, the lights pop to life. Target the gas canisters in the rear of the lab and then shoot them just as the mercs investigate. A frag next to the canisters causes an even bigger explosion, which kills more mercs.

TIP

Dive through a window as soon as you activate the lights to avoid detection. Target the mercs as you hang from the windows. By staying on the ledge, you can also avoid turning any more lights deeper in the lab.

The next lab with smart lighting is separated from your current location by a corridor that is not attached to any lighting system. However, the mercs turn the lights in the corridor on. Drop an EMP to turn them back off. Use that corridor to advance on the exterior of the lab. Mercs move through the lab, looking for you. A lone merc stays in the corridor just outside the lab, just around the corner. Use remote mines to booby trap the corridor. Get spotted and the lead the mercs to their deaths.

CAUTION

The glass in the labs is bulletproof. If shot, it does not break

The best lure to a mine trap is your standing profile. Give the mercs a sense of hope and they come running.

Prima Official Game Guide   84

MISSION 06: WHITE BOX TECHNOLOGIES

After the mercs are down, enter the room and cross the lab to locate an orange pipe. Climb the pipe to reach the ceiling of Robertson's office. Alternately you can use the calkwalk. There is no direct entrance for you. You can only enter through the ceiling. Once inside the office, Grim comes back over the earpiece.

nother band
 mercs waits
 you beyond
 next set of
ouble doors.
he snake cam
lps identify
eir positions. Have an execution? Mark your targets and then
e the window to circle the room from the outside and take
ur shots. The windows looking into the room with the mercs
e closed, though, so you need to quietly open one to get
ean shots.

ROBERTSON'S OFFICE

Inside Robertson's office, Grim tells you to make the room a "hostile environment for uninvited guests." She needs you to open a link between Robertson's computer and her terminal and know that as soon as the connection is made, Black Arrow will be all over that office. You must set up traps for the incoming mercs. There are three ways into the office: the elevator and the two doors on the wall opposite Robertson's desk.

*nd here they come to investigate the windows. Yank one right
out of the window for an easy kill.*

There is a weapons stash inside Robertson's office that provides you with a steady stream of gadgets. If you ever run out of EMP blasts, drop down between enemy waves and quickly access the weapons stash for a restock on spent supplies.

 TIP

With the exception of the elevator, place mines a few feet from the entrances. If you place one too close to a door, the blast may be blunted by the narrow entrance and the body of the first merc through it.

When mercs look out windows, they often leave their heads exposed. Those make perfect targets.

 NOTE

Mercs enter the office in multiple waves through the same entrances. After they set off one mine, drop another at the entrance so the next batch is treated to the same surprise.

After setting your traps, access Robertson's computers. The EMP data is a plum find. You hack the terminal to give Grim access, but she cannot download everything right away. She needs time to extract all of the data. If the terminal is tampered with during the download, she will permanently lose access. The alarms that started going off as soon as the hack was initiated means mercs are en route. You must hold off the multiple waves of mercs that enter the office. If one merc reaches the computer, the mission is a failure.

⊤ TIP

Place a mine in the walkway between the two doors. Mercs use that passage to cross the room.

The first batch of mercs always comes through the elevator. Watch the floor numbers to track the ascent of the mercs from the first floor.

A pipe goes along the office ceiling. Climb up to the ceiling to get a clean visual on all entrances. This lets you get the drop on mercs not killed by your  mines as they follow the first or second thug through the door.

Shoot the mercs when they are looking in opposite directions. That will keep the "surviving" merc from marking your position on the pipe.

◀◀◀◀ ⓒ CAUTION

These mercs wear bulletproof vests, so they can withstand one or two shots to the chest. Aim for the head to get a single-shot kill.

⊤ TIP

Perform a Death from Above on the last merc in a batch to get an execution.

You can also use the upper and lower windows to move around the office during the fight. You can hang on the ledges from inside and outside. This gives you a big advantage against the waves and works for vanish and flanking.

Use the weapons stash in the middle of the room, next to the desk, to refill spent mines.

An EMP grenade will not disrupt the connection. Use it to turn out the lights and stun nearby mercs.

Remote mines can be used as grenades in a pinch. Toss one into the middle of some mercs and then immediately hit the detonator.

MISSION 06: WHITE BOX TECHNOLOGIES

im announces e status of e download roughout the ttle. When she ys the download at 80 percent, e mercs turn up e juice. Instead coming in one entrance at a time, they start filtering into the ice via multiple entry points at once, such as the elevator and e of the doors, or both of the doors together. You can easily ver those from the pipe, but you must be speedy with your ots or with dropping grenades.

 TIP

f a merc gets oo close to he computer, ob a flashbang t his feet to lind him or eploy an EMP last. Then entilate him.

If you run out of mines and cannot reach the weapons stash, use Death from Above to smash one of the mercs and then seek refuge behind the

sk. Use the execution to target multiple mercs and buy Grim me additional time.

As soon as the data download is complete, the flow of mercs stops. Grim has bad news, though. Somebody on the first floor of White Box has managed

start a trace on Grim's computer. You must race downstairs d stop that person from completing the trace, otherwise t only will Grim's cover be blown, but so will Sarah's. Use the irs in the office to rush to the first floor of White Box, down the loading bay.

Grab the pipe that runs next to the stairs and slide down to the roof of one of the EMP test labs next to the loading bay.

LOADING BAY

One last batch of mercs attempts to stop you in the loading bay next to the lab. As you enter the bay, the lights flicker on. An EMP grenade or a squeeze from

your portable generator turns them back off. Use the cover to run across the room and leap up onto the pipe on the opposite wall. You need to use the pipes along the ceiling to take out the incoming mercs.

From the ceiling, shoot the red gas canisters to blast the incoming mercs.

 **CAUTION**

Do not shoot the gas canisters directly below you. You need to save those for your escape.

The canister under the landing on the far side of the room releases a blast powerful enough to kill the mercs standing above it.

red gas canisters near the door to shatter them before they get too far into the bay.

Cross the bay to reach the landing against the back wall, near the security station. An EMP generator there will destroy all systems on site, thus stopping the trace before Black Arrow can locate Grim. There are three Black Arrow mercs guarding the EMP detonator on the ledge. Use the pipe to close in on them. To keep them from seeing you, have a flashbang or EMP blast ready. Use the shadows of the ceiling to score headshots on the mercs and clear a path to the EMP detonator that will cover Grim's tracks.

Once on the landing, access the EMP generator to kill the trace and fry Robertson at the security desk.

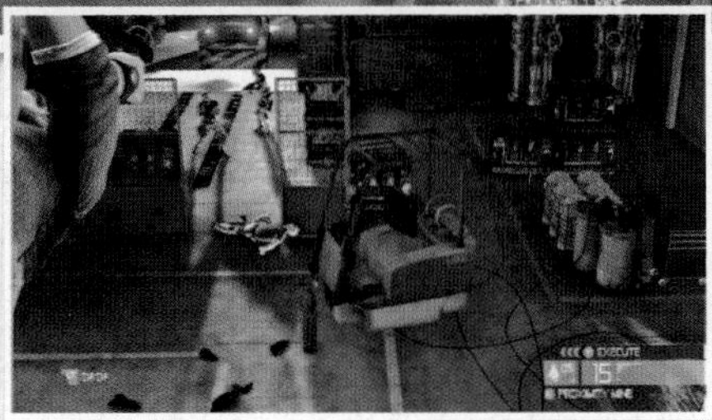

After you fire the EMP and kill Robertson, Black Arrow reinforcements attempt to retake White Box. Scramble back up to the pipes overlooking the bay. The loading dock doors open and a small crew rushes in. Shoot the

TIP

Look for flashlight beams to see any incoming mercs before they actually step through the loading bay door.

Use remote mines to drop the second wave of mercs that w[...] through the loading dock door.

Stay up on the pipe until you no longer see any mercs entering the loading dock. When the music dies down, you know the las[t] of the Black Arrow thugs have been dispatched and you can drop to the floor without worry of being shot. Leave the facility and cross the parking lot to return to your car and end the mission.

KNOWN INTEL

Fisher now has a new name: Lucius Galliard. He is apparently the owner of White Box Technologies and Black Arrow. Scientists at White Box Technologies have created at least one EMP device that is no longer in the building. Where these devices are headed and for what use is still unknown, but there is little doubt now that Black Arrow is not looking out for America's best interests and must be stopped. As for Reed, it is increasingly obvious that the director of Third Echelon is up to his neck in something ugly, too, especially because he was seen at the Price Airfield commanding Black Arrow officers. Fisher must figure out how all of these threads—Reed, Galliard, EMP devices—tie together.

MISSION 07: LINCOLN MEMORIAL

OVERVIEW

e intelligence gathered at White Box contains a name that
im recognized: Lucius Galliard. Though Grim does not
ow exactly what role Galliard plays in this ever-expanding
nspiracy, she knows he's a businessman Reed worked
h. Grim knows that the head of Third Echelon and
lliard are scheduled to meet the morning of a
speech by the vice president. Coincidentally,
lliard's business is providing security and event
ordination for the speech. Under orders from
president, Fisher needs to be on-site for the
eech to trail Reed and Galliard and gather
ditional intel about their collaboration.

LINCOLN MEMORIAL

LEGEND

1. PRESS BOOTH
2. LINCOLN MEMORIAL
3. LUCIUS GALLIARD
4. STREET CAFE
5. WAVE 1 OF ENEMIES
6. WAVE 2 OF ENEMIES
7. WAVE 3 OF ENEMIES

EXIT

START

STRATEGY

The first half of this mission is very straightforward. You are to listen in on the conversation between Reed and Galliard, gathering intel for Grim, who will assist you with using some digital eavesdropping equipment. However, after the conversation between Reed and Galliard ends, the scene suddenly turns hot and a basic intel-collection mission turns into a chase and a firefight. Only at the end of this mission will you have an opportunity to pivot between stealth and action tactics.

THE MEMORIAL

When the mission begins you receive direct orders from the president to listen in to the conversation between Reed and Galliard. You propose bugging the memorial, but the president says Galliard's operation scrubbed the site in advance of the speech. Fortunately, Grim has an alternate method for eavesdropping on the co-conspirators. The camera equipment for the speech is still in place. The cameras are tethered to directional mics. Those can be used to listen in any conversation—but only if the camera is pointed directly at the speaker and there is nothing between the source and the mic to cause interference. You can operate the cameras from the press booth.

Enter the press booth above the stage to access the cameras with Grim.

Once in the press booth, hack the camera controls so Grim ca listen in on the feed and help you get the best possible signal from the directional mics.

The mics are strong, but they are linked to the focus of the cameras. To get the conversation on tape, you must not only point the right camera at  Reed and Galliard, but you must also zoom in to get them right in frame. The pair will move around during the conversation, so you must cycle through the three cameras and zoom in and ou to get the best feed.

Start with camera 3. Zoom in on Reed and Galliard on the steps of the memorial. Whatever operation they are planning, it is less than 24 hours  out and Reed is not happy with Galliard. Galliard assumes Ree is frustrated with Black Arrow's failure to kill you, but Reed has another more pressing concern, and it involves the vice president himself.

N NOTE

The camera cannot pick up conversation if the subject is facing to either side, no matter how pretty they look in frame or in focus.

MISSION 07: LINCOLN MEMORIAL

hen Reed and alliard start to alk, move to amera 2 inside e memorial. oom in to get direct shot their faces. ere is some ncern over the vice president's dedication. Is he part of this eration? However, a new name enters the conversation that rprises everybody listening in: Megiddo. Is Megiddo a code me for a person? An organization? Either way, it seems egiddo is the top of the pyramid and Galliard is a direct link them.

rcle to camera 1 as the pair start walking again. Reed is w expressing irritation that Galliard is in America and not aris. Reed tells Galliard that he cannot guarantee his safety nce the operation is underway. Galliard says he doesn't need eed's help and the two men part ways, both agitated from the ncounter. You now disengage from the cameras.

MEGIDDO

Who or what is Megiddo? Though the identity of Megiddo remains hidden for now, the history of the name and its significance in apocalyptic prophecy offers hints that the group has a sinister agenda. Megiddo is a site in ancient Israel, located in the Jezreel Valley. Three major battles in history unfolded at Megiddo, from a 15th century war between Egyptian armies and the Canaanites to a 1918 battle between the British and Ottoman Empires. The word Megiddo is also the source of the word Armageddon, which is the name for the prophesied "final battle" between the forces of heaven and evil that appears in many faiths.

As the two men part ways, Grim recommends going after Reed, but you think tailing Galliard is a better plan. The president concurs. She would like to know more about this Megiddo that Galliard spoke of. Grim calls Galliard from a Third Echelon phone to stall him. She says that Reed has reconsidered their conversation and would like to pursue the matter further. She's trying to remain vague so as not to give away the game. Galliard bites and remains at the memorial while talking to Grim. This gives you time to slip out of the media booth and walk up the steps of the Lincoln Memorial.

GALLIARD

Sneak up on Galliard as he waits on the phone. Grab him from behind to start the interrogation. You immediately wrap your hand around Galliard's neck and hold him in a vice-like grip. Galliard at first refuses to disclose his relationship with Reed, but you know how to turn on the spigot of information. Lead Galliard to one of the objects inside the memorial, such as the control panel, the bank of monitors, one of the barricades, or the stack of crates. Smashing Galliard into each object results in a different...action.

P.E.C. CHALLENGE

Smash Galliard into three different objects during this interrogation to earn the Effective Interrogation award.

Galliard tells you that Reed and Third Echelon are not the biggest fish in the pond. In fact, he is only using them because they are the most convenient tools for the operation. Another round of "questioning" produces better results. Galliard says that Reed wants Galliard out of town because once the EMPs go off, Reed wants to assert control. There are three EMPs positioned around the capital.

Galliard doesn't know where the three EMPs are located, though. That's by design. Compartmentalize information so that if one person is compromised,

Follow the shooter into the large VIP tent to the right of the stage. The shooter pauses and turns to fire on you. Dive into cover to avoid getting shot. When the shooter stops to reload rush him. He takes off running again, but at least he isn't shooting at you.

Follow the shooter over a fence and through another tent. The shooter ducks between a pair of equipment trucks. You can hear police converging on the

site. Grim tells you that you are not to use lethal force against any police. So, when you do encounter the police, try to run by them as they reload their pistols or just barrel into them to knock them off balance.

they cannot bring down the entire operation. You try to draw the identity of Megiddo out of him. Galliard tells you they are the ones that run DC, Moscow, Beijing, and any power center in the world. However, before Galliard can tell you exactly what is about to transpire with Megiddo, he gets a bullet to the back. The shooter flees the memorial. You must give chase.

PURSUIT

The president orders you to chase down Galliard's murderer. You must run between the columns of the Lincoln Memorial and down the steps to keep the shooter in sight. Grim has eyes in the sky and will help you follow the shooter as he tries to escape. Listen to her directions. She will keep you from losing the killer.

Keep pursuing the shooter over some crates and between more tents. The shooter is fast and manages to keep one step ahead, but Grim's directions make sure you do not lose him during the chase.

As you circle the memorial, the shooter stops and opens fire. Dive behind a crate or barricade and move up when the shooter reloads to make him run again.

MISSION 07: LINCOLN MEMORIAL

e shooter runs o another large ent. Chase the hooter through the temporary dividers.

rush past another pair of cops, knocking them to the ground as you pursue the shooter through a TV truck.

de under the t truck and n pursue the oter across usy street. m hears that e police are ling back. That's d—fewer guns nted at you. Now keep running after the shooter, chasing n through a small cafe.

e shooter reaches his car before you can catch up to him— he's not going to escape. He starts his engine. The car turns into a fireball...another example of compartmentalization within Megiddo. Grim tells you to get ready for another fight. Third Echelon agents are converging on your location. A secret service agent is en route to get you out of there, but he's still a couple minutes away. You must hold off the Third Echelon agents until your ride arrives.

CAFE

The Third Echelon agents come in three waves. As soon as you draw your pistol, find cover. The planters in the courtyard next to the cafe are a good place to start if you decide to take these goons head-on. The first wave consists of two agents. One comes right through the middle of the courtyard and is an easy kill. The second agent, though, is sneakier. He flanks through the cafe itself.

Catch the agent on the stairs leading up to the outdoor seating of the cafe. If you rush him, the takedown earns you an execution.

Grim warns of the second wave of agents. Unlike the first set, which were aggressive to the point of being suicidal, the second wave uses flashbangs to disorient you in hopes of preventing you from tracking their positions. They come through the cafe. If you stay in the courtyard, switch so your back is facing away from the cafe. If your back is to the street, you can be picked off.

Get spotted at the base of the stairs leading to the second floor of the cafe. The LKP leads the agents right to you. Either shoot them as they come up the stairs or hang over the railing outside the second story windows and plug them as they reach the top of the steps.

Use the stairs as a chokepoint. As the agents try to advance on you, mark them for execution and take them out.

The third wave of agents comes from the street across from the cafe. There are three of them in this wave. If you are playing offense, then rush out to one of the planters and track the agents coming out of their truck. Tag them for kills if you have executions. Let them rush toward

Shooting agents from the window overlooking the courtyard issues a new LKP. It's another great lure. Hang in the back of the cafe and shoot the agents as they investigate.

the cafe and then blast them from behind. If one gets close to your position, pop up and kill them with a hand-to-hand attack. It happens so fast the other agents won't see it until it's too late. By that point, you have an execution to use on them.

Grim comes over the air after the third wave. Your ride has arrived. The secret service is waiting in a black SUV on the bridge behind the cafe. There is a fourth wave of Third Echelon agents about to storm the cafe. Run along the side of the cafe away from the kitchen and dive toward the SUV to escape before the Third Echelon agents surround your position. When you reach the SUV, the mission ends.

P.E.C. CHALLENGE

Pop up from one of the cafe windows and score a clean shot to the face to earn the Stealth Headshot award.

If you are trying to survive the assault via stealth tactics, use LKP to lure the Third Echelon agents into bad situations. Get spotted someplace you

can see from the windows of the cafe, such as on the narrow steps leading to the courtyard. Scurry up the drainpipe to the second story or leap through a kitchen window and rush up the steps. Watch the agents converge on your LKP and then blast them.

◉ KNOWN INTEL

Several things were established in this mission. Fisher now has the name of the organization pulling the strings on the operation involving Reed and Galliard: Megiddo. Megiddo's agents have positioned three EMP devices around Washington DC, and they are set to go off in several hours. When they do, Fisher knows that all hell will break loose in the city. Fisher must discover the locations of all three EMP devices so he can disable them before they knock out DC's electrical grid.

Additional intel was acquired, too. There appears to be some sort of rift between the president and her vice president. The vice president has Reed's admiration, so it is likely that the vice president is responsible for stonewalling the president's investigation into Third Echelon. But is the vice president just a pawn in this operation or is he privy to Megiddo's plans?

MISSION 08: THIRD ECHELON HQ

OVERVIEW

ith Galliard dead, Fisher has only one more lead to chase down on Megiddo and the EMPs: Tom Reed, the director of Third
helon. Fisher must return to his former employer, not as a celebrated hero but as the villain, and infiltrate the building to find
ed and discover what he is planning to unleash on the capital tonight.

Lower   **Upper**   **Middle**

THIRD ECHELON HQ (A)

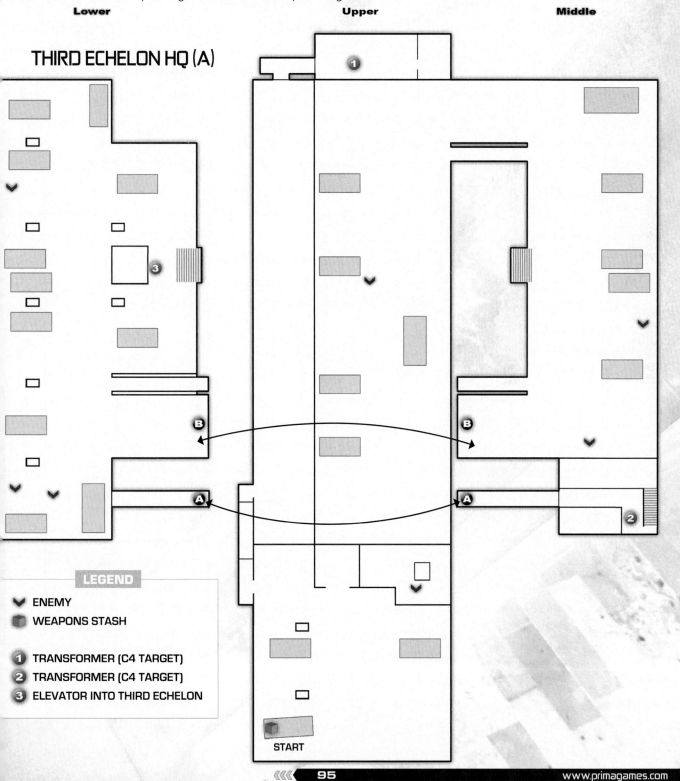

LEGEND

- ⌄ ENEMY
- ⬢ WEAPONS STASH

- ① TRANSFORMER (C4 TARGET)
- ② TRANSFORMER (C4 TARGET)
- ③ ELEVATOR INTO THIRD ECHELON

START

TOM CLANCY'S SPLINTER CELL CONVICTION

THIRD ECHELON HQ (B)

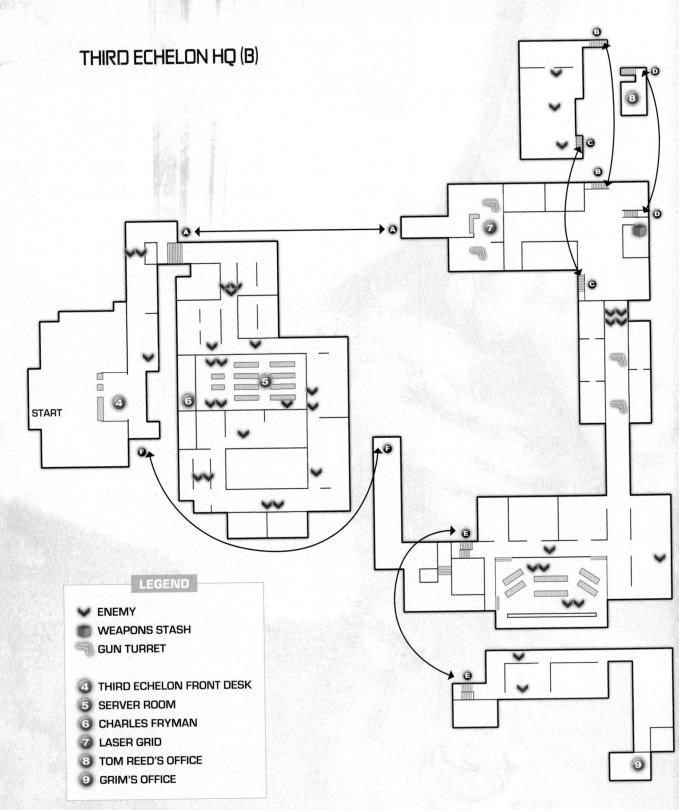

START

LEGEND

- ⌄ ENEMY
- 🧊 WEAPONS STASH
- 🔫 GUN TURRET

- ④ THIRD ECHELON FRONT DESK
- ⑤ SERVER ROOM
- ⑥ CHARLES FRYMAN
- ⑦ LASER GRID
- ⑧ TOM REED'S OFFICE
- ⑨ GRIM'S OFFICE

MISSION 08: THIRD ECHELON HQ

STRATEGY

...eaking into the nation's most secretive intelligence division
...l not be easy—there's no shortage of Third Echelon agents
...hunt you. Fortunately, they do not have the same training
...you. They are crack shots, but fail in the art of stealth. So, if
...u plan to take the resistance head-on with force, expect to
...t what you give. However, with stealth tactics you can always
...aintain the advantage.

...e first half of this mission just requires getting into the
...lding via the parking garage. You must remain out of sight
...ile planting C4 charges on two power generators. If you
...e spotted, Third Echelon goes on lockdown and massive
...curity doors slam shut. You can break into a lot of things,
...t you're no miracle worker, so stick to the shadows in the
...rking garage.

ARKING GARAGE NTRANCE

...the beginning of the mission, you find yourself just outside
...e initial checkpoint at the Third Echelon garage. Refresh your
...dout at the weapons stash in your trunk. (Make sure you bring
...ilenced pistol.) Then, check out the small security office next
...the garage entry. Two agents are inside the office, chatting.
...u need to pass through the office to access the garage itself
...cause a set of large gates blocks your direct access.

CAUTION

...You cannot damage any of the security cameras in this
...mission or else the whole system goes on high alert. Do not
...even deploy an EMP near a camera.

...e the hole in the
...f of the security
...ce to access
...e garage. Taking
...t two guards in
...id succession
...hout one calling
...help is hard.
...re one out of
...office by walking in their line of sight. As soon as you see
...white arc of being almost noticed, rush into the shadows.

One of the two guards says he needs to go check something
out, and he comes through the door to investigate the garage.

*Scramble to the roof of the security office. If both agents are
still inside and you do not have a Mark and Execute, mark one
of the guards and perform a Death from Above on the other.
As soon as you smash the first guard, execute the second. If
you hit the execute as soon as it becomes available, you will
avoid detection.*

*If one of the guards stepped out of the office to patrol the
garage entrance, wait for him to turn his back and take him
out with a silenced pistol. You can now use the door inside the
office to access the main garage.*

PARKING GARAGE LEVEL 1

As you sneak into
the first level of
the garage, Grim
pops over the
earpiece. She
needs you to hurry
it up. Her contact
inside Third
Echelon—Charles

Fryman—can help you find what you are looking for, but security
is searching for him. He is located near the server room. You
have to find him as soon as possible.

Use the pipes that stretch across the garage ceiling to survey the scene. There are multiple guards. At least one patrols the first level, and you can spot two more on the floor below. There are multiple security cameras in the garage, too. Use the moving pools of light under the cameras to avoid detection.

> **TIP**
>
> Always slide down from the pipes. If you drop to the floor, your impact garners attention.

Watch out for the guard moving right up the middle of the garage. Duck away from him behind a small car or hang over a railing to avoid detection.

Cross to the right side of the garage and use the large van as cover to sneak past the guard.

Slide along the railings on the left side to get behind the gua and then make a break under the security camera's watch slip into the transformer room.

> **TIP**
>
> Shut the door to the transformer room behind you. An open door will only attract attention.

Plant the C4 on the transformer. You now need to access the second transformer on the level below. There are two routes. Either exit the

transformer room through the door and sneak down the ran or crouch and slip through the narrow passage to the left of the transformer. The narrow passage drops you off right into the shadows, making it an ideal way to reach the lower level of the garage. Just watch the guard patrolling the right wall the garage and make sure he is on the far side of the garage before you drop down. Your footfall will make a little noise.

PARKING GARAGE LEVEL 2

Take cover behind one of the cars or a support pillar immediately. There is a strong chance one of the guards on the lower level will start walking along

the right wall. He has a flashlight mounted on his shotgun. If he catches even a shoe in that beam, he starts shooting. Kee hidden until the guard walks within striking distance. Jump ou and seize him. Pull him into a human shield position and then dump his body in a dark corner, such as below the vent you dropped through.

MISSION 08: THIRD ECHELON HQ

P.E.C. CHALLENGE

Wait until the guard is completely out of the light so when you do grab him, you get a Shadow Takedown.

Continue sneaking along the ground, sticking to the shadows. There is another guard in the headlights of a car at the far end of the garage. Rush up when he is not looking and take him down. If you drop the body where he stands, shoot out the headlights to cast the body in shadow.

Cross the back wall of the garage and duck into a vent obscured by the pick-up truck.

Place the C4 on the second transformer and then climb the stairs behind you.

Enter the garage again. There are a few fluorescent lights along the ceiling to the right and a guard is typically patrolling directly beneath them. Shoot out the closest light when the guard has his back turned, and then advance to one of the parked cars. Either wait for the guard to approach and draw him into a stealth kill, or wait until he is in the shadows and then drop him with a headshot.

CAUTION

Look out for a single guard patrolling the wall along the elevator entrance. Wait for him to peer over the wall before making your move, whether it's a kill or just slipping by.

After eliminating the guard, run around the path of the surveillance camera and then duck into the elevator emblazoned with the Third Echelon logo. Enjoy the ride up into Third Echelon's headquarters, remembering past assignments done on behalf of this branch before it was compromised by men like Reed.

THIRD ECHELON ENTRANCE

The elevator deposits you in the spacious Third Echelon lobby. Stride across the lobby and speak to the receptionist. She denies you entry, but when you set off that C4 and cut the main power, she loses interest in keeping you out. Jump over her desk as she dives underneath it. You now need to run through the hall behind her to avoid getting locked out by another series of security gates.

Guards step out of the hall as you rush under the gates. Run into them to knock them off-balance or drop a flashbang to throw them off their game. You need to get under that last gate before it drops down.

(T) TIP

Catch the last guard with a close kill to earn an execution before going into the main office. There are several patrols inside. Having an execution at the ready is a serious help.

Grim tells you to meet Fryman in the server room office.

Sneak up to the first corner and peer down the hallway to see the first patrol of agents. There are two in the main hall and at least one inspecting the rooms on each side. There are entirely too many lights to effectively mount a counteroffensive. Use an EMP grenade or the portable EMP to darken the area so you can move on the agents under cover of shadows. In the darkness, you can clean out the agents with direct attacks, plot an execution, or jump up to the rafters overhead and sneak past the guards.

◀◀◀◀ (C) CAUTION

Walk slowly in the rafters above the offices. Fast or sudden movements generate noise.

Going for action? After turning out the lights, move through the offices and target the agents. They move slowly as they sweep the area for any sign of you, giving you ample opportunities to line up headshots. When the lights flicker back on, duck into cover behind a desk or table and continue methodically taking down the agents.

Watch the patrol patterns. Agents weave around desks when they walk. Wait near a desk so an agent will walk by you as he starts his search and then jump out to take him into a close kill.

The agents are armed with machine guns, so the usefulness of a human shield is limited. Still, it is a good way to get out o[f] a sticky situation if you find yourself completely exposed.

MISSION 08: THIRD ECHELON HQ

Many of the walls in the office have multiple entry points. Use LKP to make the agents look at one while you move to the other and gun them down from behind.

e server room is in the middle of the office, but it is not easily accessible. The plate glass walls are bulletproof. You must rcle around the room to locate the entrance. Unfortunately, this puts you in the direct path of another patrol.

alth will get
to the server
m with less
ger, but is
ch slower
n if you make
reak for it with
r guns blazing.
u want to
down these
nts, arm a
chine gun (take
from a dead
nt if you do
have one) and
t blasting. You
st use your

LKP to survive, though. Pop up and shoot an agent while the others are not looking. The noise whips their heads around. Duck back down and flank the other agents, popping up to shoot when they direct their fire at your LKP.

A direct assault on the guards does not mean just standing in the middle of the room and shooting. You must seek cover, otherwise you will be surrounded and shot within seconds. (If you do get surrounded, use an execution to increase your odds of survival or drop a flashbang

to blind everybody.) You must also repeatedly reload because your accuracy with a machine gun is not nearly as strong as it is with a pistol. Your sprays empty clips. Reload between each kill so you are never caught empty.

If you are moving on the server room with stealth, use the bodies of the agents to your advantage.

After snatching up an agent into a close kill, dispose of the body in the shadows if you are facing down multiple guards. If one of them catches sight of the body, they all come running with itchy trigger fingers. But if you leave a body out in a space between cubicles for a single guard, you've created an effective trap. The agent will come to look. When they peer down at the guard, take your headshot.

> **TIP**
>
> While you shouldn't be throwing EMPs around like holiday candy, don't be afraid to use them regularly. EMPs are a great tool for turning an entire area into a shadowy playground for you to strike.

When you break from Fryman, try out the goggles. You can ▢ through the entire server room—and see a new patrol inf▢ trating the room. They are hunting for you.

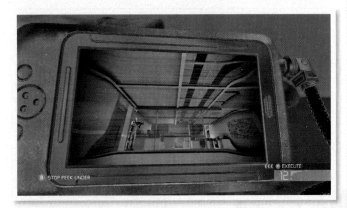

Use offices and conference rooms for cover when staking out the agents. Peek under the doors with snake cams to mark targets and track agents.

The server roo▢ is a small spa▢ It's difficult t▢ see all angles, ▢ agents can sne▢ up on you wh▢ you are target▢ another. It's be▢ to hit them fr▢ the ceiling. Ju▢ up to the ledge in the server office and then pull yourself on▢ of the servers.*

Use the red door to access the server room. Fryman is in the narrow office in the back of the room.

SERVER ROOM

Locate Fryman cowering in the back of the server room. He claims that he was a major fan of you back when you worked at Third Echelon. Fryman

offers you a set of high frequency sonar goggles. These goggles send out a pulse that maps the immediate vicinity, allowing you to not only see in the dark, but also see through walls. Fryman added an extra goody to the goggles: you can see laser tripwires, too. Apparently several rooms in Third Echelon are protected by laser grids attached to gun turrets that automatically target the beam that was broken.

Sneak along the servers and pop the agents in the head when they are looking away so your position is not discovered.

While you can use your LKP to get them to look elsewhere, ▢ are far better off not being detected at all. If your goggles sh▢ at least one agent hanging back outside the server room, dr▢ to the floor and get spotted so your LKP lures them into the ▢ room. Once they are in the room, flank them as they close in ▢ your LKP.

MISSION 08: THIRD ECHELON HQ

EADING TO REED'S OFFICE

The sonar goggles are extra-effective while you are in the ceiling. You can see much farther.

ur next stop is Reed's office. This requires you to backtrack rough the office, leaving the server room through the same or you entered. The first hall is empty. Use the cubicles cover when advancing to the bend in the office, near e conference rooms. When you turn the corner, you can e movement from another patrol at the far end of the bicle farm.

Drop the agents with a silenced pistol to thin the herd without being spotted.

Use your sonar goggles to note their patrol patterns.

ese agents are
re aggressive,
consider
cking to stealth
avoid detection
ile moving to
ed's office.
mp up to
cess the rafters

The ceilings are
not all connected.
You must drop
down to the floor
from time to time
and then advance
to the next section
of rafters to
resume your crawl
toward Reed's
office. When you
must drop down
to the floor to
advance, pop an
EMP or shoot out
some lights to
create additional

ove the cubicles and then track the agents as they shine eir flashlights into the shadows on the floor.

cover. If you are spotted while pulling yourself up to the ceiling, the agents will open fire and bring you down.

CAUTION

Move slowly through the rafters to avoid detection. If the agents figure out you are above them, they open fire. The ceiling offers zero shielding from their bullets.

Continue through the cubicle corridor until you reach a wide set of stairs leading up to the next floor of Third Echelon.

LASER GRID

The reception area in front of Reed's office has been rigged with the laser grid and machine gun turret defenses Fryman described. You must navigate

through the beams to avoid getting cut down by the ceiling-mounted turret. You cannot use an EMP to take this system out, nor destroy the turret with gunfire. The only way through the room is to slip on your sonar goggles and deftly maneuver through the beams. Here's how to survive without 88 holes in your chest:

Crawl under the first moving beam when it reaches the top of its climb. Then slip under the next pair as they do the same thing.

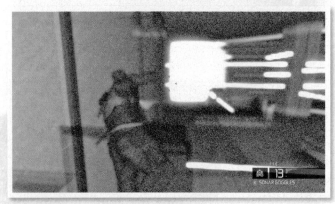

The next beam is on the floor. There is nothing to grab above it. Jump over the planter against the wall to avoid the beam.

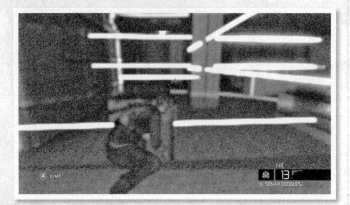

Crawl under the next beam and then vault over the planter in the middle of the walkway to avoid another floor beam.

After ducking under another moving beam, jump up and ho the ledge on the wall to shimmy over a series of low beams

Duck under the next pair of beams as you close in on the ba visible wall map.

The last set of beams moves around. Watch for the beams move toward the edges of the room, creating a "hole" you c crawl through.

Jump over the security gate to enter the lobby outside Reed's office. Cross the lobby and climb the stairs to confront the man standing in the office.

MISSION 08: THIRD ECHELON HQ

REED'S OFFICE

...driy Kobin. ...hat is he doing ...re? Why is ...e man who ...s supposedly ...ed to kill your ...ughter standing ...he office of the ...ector of Third ...helon? Interrogate Kobin to get your answers. You kick him ...er a railing, smashing his body on the conference table below. ...s gets him talking.

...bin spills the ...tire operation. ...der direction ...m Megiddo, ...ed is planning ...unleash the ...ree EMPs ...und DC tonight ...knock out ...e power. While the grid is down and chaos ensues, Reed is ...nning to kill the president. Further interrogation reveals that ...e president has been targeted because she refuses to join ...egiddo. However, the vice president has. Once the president ...s been replaced, Reed will get a medal, a promotion, and a ...more power.

...bin also confirms that the hit on your daughter was at the ...quest of Third Echelon. He provided the body that matched ...e photo he was given. Kobin eventually passes out from the ...ating he's taken. You must now reach Grim's office to set up ...secure conference call with her and get to the bottom of why ...ur daughter somehow got involved in all of this.

 TIP

...Use the weapons stash in Reed's office to refresh your loadout ...and spend any acquired P.E.C. Challenge points.

Three agents crash through the ceiling to stop you from escaping Reed's office. These are highly trained specialists—not the mid-level agents you have been dealing with so far. These agents are well armed, know stealth tactics, and have sonar goggles similar to yours. You must take them out before moving on to Grim's office.

Throw a grenade up to the landing above Reed's office. Even if you do not kill any of the agents, they still turn to look at where it dropped.

Creep up the stairs and shoot the agents with a silenced weapon while their backs are turned.

Or mark the three agents for execution and then lay them out as they try to rush downstairs to find you.

After the three agents are downed, a security barricade raises to the left of Reed's office. Four agents are coming down the corridor. Seek cover and

plug them as they step into the lobby. The corridor beyond them is protected with laser tripwires and turrets, so use your goggles again to pass through the gauntlet.

Slide over to th
partial wall tha
overlooks the n
room. A laser
sweeps acros.
the open spac
between the w
and the ceiling
Wait for the las
to pass and the
vault through
the space.

The room is clean, but another laser sweeps across the ceiling. Drop to the floor and cross the room. Jump up on th partial wall on the far side of the table and hang until the lase passes by.

P.E.C. CHALLENGE

The agents move slowly enough through the gate for you to draw a bead on them. Your headshot from the shadows awards you a Stealth Headshot.

The main corridor is blocked off by an impenetrable wall of laser beams. There is no way to get to other end of the corridor without ducking into the

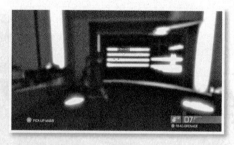

conference rooms and offices on the right side of the hall. Slip through the first door and then follow these directions to safely maneuver through the beams:

Jump past the laser and then shimmy to the pipe that runs along the ceiling. Crawl along the pipe over the room full of lasers and then drop down on the other side. Exit through th door to enter the main corridor again. You are now past the laser gauntlet.

GRIM'S OFFICE

Grim needs you to see something in her office. You must slip past one more patrol to reach her digs, which overlook a command center

After entering the conference room, scurry up the far wall and grab the ledge to cross over the beams in the center of the room.

MISSION 08: THIRD ECHELON HQ

ow massive banks of maps and monitors. Several agents sweeping through the desks, slashing at the darkness with ir flashlight beams. Slip into the shadows to avoid being tted. An EMP pulse (grenade or via your portable generator) nguishes their lights and the rows of lights that line the halls rounding the command center.

Use the sonar goggles to spot all of the agents.

op off a shot or two at the agents from the nearby cubicle rm. The agents rush to investigate your LKP. Either target them from behind or just slip around them.

Alternately, sneak up and nab one to use as a human shield while you hunt the other agents in the command center.

Climb the stairs on the far side of the command center. Three more red-goggled agents drop into the area and start sweeping the hall and several

smaller rooms for you. There is nowhere to hide in the hall, so dive into the rooms and use LKP to lure the agents into narrow doors where you can easily grab them into close kills.

Grim's office is at the end of the hall. When you enter the office, move to her desk and activate the telepresence to initiate a conference call with Grim while she is at an undisclosed location. You pressed Grim for answers about Sarah. Why was her death faked?

Grim tells you that it was actually Lambert's idea. He did it in hopes of protecting you. Grim plays you a recording Lambert left before his death. Lambert had heard of a credible threat against Sarah's life by a mole within Third Echelon. To prevent you from being compromised by somebody threatening Sarah, Lambert took her out of the equation by faking her death. You'd suffer her loss, but at least Sarah would be safe.

Lambert contracted Kobin to come up with a body to stand in for Sarah and then took advantage of your grief for Third Echelon, funneling you deep undercover to penetrate a domestic terrorist cell. You go berserk, kicking over chairs and throwing things around Grim's office.

But Grim talks you back with news about the EMPs. She has new data that can help with deactivating the weapons. Analysts have determined the best locations to place the EMPs. Grim says one of them is near Sarah's apartment. There is only time to disable one of the EMPs and Grim says that's the one you should hunt down and deactivate. In the meantime, Grim will go to the White House with Reed and try to save the president.

News about Sarah throws you into another rage. Use this heightened condition to target the last of the agents steaming toward Grim's office. You must get out of the building as soon as possible before Reed has the place blown up to cover his tracks. Follow the path   through the office, directed by the closing security gates. Drop any incoming agents with executions before they can attack. Don't overreach and try to fill up the markers—just take the kills as they present themselves.

Take the Third Echelon security in the stairwell as you see them. You may have heightened killing power, but you are not invincible. You cannot wait for multiple agents to crowd these narrow spaces and expect not to be shot.

RAGE

Fisher doesn't necessarily have a temper, but when you attack his only weak spot, he goes berserk. That Achilles heel is his daughter. While furious, your senses are heightened. The screen turns a slight orange hue, which makes it easier to pick up enemies. The action slows to a crawl, too, letting you move faster than your enemies. Best of all, not only is any enemy you see automatically marked, but you have unlimited executions.

CAUTION

Rage does not mean invincible. You can still be shot and killed while on the warpath.

Three agents wait for you near the front desk. Look for two to flank the wide passage back into the main Third Echelon lobby. Execute them to clear a path to the exit. Leap over the desk and jump into the empty elevator shaft to disappear as the bomb goes off.

KNOWN INTEL

Fisher knows for certain that his daughter is alive but is devastated to find out that his friend Lambert is the person behind her faked death. That Lambert "killed" Sarah to get Fisher to agree to a potential suicide mission is particularly distressing. Fortunately, the reunion will happen soon—Fisher just needs to help stop at least one of the EMPs to weaken Megiddo's plan to take out the President of the United States and replace her with a puppet.

MISSION 09: MICHIGAN AVE. RESERVOIR

OVERVIEW

Showers of sparks bounce off the pavement behind Fisher as he runs from the inferno enveloping Third Echelon's headquarters in DC. He was torn by old allegiances. He helped build Third Echelon with his old friend Lambert—the person he put a bullet into so as not to blow his deep cover against domestic terrorists during his last assignment for Third Echelon. But that friend had lied to him about his daughter's death and used that grief to get him to take the assignment in the first place. Perhaps the destruction of Third Echelon, especially now that it is under the stewardship of a rat like Reed, is for the best.

Grim threw Fisher a lifeline before Third Echelon went up in flames. There's no time to stop all three EMPs before the scheduled blasts, so Grim pointed Fisher to the one going off closest to Sarah. He may not be able to save the city, but he could at least try to save his daughter from the horror about to be visited on DC by Megiddo.

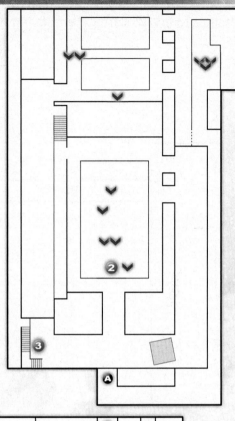

MICHIGAN AVE. RESERVOIR (A)

LEGEND

⋁	ENEMY
▢	WEAPONS STASH
①	BLACK ARROW INTERROGATION
②	WHITE BOX SCIENTIST
③	HOLE TO SURFACE

START

MICHIGAN AVE. RESERVOIR (B)

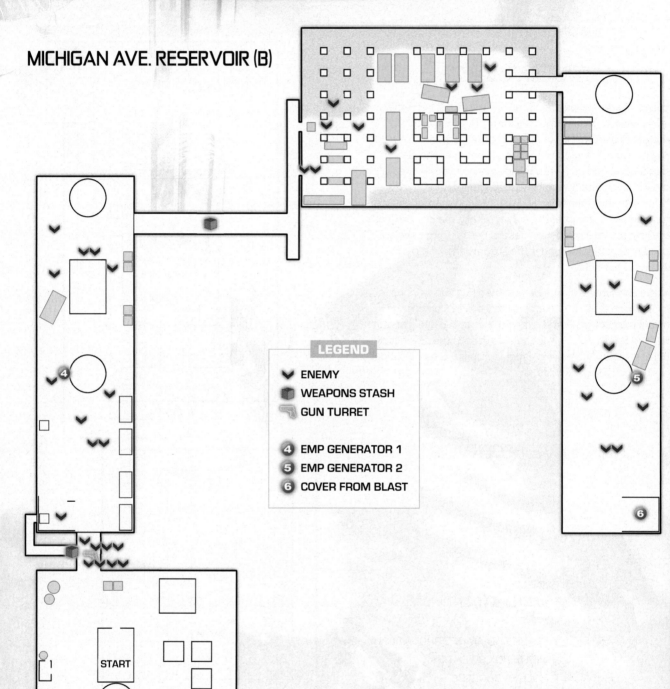

LEGEND

- ▾ ENEMY
- ▨ WEAPONS STASH
- ⌐ GUN TURRET

- ④ EMP GENERATOR 1
- ⑤ EMP GENERATOR 2
- ⑥ COVER FROM BLAST

START

MISSION 09: MICHIGAN AVE. RESERVOIR

STRATEGY

...s mission is split in two halves. In the front half of the ...ssion, you must infiltrate a warehouse near the reservoir ...ere the EMP is located to rescue one of the scientists ...napped from White Box. Hopefully, she can help you disable ...e EMP. Once you eliminate her captors, she fills you in on ...e generators that charge the EMP. There are two of them, ...d both must be destroyed at the same time. If only one is ...rgeted, the other generator juices the EMP as a fail-safe.

...e back half of the mission offers an even split between ...ealth and action. You must cut through several groups of ...ck Arrow thugs to reach the generators that power the ...MP. At times, they will overwhelm you 10 to one. Use stealth ...ctics to chisel those odds closer to your favor before taking ...t the remainder of the patrols with gunplay.

NTERROGATE BLACK RROW OFFICER

...u must gather intelligence on the Black Arrow presence ...fore making a move on the EMP. You park your car close to a ...rehouse with Black Arrow activity. Access the weapons stash ...your trunk to choose your loadout and then slink along the ...nce until you hear chatter from the Black Arrow mercs. They ...e just inside the chain link fence, next to the pick-up truck.

...ait until the ...ercs are looking ...ay and then ...vance to the ...ncrete block ...xt to the truck. ...om here, you ...n either slink ...rough the ...e in the fence and flank from the side or target the mercs ...m behind.

> **CAUTION**
> If the officer by the tree spots you, he'll shoot you. And although you can't shoot him, you can kill him with a grenade, but it'll end your mission if you do.

You have time to drop two of the mercs before the third gets his act together. Let him see you to establish an LKP.

As the third merc investigates the LKP, slip through the hole in the fence and flank him. If you move low and slow, he'll never see you coming.

The officer opens fire in all directions as you close in on his position next to the tree. Shoot the lights out around him to create shadows. Then, use LKP to keep him guessing. Let him see you next to the front of the truck by the tree. Slip around the truck and the brick wall as the officer empties clip after clip into the shadows.

TOM CLANCY'S SPLINTER CELL CONVICTION

Jump the officer from behind to start the interrogation.

It takes a few smacks to get the officer talking. Move him around the area beneath the tree, cracking his head into different objects such as the

truck's wheel well or the old air conditioner. Despite each line of "questioning," the officer claims to have no idea how to disable the EMP—and judging by the guy's haircut, science may not be his strong suit. But slamming a knife into his hand gets him to spill about the scientist from White Box inside the warehouse. She knows how it works and she is scheduled for disposal after the EMP is fired. You must save her.

P.E.C. CHALLENGE

Be sure to slam the officer into the truck, the refrigerator, and the brick wall to get the Effective Interrogation award.

WAREHOUSE

There are two ways into the warehouse behind you: a door to the right and a window on the left. There is no immediate resistance at either entrance, but the window will allow you to take the entire room by stealth.

CAUTION

With the EMP set to go off, the mercs have started using chemical lights that cannot be shot or disabled.

Jump through the window and shimmy up the nearby pipe. From the pipe, you can survey the room. Multiple mercs patrol the floor. Watch for three to coalesce to the right. You should have an execution ready from the interrogation with the officer. Mark the three mercs for execution...

...or look above them. There is an EMP device hanging over them. Shoot the chain holding up the EMP to drop it on the mercs. This puts the entire room in a panic, but it is unlikely that any of them will look up at the pipes to see if there a super spy crawling around the ceiling.

Mark the other mercs on the far side of the room so when they run to check out the fallen EMP, they run right into range for an execution.

If there are survivors in the room following the EMP drop, hit one with a Death from Above and then immediately seek cover near one of the plated railings

MISSION 09: MICHIGAN AVE. RESERVOIR

crates and hunt them one-by-one. The chemical lights flood
e walkways with light, but you can still hide in the shadows
eated by walls and cover.

(T) TIP

here are underground pits with tunnels under this warehouse.
eel free to use them to vanish and sneak up on your
pponents.

ou choose to take the warehouse by force, use the door
the exterior of the building to enter a small room. Then,
eep up to the openings that look inside the chamber with
e hanging EMP. Mark targets for execution or fall back and
vise a strategy for bringing them to you.

ere is a light
side the small
om. It is not
emical. Shoot
ut to get
tention from a
ngle merc. He
ters the room
investigate.

ke him hostage as a human shield if you want to move into
e warehouse and start shooting. Otherwise, dump him in a
rk corner so he is not seen by the other mercs.

*Going hard on the warehouse? Execute to thin the herd
and give away your position. The other mercs will seek out
your position.*

(T) TIP

Because there are two openings into your small room, prime
one of them with a mine so nobody can sneak up on you with
impunity.

Use your LKP
as a lure to get
the mercs to
concentrate on one
of the openings in
the small room.
When you see their
flashlight beams
approach one of the openings, circle around to shoot them
from behind as they investigate the LKP.

Once the warehouse is clear, enter the back room beneath the
chemical light. There are frags and flashbangs on the crate in
the back office. After collecting the weapons, jump up to the
pipe along the ceiling and shimmy over the wall to the right. The
pipe extends down a vertical shaft. The scientist is in the sewer
tunnels beneath the warehouse. Drop down to find her.

SCIENTIST

At the bottom of the pipe, drop down to the tunnels and then
follow the long corridor until you hear chatter. Peek through the
space between some of the water pipes to see the Black Arrow
thugs harassing the kidnapped scientist. You cannot shoot
them from here. That would put the scientist at risk. But her
time is limited. You must rush to her rescue before the Black
Arrow thugs kill her.

There are mercs dead ahead. Sneak up to the corner looking into the clearing where the trio is discussing their next move. If you have an execution, mark and kill. If not, set a trap to kill all three within seconds. Drop a remote mine in the narrow opening between you and the mercs.

Then, lean out and shoot one. The mercs spot your LKP and start to move on you. Run to the nearby pipe and climb it. When the mercs step too close to the remote mine, blow it up. Hopefully, both were flattened, but if not, use the pipe as a vantage point to take out the third merc.

Explosions attract attention. Stay on the pipe. Reinforcements are on the way. From the pipe, you can cut down any additional mercs that inspect the carnage.

Use the pipe extending across the ceiling to slide over the next room. Additional mercs are looking for you. Mark them for execution and then drop down for a Death from Above on the closest merc. Now you have the execution needed to finish off the other mercs before they turn their machine guns on you.

When you round the corner and close in on the scientist, the clock starts ticking. You have just one minute to kill the mercs around the scientist and save her from execution. There are stairs for dropping in on the mercs or you can slink along the ground floor and attack from the doors.

CAUTION

Do not use frag grenades or mines in this room. You may accidentally kill the scientist.

The stairs provide the best killing angle on the mercs holding the scientist. While they look for you on the ground floor, you can target at least two of them from above before they get wise to your position.

Get spotted at one of the doors on the ground floor. While the merc looks at your LKP, use another door to flank.

MISSION 09: MICHIGAN AVE. RESERVOIR

...hen all of the ...rcs are down, ...roach the ...ientist. She tells ...u exactly how to ...able the EMP. ...o generators ...ce the EMP. Only ...e is required to power it for the blast. If you want to take out ...e EMP, you must destroy both generators at the same time ...deny it power.

Refresh your loadout at the ...eapons stash just ...yond the scientist ...before pulling ...urself up to the ...rface to track the ...MP generators.

...er questioning ...e scientist, ...ease her and ...en follow the ...nnel behind her. ...cend the stairs ...d then jump ...the wall to pull ...urself toward the surface.

...ck Arrow has a serious concentration of mercs around ...e EMP site. It almost looks like a small army. You must get ...rough these and close in on both generators and mark them ... Vic. Vic will fly in via chopper once the second generator ...s been marked and then destroy them both with missiles to ...arantee neither juices the EMP. He'll have Sarah onboard, ..., so you better work fast.

...IRST GENERATOR

...hen you reach the surface, you are looking up through a hole ...the floor of a small storehouse. Several Black Arrow thugs ...e fanning across the area. One false move will bring them all ...wn on your position. There is a single guard looking around ...e storehouse. Stay low and wait until his back is turned. If you

...can get a clean headshot, take it. Otherwise, jump up and grab him for a hand-to-hand kill, banking a Mark and Execution.

Killing the first merc may draw attention to the storehouse. Jump up on the pipes and climb to the ceiling. If several PMCs push through the door, you can either take them out with a remote mine or frag. If you have a banked execution, mark these thugs and wipe them out.

Hop through one of the windows on the right side of the storehouse and take immediate cover. Multiple mercs are now surrounding the storehouse. Watch for them to come from both sides. If at any time you can eliminate a guard with a close kill, do it. Mark and

Execute is perfect for clearing out the remainder of the PMCs spreading across the yard surrounding the storehouse. Stay in cover, away from the tunnel though, because there is an auto-turret inside that will chew you up if you're spotted. You do not want to deal with guards and the turret at the same time.

You have a serious problem at the lighted tunnel opposite the storehouse. Not only is there a merc inside, but also an auto-targeting machine gun turret.

You must disable that turret. It's shielded, so an EMP burst will not work. Instead, lob a frag grenade into the tunnel. The explosion disarms the turret and kills the nearby merc.

Climb down the ledge beyond the weapons stash and follow the tunnel until you locate another ladder. This leads up to the clearing next to the first generator. Be warned: several mercs patrol the area directly above the ladder. Your sonar goggles give you a peek at their locations. Watch their patrol patterns and then move when the coast is clear at the top of the ladder.

Mark the mercs near generator one, even if you aren't plann to use an execution. This will at least help you keep track of targets.

Silly mercs, standing by a fuel drum. Punish them for not observing their surroundings while Sam Fisher is afoot.

⟨T⟩ TIP

Shoot out the lights on the parked ATV to create additional shadows to use if you do not have an execution and must slir closer to take out the mercs.

When the rest of the mercs are down, approach the generator. You are in plain sight right now, but nobody is around to disturb you while you mark the generator for  Vic. The second generator is on the other side of the reservo You must slip through a tunnel connecting the two sites, but first you must deal with an incoming Black Arrow patrol. Approach the building with "Locate Second Generator" painte on the side of it and take cover. The next patrol is on the othe side of the building.

The explosion may not kill many mercs, but it causes confusion. While the mercs swarm the area of the explosion, pepper them with frag grenades.

Tossing those frags (or taking shots) at the mercs near the explosion site draws a little attention. You are likely to have a visitor. Sit in the shadows and then grab him when he approaches the ladder. Use the merc as a human shield and target the other mercs near the generator.

The mercs split up. One usually ducks into the building while others come around the left side. Hide at the carts to plan your shots.

MISSION 09: MICHIGAN AVE. RESERVOIR

TUNNEL

When you enter the tunnel beneath the reservoir, seek out the weapons stash next to the fleet of Black Arrow Humvees and trucks. These mercs are ready for war. The corridor on the far side of the fleet leads off to the right. The corridor is narrow with two doors. There are mercs at the first door so do not blindly run past it (located halfway down the corridor) or else you will have mercs on you.

The fuel tank on the forklift outside the storehouse is a perfect bomb. Plant a sticky cam on the tank and make noise to attract mercs. When you see one appear in the sticky cam monitor, blow the cam to ignite the tank and eliminate any nearby PMCs.

Wait at the edge of the first door for the mercs to turn their backs. Run by the door, but then let out a shot to get their attention. This leaves behind a LKP. Use the second door as cover to cut down the mercs checking your LKP. The splash damage from mine or grenade should do the trick.

(T) TIP

Return to the weapons stash often, refilling spent grenades or Portable EMP blasts. Once you leave this area, there are no more weapons stashes in the mission.

Grab a merc by the carts to bank an execution in anticipation of either clearing out the rest of the patrol or infiltrating the tunnel.

Look for a fuel drum inside the second door. Watch the merc patrols via sonar goggles and then shoot the drum when more than one is close to it.

Set up a trap by placing a remote mine at the corner of the building near the tunnel. Lure the mercs in with LKP and blast them off their feet.

Enter the room after the dust clears. A flashbang keeps the mercs back as you move to the left into the shadows. If you leave behind a LKP, don't worry about it. You're about to announce yourself in a bigger way.

Always use your sonar goggles to check for survivors after a big explosion. You may have missed one or two mercs that were just outside the blast radius.

There's nothing like luring a merc out with LKP—right into an expertly placed mine.

Continue deeper into the tunnel; you're almost to the other side. Duck into the small room among the trucks and slink up to the door looking out on several mercs taking up positions around tires. Lob a frag into the mix to get their attention and leave behind an LKP. Now, you can stick to the door and try to pick off the mercs, but with that LKP at the door, you're safer backing out of the small room and flanking to the left around the trucks. Exit the tunnel via the ramp and make your move on the second generator.

SECOND GENERATOR

Vic isn't the only person in the vicinity with a chopper. Black Arrow is determined to take you out once and for all, so they have put a bird in the air circling the second generator. This chopper cannot be taken down by gunfire, grenades, or an EMP pulse. You must avoid it as you move up on the generato. Never stray far from cover because when the chopper circles around and gets you in its floodlight, it unleashes a storm of bullets. If caught, you're shredded within seconds. However, th chopper can only fire in bursts. If you wait until those pauses t move, you can survive moving up through the area, even if the chopper floodlight detects you.

Even though the chopper cannot be laid low by EMPs, the mercs can. Use EMP blasts to temporarily disable the mercs so you can advance with only the chopper to worry about.

The central tower is a great vantage point for spotting incoming mercs as well as avoiding chopper fire.

MISSION 09: MICHIGAN AVE. RESERVOIR

eep up to
e old metal
rts. They are
cellent cover
m the chopper
d the mercs.
e grenades
d mines to take out the mercs at the building dead ahead.
hen you see an opening, advance to the sandbags to keep
Iden from the chopper. Drop the incoming mercs with mines
d grenades if possible—otherwise, take them out with bullets.

◄◄◄ ⓒCAUTION

| The building does not last long against the chopper if you try to seek refuge inside of it. |  |

e mercs make
e last push as
u approach
e tower with
e second
nerator.
e the crates

and the tower itself as cover from the chopper and target
the rushing mercs headed in your direction. You must circle
the tower to the right to access the generator, which leads
you straight through enemy territory. Never stand in the
open—that's a quick death. Use cover, running only when the
chopper's floodlight sweeps elsewhere.

*Use the tower encasing the second EMP generator as cover to
eliminate the Black Arrow guards on each side of the objective.
The tower protects you from the chopper.*

After you mark the second generator, Vic swoops in to save the
day. He shoots down the menacing Black Arrow chopper. Once
you have the signal, flee from the second generator and take
cover as Vic hammers both sites with missiles, successfully
disabling this EMP.

TOM CLANCY'S SPLINTER CELL CONVICTION

Vic lands to pick you up. Sarah is onboard. Run to the chopper to meet her embrace. This has been three years in the coming, but with Black Arrow still poised to strike the White House with Third Echelon's back-up, there is little time for the reunion. You must hitch a ride to 1600 Pennsylvania Ave., to catch up with Grim as she tries to rescue the president from Reed's nefarious power-grab.

KNOWN INTEL

While flying to the White House, you witness the spectacular power of the two remaining EMPs. The pulses, directed at the power center of the United States, knock out all electricity in the downtown area. Sarah cannot help but feel for the citizens of DC who have no idea what's happening—or what's coming.

Vic, on the other hand, is more concerned about the missile heading toward his chopper from air defenses around the White House. Black Arrow moved into position faster than expected. The chopper is hit. Vic guides it into a "soft" crash landing downtown. Everybody onboard survives, but Fisher must leave his daughter again and make his way to the White House to stop Reed.

MISSION 10: DOWNTOWN DISTRICT

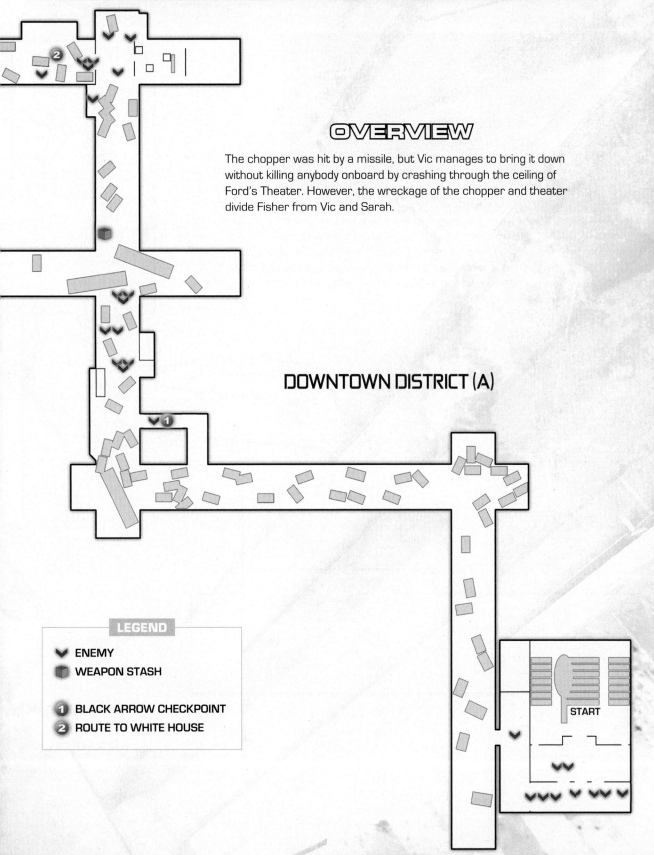

OVERVIEW

The chopper was hit by a missile, but Vic manages to bring it down without killing anybody onboard by crashing through the ceiling of Ford's Theater. However, the wreckage of the chopper and theater divide Fisher from Vic and Sarah.

DOWNTOWN DISTRICT (A)

LEGEND

- ⌄ ENEMY
- ◧ WEAPON STASH

- ① BLACK ARROW CHECKPOINT
- ② ROUTE TO WHITE HOUSE

START

TOM CLANCY'S SPLINTER CELL CONVICTION

Fisher is hesitant to leave Sarah behind and get to the White House—he's lost her once before and would rather not do it again. But Sarah encourages him to go. She knows her father is the only person who can stop the coup about to take place under the cover of darkness.

EXIT

5

4

3

START

LEGEND

⌄ ENEMY

3 WHITE HOUSE GATE

4 GATEHOUSE

5 WHITE HOUSE LAWN

MISSION 10: DOWNTOWN DISTRICT

STRATEGY

egiddo's plan to assume the power of the presidency is most complete. You must leave Sarah behind and fight your ay to the White House to stop Reed. The streets are filled th panicked citizens, terrified not only of the loss of electricity, t also the arrival of a paramilitary force that's acting like it's placing the Army.

rtunately, you are not too far from the White House. After shing through the streets, you must cross the White House wn and gardens to access the building. Black Arrow is heavily ncentrated around the White House, so expect a lot of sistance not only at the gates to the grounds, but also the wn itself. You must employ stealth to survive. You are simply tgunned and will not survive a forward assault.

THE THEATER

ter accepting at you must ave Sarah, get ady for Black row mercs nverging on e theater. They acked your ash and want make sure you're dead. Sneak up to any of the three doors oking into the lobby to observe the mercs infiltrating the ilding. You have the advantage, but not for long. Act fast to ke down as many as possible by lobbing frags into the lobby they pour through the doors.

P.E.C. CHALLENGE

Dropping a frag in the middle of at least three enemies in close quarters like the lobby results in the 3X Frag award.

Throwing frags reveals your osition, but if you old your ground, you can lunge ut and grab an ggressive merc attempting to nter the theater.

Use a Mark and ecute earned via hand-to-hand kill eliminate Black Arrow thugs.

Gun down any surviving mercs from the doorway. Use your sonar goggles to check for any potential stragglers. When the coast is clear, move through the lobby into the streets outside.

THE STREET

It's hard to believe that Washington DC could ever look like a war zone, but the damage caused by the EMP blast has done just that. Abandoned cars are everywhere, smashed into poles and storefronts when the pulse killed their engines. Fires rage in apartments. Emergency services try to help those they can, but the amount of death and destruction is overwhelming, especially when they are denied all but the basic tools of their trade.

Walk through the survivors, stopping only when an exploding gas tank blocks the street and forces you into an alley.

A Black Arrow thug is maintaining a checkpoint, trying to push civilians as far back from the White House as possible. A harassed citizen occupies the attention of the merc, allowing you cover to sneak up on the checkpoint. As soon as the dejected citizen leaves, strike to earn an execution.

If you shoot before the citizen leaves, he yells out in surprise, which gets the attention of the mercs around the corner. This feeds them into the narrow alley, which is an excellent chokepoint.

Shimmy up the pipe and hold on to the ledge as more mercs rush the alley. Mark and execute or drop down for Death from Above.

Use the tunnels under the street to get behind the mercs and surprise them from the intersection where they parked their trucks. Grab one for a hand-to-hand kill and use the Mark and Execute to thin their numbers.

You can either advance on the mercs from the street or remain on the ledge and use the high ground. The only catch is that if you are spotted up there, you're a sitting duck. Everybody in the street will know exactly where you are until you deploy countermeasures, such as a flashbang. However, the height advantage does have its perks. You can see the entire street full of mercs and lob frags into their midst to score multiple kills.

Stay low and creep up to the next corner to spy a small Black Arrow patrol. Mark the mercs for execution and then cut them down. If you miss any, fall back and use your LKP to lead them up to the corner. When you see a helmet pop around the side of the building, open fire.

There are small tunnels running under the street, exposed by the EMP blast disrupting gas pipes. Under the street, you are invisible to the mercs. Criss-cross under their feet to keep them on their toes, popping out to take a shot or lob a grenade. Establish LKPs at the holes leading

into the tunnels to distract the guards, playing a little Cat and Mouse with them. While they investigate your LKP at one hole, you pop up from another and shoot them in the back of the head for an effortless kill.

(T) TIP

Never forget the sticky cam trap. If multiple mercs swarm, draw them into one central location by throwing a sticky cam in a well-trafficked route. Use the noise function to draw them near and then blc the sticky cam to eliminate anybody that gets too close.

Advance to the white compact car farther up the block to observe the next patrol. They have established a sandbag barricade. Launch a frag or mine into their midst.

While the mercs recover from the explosion, move to the truck and cut down the survivors.

Weave around the trucks in the next intersection to locate a weapon stash and restock. Then run through the next batch of citizens who cannot believe what has happened.

MISSION 10: DOWNTOWN DISTRICT

‌NTERSECTION

‌mb up the fire
‌‌ape ladder on
‌ right side of
‌ intersection to
‌serve the crowd
‌hering around
‌ checkpoint.
‌en in on the

‌e Black Arrow boilerplate while plotting your course of
‌ion. You must kill these mercs to gain access to the street
‌ind them, but you cannot allow any civilian casualties.

> **TIP**
>
> ‌ways seek high ground to mount assaults, whether you are
> ‌tacking by stealth or outright gunplay.

> ◀◀◀ **CAUTION**
>
>
>
> Use no
> grenades or
> mines at first.

‌rgeting one of
‌ mercs in the
‌owd and pulling
‌ trigger causes
‌ a panic that
‌ears the crowd.
‌w you can use
‌ugher tactics
‌ch as grenades.

‌he panic of the
‌owd allows you
‌ disappear for
‌ second. Drop
‌ frag into the
‌ercs to kill at
‌east three of
‌hem and bank
‌other 3X Frag
‌.E.C. Challenge.

‌p down to the
‌eet and use
‌ cars and walls
‌cover when
‌acking the
‌ckpoint. If you
‌e any more
‌gs, throw them

at your attackers
to clear out
the checkpoint.
Otherwise, target
them with your
guns and pick
them off from
the safety of the
shadows.

*Use sticky cams
not only to monitor
the mercs in the
busy intersection,
but also to pull
them in and blast
their faces off.*

*There are more
tunnels beneath
the busy inter-
section. Elude the
mercs by darting
into the tunnels,
keeping them
guessing.*

When the
checkpoint is
emptied of mercs,
pass through the
gates and step
around the Black
Arrow gear to
make a beeline for
the White House.

You have a country to save, even if it no longer gives a damn
about you.

> **TIP**
>
> After clearing out the intersection, head back to the weapons
> stash to restock your grenades and mines.

WHITE HOUSE EXTERIOR

Under orders
from Megiddo,
Reed and Black
Arrow wasted
no time making
their move on
the White House.
As you approach

the White House perimeter, you see smoke rising from the
building. Bodies slump on balconies. Reaching the White
House requires running down the winding lane leading to the

columned entrance. That road is lined with Black Arrow patrols. But before you can make a move on the lawn, you must break through the Black Arrow checkpoint at the White House gates.

GATES

On a night that's gone so wrong, fortune manages to finally smile on you. The EMP pulse knocked out all electricity, requiring the

use of gas-powered generators. Black Arrow has a fuel tanker parked near the gates. That is your ticket into the grounds. Target the bright red tanker and pump it with bullets. The explosion blows the gates off their hinges and kills every single Black Arrow merc on the street. There are still survivors inside the gates, but you just created an incredible diversion.

The mercs know that gas truck didn't explode on its own. Reinforcements filter across the street to investigate. Tag them as they approach to keep track of

the mercs and then shoot them one by one to clear out the initial wave.

As you close in on the gate, more Black Arrow thugs emerge from the White House grounds. Stay to the right of the entrance and pick them off as they run by.

Infiltrate the gatehouse from the street. Plug the mercs looking at the blown gates and then slip into the gatehouse via an open window on the back wall.

CAUTION

A frontal assault here is possible, but stealth measures will guarantee your extended survival.

At least one merc is inside the gatehouse. Slip through the shadows to approach the merc from behind. Blast the merc in the back of the head and then quickly target the first visible merc on the road outside. This alerts the rest of the mercs that you are in

the gatehouse, but placing a remote mine on the door sets trap. As the mercs chase your LKP, you shatter them with t detonation.

If you move fast (using the cover of a flashbang or EMP blast helps), climb on top of the gatehouse. From up there, you can target the mercs with frags or a powerful rifle.
Just make sure you aren't spotted because if the mercs s you, they communicate your position and then you must u another diversion tool to get back down.

GARDEN ROAD

The road through the White House garden is even thicker with Black Arrow scum. As you approach the parked Humvee in the middle of the road, duck into

cover off to the right to watch the advancing patrol. They are spreading out to hunt you. If you have a grenade, blast them all before they fan out. If you lack explosives, you can use the shrubs and truck as cover to take them out one at a time.

Stay in cover to avoid being detected while hunting the mercs from the bushes.

MISSION 10: DOWNTOWN DISTRICT

CAUTION

Bushes do not absorb bullets—they pass right through them.

Grab one of the mercs for a close kill so you have an execution at the ready.

NOTE

A human shield is always of good use when dealing with multiple attackers, but it is incredibly difficult to be stealthy while holding a squirming man.

As you come to the White House lawn, look for even more mercs to push down the road. The lawn is a parking lot for Black Arrow vehicles, from personnel carriers to satellite trucks. Dive into cover before the mercs see you. There are several of them and if you want to survive, you need the element of surprise.

TIP

Got a grenade or mine? Toss it into the incoming group for a massive kill.

Advance to the trucks for cover and target the mercs from the shadows. They are partially trained on the road, so use that to flank.

It is easy to be overwhelmed by the sheer number of mercs in the lawn area, plus they are ultra-aggressive. Without any sense of fear to keep them back, you need to use human shields to avoid getting blasted. Plus, the Mark and Execute granted by the human shield thins the herd by at least two per use. You can get more depending on the sidearm you use.

Grim comes over the earpiece. She needs you in the White House—now. You tell her that you're coming through the front door, but she tells you it has been completely locked down. You need to enter the White House through the garden door to the right. Grim unlocks the door. However, as you approach the front of the building to break for the garden door, a final batch of mercs spreads out.

Flank the incoming mercs by hiding behind the bushes near the steps leading to the front door. Do not use the landing above you. There is no cover up there; you will be a sitting duck.

Use cover to sneak up to the face of the White House. Cut down any remaining mercs from the shadows or use an execution to eliminate them in batches.

The garden door is at the end of a long path along the side of the White House. The bodies of slain Secret Service agents litter the path. If these elite guards could not stop Reed's plan, then you are truly the president's last chance. You are this country's last chance. Enter the White House and fight your way to the Oval Office where you hope you can stop Reed before he does the unthinkable.

MISSION 11: WHITE HOUSE

OVERVIEW

When Fisher finally breached the White House, he found a scene of pure horror. The American seat of power had been successfully infiltrated and taken hostage by an outside force. In this case, Tom Reed had used a select cabal of trusted associates to do the ultimate dirty work, slaughtering White House staff and the president's last line of defense: the Secret Service. While Black Arrow mercenaries continued to lock down the immediate area around the White House, Fisher moved on the Oval Office in an effort to stop Reed. Cut the head off the snake and the body will die. The only problem is that while this operation is a snake, Megiddo is a multi-headed hydra.

WHITE HOUSE (A)

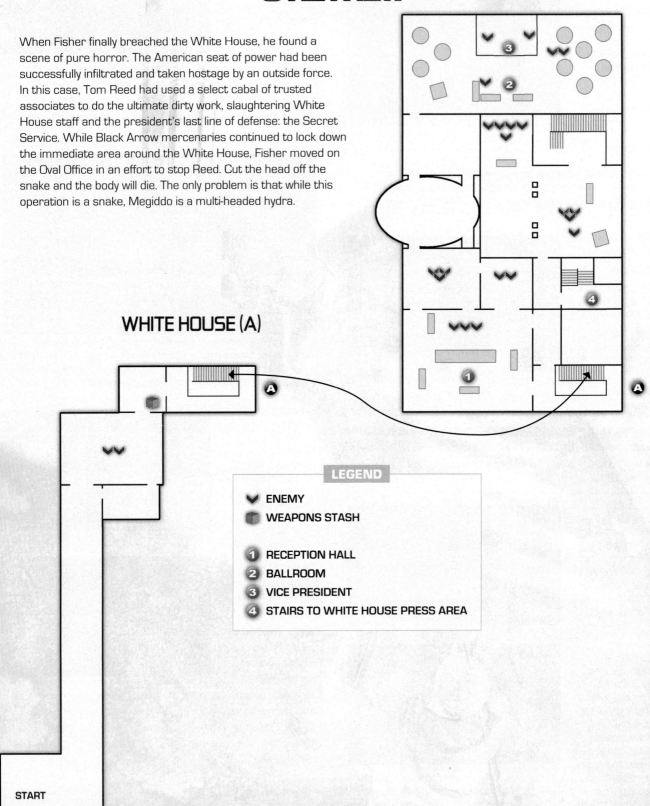

LEGEND

⌄ ENEMY

▣ WEAPONS STASH

① RECEPTION HALL
② BALLROOM
③ VICE PRESIDENT
④ STAIRS TO WHITE HOUSE PRESS AREA

START

MISSION 11: WHITE HOUSE

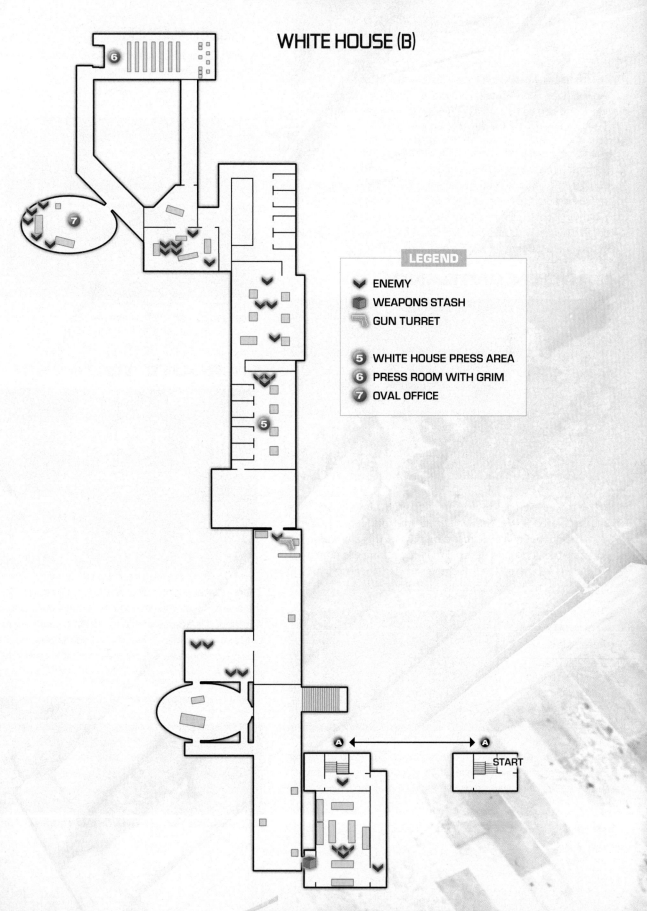

WHITE HOUSE (B)

LEGEND

⌄ ENEMY

WEAPONS STASH

GUN TURRET

5 WHITE HOUSE PRESS AREA

6 PRESS ROOM WITH GRIM

7 OVAL OFFICE

STRATEGY

You are always outnumbered, but inside the White House, you must face Third Echelon agents once trained by you. They know how to use cover and effectively flank, and they possess top of the line gear. Some of the agents even have sonar goggles like yours and can see you through walls. So, whenever you spot an agent with red lenses, know that no corner is truly safe.

The White House mission is divided into two parts. In the first half of the mission, you must secure the vice president, who is in the building and ready to take a seat behind the big desk once Reed gets to the president. In the back half of the mission, you must locate Grim at the White House press room and then determine a way to take the Oval Office back from Reed before he kills the president and completes his coup.

GARDEN ENTRANCE

When the mission begins, you are inside the White House. The bodies of fallen Secret Service agents litter the long corridor from the garden entrance to the main floor. There are several doors on the corridor's right side, but the rooms are empty. Slow up as you reach the end of the corridor, because two agents are standing watch in the next room.

There are multiple ways to take out these agents. Because they have their backs to you, you can easily target them for headshots. However, if you  shoot only one and then rush the other, you can grab the agent for a close kill and bank an execution. Of course, you can also roll a frag between their legs or toss a mine at their feet.

P.E.C. CHALLENGE

Popping one of the agents in the back of the head from the shadows results in the Stealth Headshot award.

Access the weapons stash in the next room and then climb steps to the second floor of the White House to start hunt. the vice president. He's in a ballroom.

EN ROUTE TO THE VP

There is a reception hall at the top of the stairs. As you ente the room, several White House staffers burst through the double doors across the room, fleeing from agents. The age cut them down in cold blood and then spread out in the roor looking for more survivors from the initial attack. Make yours invisible so you can mount an effective offense on these thug

<<<< **CAUTION**

These agents carry frags and will not hesitate to lob them you, even if they do not have an exact bead on your positio They rely on splash damage to do the rest.

The agents have set up chemical lights to thwart your EMF You cannot knock out any of the lights with skinny bulbs an a blue glow.

MISSION 11: WHITE HOUSE

ere are two
ys to handle
s hall. The
tion approach is
rush in and dive
hind one of the
les. Watch the
ents mill around
e room and
en shoot the
andeliers when
u spy agents
neath them.
e crashing
andelier not
y kills the agent
ught beneath

ut the resulting chaos gives you a few seconds to pull off a
adshot or two from the tables without being detected. You
ust then find a way out of the room or else the agents will
round you. Either dive through the windows to the right to
o the agents from outside or leave a LKP at the door you
ed to enter the room and funnel the agents to the stairs.

*The agents are smart enough not to run down the stairs to
hase you, but you can drop at least one or two of them from
the bottom floor as they peer over the railing.*

cause there is
thing you can
to save the
affers, you can
rush the hall
d then scramble
the brass
ing that lines
e ceiling while
e agents are
sy murdering.
ey will not
e you hanging
m the railing
the shadows
the back

corners of the room, so use those hiding spots to shoot down
the chandeliers and kill as many agents as possible before
targeting them directly.

Watch the agents spread across the room...

*...and then target loners who break from the pack for easy kills
without giving away your position.*

*Watch the agents move through the room and then drop
mines in their routes.*

TOM CLANCY'S SPLINTER CELL CONVICTION

The room beyond the hall (with the red walls) is also crawling with agents. There is too much light in there to run in and start shooting. You'll be cut down. You can roll frags into the room from the hall and then watch the fireworks or dive through a window in the reception hall and shimmy along the ledge to mount a sneak attack.

Kill some agents from the window (that chandelier hanging from the ceiling tempts) to establish an LKP and then slip back through the window in the reception hall to flank the remaining thugs.

After emptying the red room, move through a round blue room and then into a green chamber to close in on the ballroom. More evidence of Reed's rampage is everywhere, such as staffers slumped over in chairs, their lives stopped with bullets to the brain. Slow down when you reach the door on the far wall of the green chamber. The ballroom is next, as is the vice president and a significant security detail.

SECURE THE VICE PRESIDENT

Quietly slip into the ballroom. The vice president is on the stage, standing before a flag. Several agents patrol the room while two stand guard next to the VP. Climb the lighting trellis that circles the ceiling to get the drop on the agents.

Draw the agents away from the VP by blasting the chandeli on the other side of the room. When the chandelier drops, t agents move to investigate.

ⓣ TIP

Do not drop both chandeliers. A second group is coming, an you can use the other chandelier to either distract that bunc or drop it on some unlucky agents.

If you have an execution ready, mark the agents as they mo around your half of the room and then make the kill.

MISSION 11: WHITE HOUSE

Dispatch the rest of the agents by targeting them for headshots from the trellis.

rnately, slink
g the back
e ballroom,
g the tables as
r. Get close
e agents and
mark them
execution.
e sure you are
ly behind cover
then drop
quarry. This
es a LKP at
table. Dash to
ther table and
ch the agents
e the ballroom

ank your LKP. Cut the agents off as they attempt to move
our LKP.

TIP

ou used an execution in the ballroom, try to kill at least one
ent with a hand-to-hand move or a Death from Above to bank
new execution.

vice president
s glued to the
e as you drop
security detail.
e you are
e with the VP,
e to the stage
grab the
as in a choke

. The VP taunts you as you squeeze his larynx, saying you're
ing but a washed-up old agent while he is bulletproof in this
order. You toss the VP back and then show him exactly
bulletproof he really is.

Move fast after releasing the VP. A second security detail is about to burst into the ballroom through the double doors opposite the stage. Try to get

back on the lighting trellis before they enter the room, but if you don't make it, duck behind one of the tables. This is why you always want to have an execution ready. You can mark and execute at least three of the agents pushing through the door.

The chemical lights in the room cannot be snuffed by an EMP blast, but you can at least stun the agents with an EMP grenade or a flashbang and then slip out of sight. Slam the agents with a grenade and then sprint away along the trellis so the agents are left staring at your LKP when they regain their senses.

If you make it on the trellis before the agents enter the ballroom, drop a mine in their path as they investigate the VP's new limp.

Cautiously follow the red carpet into the next hall. four agents, each with sonar goggles, are about to drop into the room to your left. If they spot you, they track you no matter where you go. The only escape is to drop a flashbang and then fall back as far as possible and hope the agents temporarily let down their guard.

The elite agents throw smoke grenades that fill the corridor. Use sonar goggles to spot your targets through the smoke.

However, if you rush down the red carpet as soon as you drop the last of the VP's security detail, you can shimmy up the pipe before the agents are dropped into the room. They will not instinctively look up to the ceiling. Use this to get the drop on the agents. Kill them with well-placed mines. If you drop one right between the agents, they won't see it with their sonar goggles in time. The explosion rips through each of them.

You're not done yet. Additional agents with sonar goggles are on their way into the hall with the red carpet. Stay to the side of the door near the grand piano and catch one of the agents running through. Take him down with a close kill or hold him as a human shield to prote you from his nearby back-up.

Sonar goggles let the agents see through walls, but they cannot shoot through them, so still seek cover and use it to return fire on the agents.

KITCHEN AND TUNNEL

The plan is now to meet Grim in the White House press room and formulate a plan for saving the president. You must move through the kitchen and a tunnel to access the press area of the White House and close in on the Oval Office.

Carefully drop down the open elevator shaft and surprise the guard outside the kitchen. Grab him to earn an execution.

Use the agent as a human shield and mark the other thugs in the kitchen for execution.

MISSION 11: WHITE HOUSE

TIP

ossing frags into the kitchen via the service window also makes short work of the agents patrolling the area.

P.E.C. CHALLENGE

f the agents in the kitchen start to run for the exits to meet you in the allway, toss a flashbang into the mix and fall back to the stairs to earn he Flashbang Escape.

Use LKP to lure the agents to one of the service windows while you sneak to another window (or into the kitchen) to flank.

e hall behind
e kitchen
ds to a
nnel that
es through
basement
the White
use. There
several dead
cret Service
ents in the
nnel, shredded
an automatic
rret behind
metal gates
lfway down the
rridor. The gun
ates, looking for
arget. Watch
turret and
en it spins away, advance to the next cover in the corridor, ch as a planter or crate.

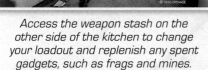

Access the weapon stash on the other side of the kitchen to change your loadout and replenish any spent gadgets, such as frags and mines.

CAUTION

The chemical lights illuminating the corridor for the turret cannot be extinguished with EMP tech.

To flank the turret, advance to the end of the corridor and then rush to the open door. There is no time to breathe a sigh of relief, though. More agents with sonar goggles are ahead.

When you approach the next room, you see multiple agents. With their sonar goggles, they can see through the walls and crates. So use yours to watch their movement patterns and then slip up to a door when their backs are turned and open fire or roll grenades at their feet.

CAUTION

LKP means nothing to these agents—they can see through walls. They know you are not at your LKP.

It's easy to start running laps around the room with the agents. To break the pattern, drop a flashbang or mine and then set it off to create a diversion. The agents will be stunned by the action, giving you a chance to slip into the room beyond this circular chamber and then hunt them from behind. Because they can see through walls, you have to sneak up from behind. Those sonar goggles do not give them eyes in the back of their heads.

P.E.C. CHALLENGE

Slipping away from these agents and then hanging tight until the heat blows over and they return to their normal patrols (visible via your sonar goggles) can result in either the Cat and Mouse or Vanish Silently awards. Or both.

Stay low and sneak through the first line of cubicles and sm offices in the blue-walled room.

After eliminating the elite agents in the library, step over their bodies and re-enter the corridor with the auto-turret. Do not rush. Slowly approach the corner leading into the hallway and crouch down.

Use your sonar goggles as you near the end of the row. Wh you see movement, duck into one of the offices so the agen run right by you.

Creep up to the corner of the statue pedestal outside the library. Lean out and roll a frag grenade at the turret to disable it and kill the merc maintaining it.

PRESS ROOM

The door at the end of the tunnel, behind the turret, leads into the press area of the White House. More Secret Service bodies reveal the sheer

brutality of Reed's assault. He planned this to go fast and hard, leaving nobody alive to tell the tale. Use the weapons stash in the room with the dead Secret Service agents and then move on to the press area.

Flank the agents after they run past you, and mow them dov as they explore the offices.

MISSION 11: WHITE HOUSE

...ditional agents ...op from the ...ling in the next ...om. They are ...t immediately ...king for you, ...ich you can use ...your advantage. ...shbangs daze ...m just as they ...d, letting you ...ect the assault. ...op a flashbang ...d then kill an ...ent or two while ...ey recoil. When ...ey start to ...aighten back up, drop another flash and keep clearing.

TIP

Use an execution to drop multiple agents with a single move. ...he room is small enough that you can easily drop two targets ...ith an execution.

...jents stunned by the flashbangs are perfect targets for hand-...-hand kills. Plus, you'll benefit from a banked execution in the next encounter.

...ough there are chemical lights in this room, you can still stun an agent with an EMP grenade rolled right under his feet.

P.E.C. CHALLENGE

An EMP grenade dropped in the laps of these guards satisfies the Stunned P.E.C. Challenge.

Sneak up to the door of the next room. The agents are involved in a last-stand firefight with Secret Service agents. Use this situation to your advantage. Circle behind the agents and take them out with frags, Mark and Execute, or any combination thereof. Peek under the door with the snake cam and mark as many as possible for execution. Then, slip into the back of the room via the nearby open door and drop the marked agents. This throws the rest in high alert, but a flashbang throws them off the trail, allowing you to slip back out into the hall.

While the agents investigate your LKP, flank the room back toward the door you peeked under and finish off the survivors.

The door at the end of the hall leads into the actual White House press room, where Grim waits for you. Reed still does not suspect her, but if she marches into the Oval Office with you at her side, Reed will kill the president and then turn his men on you. Grim has a plan, but it's going to hurt. She shoots you in the shoulder and then disarms you.

TOM CLANCY'S
SPLINTER CELL
CONVICTION

As Grim pushes you toward the Oval Office, you sure hope she's still on your side. Otherwise the last thing you see will be your blood splashed across the rug in the Oval Office.

Grim shoves you to the floor in front of Reed, who has the president surrounded by his closest agents. If the president is not dead, then you still have a chance, but only if Grim is still true to the cause you once both believed in. Reed gets in your face, furious about your interference. As he talks, mark the agents surrounding the president.

Reed reveals his plan: he is going to frame you for the president's murder by shooting her with your gun and then filling you with lead before the Army arrives to secure the White House. As Reed explains that the president was about to shut down Third Echelon, he gets too close. When prompted, reach out and grab Reed's gun. Reed doesn't see it coming and flinches, allowing you to grab his pistol and kill the marked agents. Grim assists the president as you corner Reed.

You question Reed about Megiddo. Megiddo pulled the strings to have your daughter killed so you would take the undercover assignment from Lambert that put you in a position to later kill him. With Lambert and you out of the way, Megiddo and Reed could sculpt Third Echelon into a shadow government. Just before you can pull the trigger on Reed, the Army enters the Oval Office to secure the president. The president tells the Army to back off and that the official record will show that nobody besides Grim and the president were in the Oval Office.

As ordered, the Army falls back and the president excuses herself from the Oval Office, leaving just you, Grim, and Reed. You have a choice now. You can either pull the trigger and execute Reed, or just smash his face one last time before leaving the office. He took three years of your life. Engineered the great lie about your daughter. What does he deserve? Death and mercy? If you pull the trigger, Reed slumps back on the desk. His death will not stop Megiddo but it will slow it down.

However, if you show mercy and do not summarily execute Reed, you remain a whole man. You did not stoop to that monster's level. But that doesn't mean Grim can't. As you turn your back on Reed, Grim slides behind you and puts a bullet in Reed's head. Grim understands why you didn't kill him, but she has her own reasons for wanting him dead. Grim begs you to stay to help her pick up the pieces of tonight's catastrophic events, but you are finished. You walk. But can you ever get out of the shadow of Third Echelon?

CO-OP STORY

The four-mission Co-op Story charts the assignments of special agents Archer and Kestrel, two spies involuntarily placed on the same team when four Russian EMP devices are stolen. The EMP devices in question are related to the main plot of Sam Fisher's mission, making this game mode a prequel of sorts. Archer and Kestrel must travel deep into the Russian underworld to track down the EMP devices before they are sold to the highest bidders among the lowest people.

Co-op Story cannot be played alone; it must be played with a second person. You can either play Co-Op Story online, via System Link, or split-screen. You and a friend must work together to dispatch enemy guards, circumvent dangerous security systems, and find those EMPs.

NOTE

For additional multiplayer modes, such as Face Off and Last Stand, please see the next chapter. All Deniable Ops and extra missions use the same maps as Co-op Story, although some appear in truncated form in Last Stand.

CO-OP

When you begin Co-op Story, you must set the mission parameters. If you are just starting Co-op Story for the first time with a particular friend, you must select the very first mission: St. Petersburg Banya. If your game is interrupted, you may pick up where you left off the next time you play. You can also select the mission difficulty: Rookie, Normal, and Realistic. The higher the difficulty, the more merciless the hostiles. On Rookie, for example, you may have a few extra moments to take down a guard who has spotted you before your Last Known Position is relayed to comrades. In Realistic, you have only a second to react to being revealed—and you better be ready for serious incoming fire.

Prior to your mission, select mission settings such as difficulty and gadgets in the set-up menu.

You must also select the weapons and gadgets you take into the field. You can choose two gadgets, such as frag grenades and flashbangs, or sticky cameras and remote mines. You always have sonar goggles and the portable EMP generator.

TIP

Mix up your gear so your team is prepared. Make sure each player has one explosive such as frags or mines and one distraction gadget, such as flashbangs or EMP grenades.

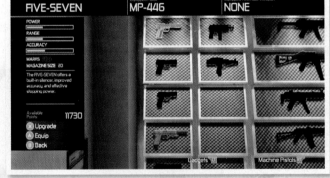

You also select two weapons: pistol and alternate weapon. Your weapon choices are limited to those unlocked in the main story or unlocked during previous co-op play successes. Finally, you select a uniform for your agent. Information about all uniforms, including how to unlock them and upgrade them, is covered in the beginning of the Deniable Ops chapter.

THE HEROES

The Co-op prequel to the events of *Conviction* stars two agents from opposite sides of the Atlantic—Archer from Third Echelon and Kestrel from Voron, Russia's top-secret spy organization. Each player assumes the role of one of these agents. Each has similar training, so there are no shortcomings to avoid. Both can mark and execute. Both can use all gadgets. Both are ruthless.

ARCHER

Archer is the code name of special agent Daniel Sloane-Suarez, a former NSA officer with an Economics degree from Harvard. Sloane-Suarez was a brilliant analyst, but he was not suited for the office. He longed to work in the field and chase down the terrorists he spied on at the NSA. Sloane-Suarez was eventually recruited by Third Echelon and placed in the agency's physical training program. He passed all training with flying colors and earned the call-sign Archer.

KESTREL

Not much is known about agent Kestrel. His real name is Mikhail Volkov, and after a hard childhood in foster care (his parents we killed in a terrorist attack), he was arrested and placed into conscription with the Russian military. Finally, Volkov found his place and excelled in the army, soon finding himself in a counterinsurgency unit charged with neutralizing Chechen guerillas. Volkov was captured and tortured by the guerillas but was eventually rescued. After Volkov recovered, he was recruited into Voron, a high-ris recon agency where he was given the call-sign Kestrel.

CO-OP STORY MODE

CO-OP MOVES

CO-OP MARK AND EXECUTE

...th Archer and Kestrel can mark and execute targets, just ...e Sam Fisher. After completing a close kill, the spies earn ...ecutions. Each player can tag targets independently, but ...hen you share a view of the same marks, you can execute ...gether and expand your range of fire. The player who initiates ...e execution waits for the other to join in. Both players then ...ke down the marked hostiles. The player that "joined" the ...ecution does not give up his banked execution.

...EVIVE

...you are shot a few times, you stumble and fall. However, ...stead of dying right away, you start to bleed out. Your ...rtner will see that you are down and that there is a time ...nit to reach you before you die for good. Your partner must ...and over you and hold the Revive button to get you back on ...ur feet. During this time, they are vulnerable to attacks. If ...n enemy approaches, they must release and engage. This ...starts the Revive meter, though.

...hile you are down, you may defend yourself. Choose Sit Up to ...ush your torso off the floor and shoot at enemies. Sitting up ...akes you an instant target. If you are shot again, you die and ...nnot be revived. This ends the mission in failure.

CHOKE HOLD

Enemies can grab you, too. However, they cannot execute. Instead, they hold you in a choke hold and slowly squeeze the life out of you. When you are being choked, a warning on your partner's screen points out your location and a timer shows how long before you lose consciousness.

While being held, you can dodge. This move quickly pulls you away from the hostile, giving your partner a clean shot at the target. However, your assailant does not let go of you while you dodge. If your partner does not kill the hostile while you are dodging, you're pulled back into the choke hold—after getting a good pistol-whipping that saps your health.

WEAPONS STASH

Each location is split into five sectors. When you make it through a sector, you encounter a duo of weapons stashes your spies may use to replenish spent supplies and change out weapons. Once both of you reach a weapons stash, you may not backtrack into the previous area. However, you may return to these weapons stashes as many times as you like before moving on to the next sector.

ST. PETERSBURG BANYA

As you approach St. Petersburg, you receive basic intel for the mission. A rogue element of the Russian military has stolen four EMP devices, intending to sell them on the black market. Andre Kobin, a Third Echelon contact, has tracked the devices to Lesovsky. Lesovsky is brokering the deal, using his underworld connection to locate a buyer. Your objective is to eliminate Lesovsky and steal his contact list.

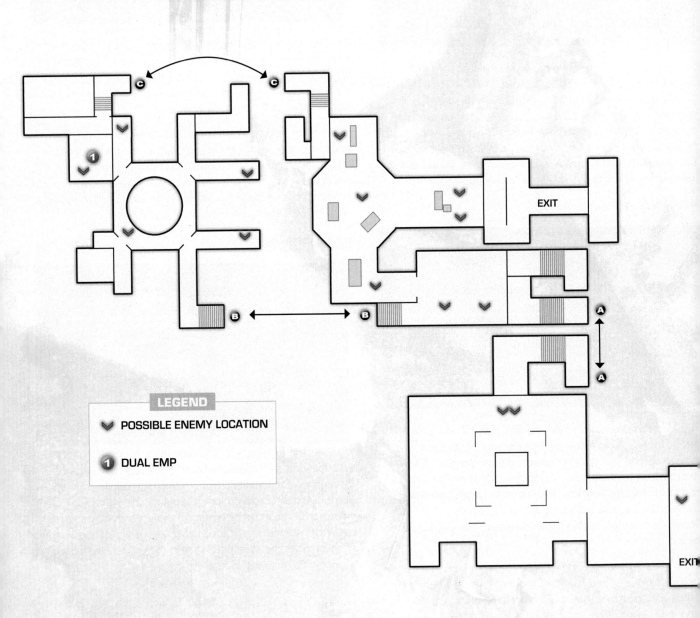

LEGEND

⌄ POSSIBLE ENEMY LOCATION

1 DUAL EMP

ST. PETERSBURG BANYA

ECTOR 1 STRATEGY

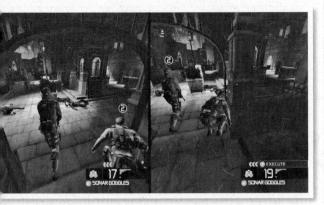

hen you approach the banya, you must take down the drunk
unding on the outer gate in order to score an execution.
you enter the grounds, use a co-op execution as a test so
ch of you are comfortable with the timing of sharing marked
rgets and taking them down. After sweeping through the
urtyard, enter the banya.

it up. One of you enters through the ground level door
ile the other shimmies up the pipe and enters through the
ndow. Work together to clear targets and converge in the
om visible through the window.

 TIP

Communicate! Talk over strategies and routes with your co-op
artner. Splitting up lets you cover more ground. However,
here are definitely going to be situations where you can use
ouble the firepower on the same enemies.

Once inside the banya, cross the empty circular lobby and
move up to the second floor. A room on the far side of the
balcony is bathed in blue light. Enter this room and use your
EMPs together to fry the lights in the banya. Make sure the
thug guarding the EMP spot is dead and then pump your EMPs
together. This extinguishes all of the lights.

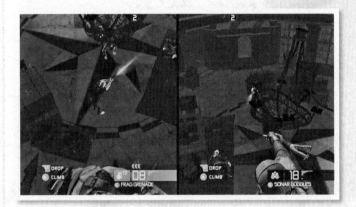

Now, backtrack to the circular foyer. Enemies are crowding the
foyer, looking for who killed the lights. Drop the chandelier on
their heads by shooting the chain that holds it up. Hang over
the edge of the balcony and shoot the thugs as they mill below
and when the coast is clear, move on to the first weapons
stash, which is your checkpoint.

 TIP

Lob frags down on the thugs in the foyer. And even though
the lights are out, EMP grenades or the generator pulses are
still effective at stunning hostiles, giving you breathing room to
either escape or close in for a hand-to-hand kill.

ST. PETERSBURG BANYA—SECTOR 2

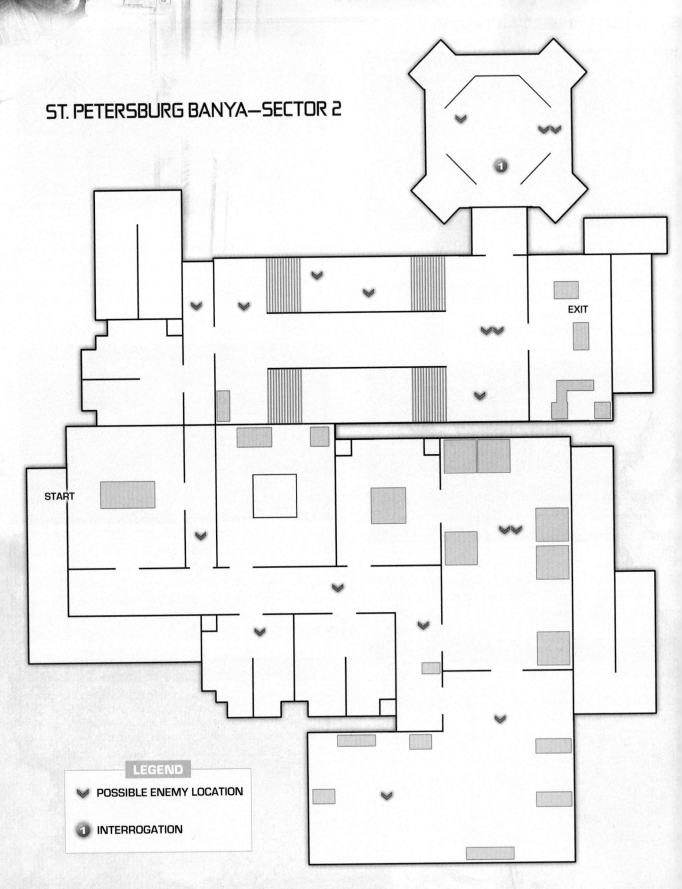

EXIT

START

LEGEND

POSSIBLE ENEMY LOCATION

1 INTERROGATION

ST. PETERSBURG BANYA

ECTOR 2 STRATEGY

e next sector is the bathhouse. In here, you are seeking one Lesovsky's goons. But first, you must push through an easy zen thugs in a series of smaller bathing rooms. Stay low or awl along the pipes in the ceiling, carefully monitoring the ards spreading out through the bathhouse.

TIP

Definitely split up in the bathhouse and take the rooms ogether: one on the floor, one in the ceiling.

As you close in on the large room in the bathhouse with the ornate wall, close ranks to take the next group of thugs together.

Inside the large bathing room, split up and perform a Co-op xecute to take down most of the guards. Stay in the shadows so you are not spotted.

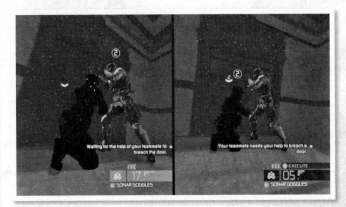

Beyond the ornate wall, you may team up to breach a locked door. You encounter these from time to time in co-op. Both of you must flank the door and then force it open with pry bars. However, before throwing open the door, peek under it and target some of the thugs inside. Your main target for this sector is just beyond—you cannot miss him. He's the big fella in the towel.

Breach the bathhouse and take down the guards or rush your target.

After clearing out the bathhouse, backtrack through the bathing rooms and break through the door marked as your objective. Use the ornate wall for cover or hang from it to take down the guards coming to investigate the fracas beyond the breached door.

ST. PETERSBURG BANYA—SECTOR 3

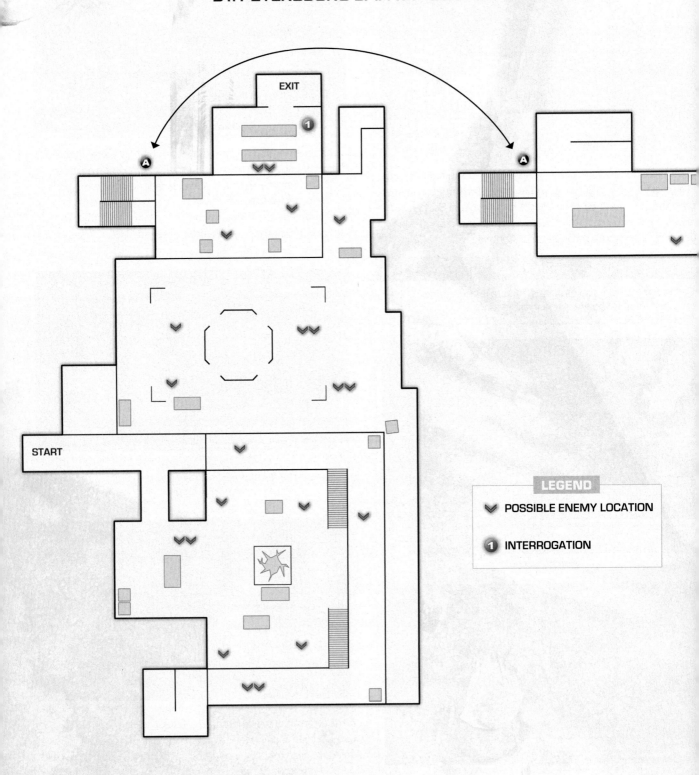

EXIT

1

A

A

START

ST. PETERSBURG BANYA

ECTOR 3 STRATEGY

Clear out the lighted room on the opposite side of the gazebo. Use the windows as cover while targeting the thugs within.

next sector leads you deeper into the banya. Slink into a
-level foyer and immediate start shooting the lights out.
h player should take a different direction around the base
he room to put out the lights as fast as possible. If either
ou get spotted, just hit the EMP to stun your enemies and
them down. After clearing the thugs on the bottom floor,
end the stairs and sweep through the balcony, using the
rs as cover.

> **TIP**
>
> nsistently work together to take out lights when either of you
> directly threatened.

Breach the door inside together to surprise another group of thugs.

up up again and slip through the open window on the
cond floor of the foyer. There are several guards in the yard
outside, moving around the central gazebo. If one of you
frags or mines, let that player go first and shimmy up to
edge of the building and pepper the ground with ordnance.
refully drop to the ground and sweep across the yard.

After executing the thug inside, you must zero in on Boris, one of Lesovsky's lieutenants. Interrogate the lieutenant to get information on the whereabouts of his boss. Move around the kitchen and slam Boris into different objects, such as planting his face on the hot stove. Once the interrogation is over, move on to the next sector.

> **TIP**
>
> se the roof of the gazebo as cover. You can pull yourself up
> to the shadows and pick off guards without them noticing you.

ST. PETERSBURG BANYA—SECTOR 4

SECTOR 4 STRATEG

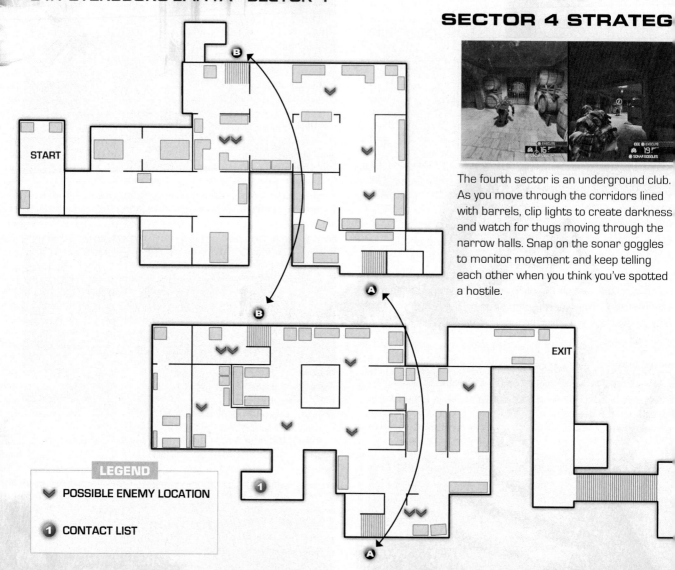

The fourth sector is an underground club. As you move through the corridors lined with barrels, clip lights to create darkness and watch for thugs moving through the narrow halls. Snap on the sonar goggles to monitor movement and keep telling each other when you think you've spotted a hostile.

LEGEND

⌄ POSSIBLE ENEMY LOCATION

① CONTACT LIST

Downstairs from the barrels is a dance club and several small bedrooms, each occupied by passed out prostitutes. Work together

to brush through the thugs. While one of you clears out the balcony over the club and the stairs leading down to the dance floor, the other can clean out the area around the bar and look for any movement among the bedrooms.

 TIP

Use the bar on the bottom floor as cover when clearing out the club.

After emptying the club, break into Lesovsky's office and ste his contact list from his desk. Now move on to the next secto

ST. PETERSBURG BANYA

ST. PETERSBURG BANYA—SECTOR 5

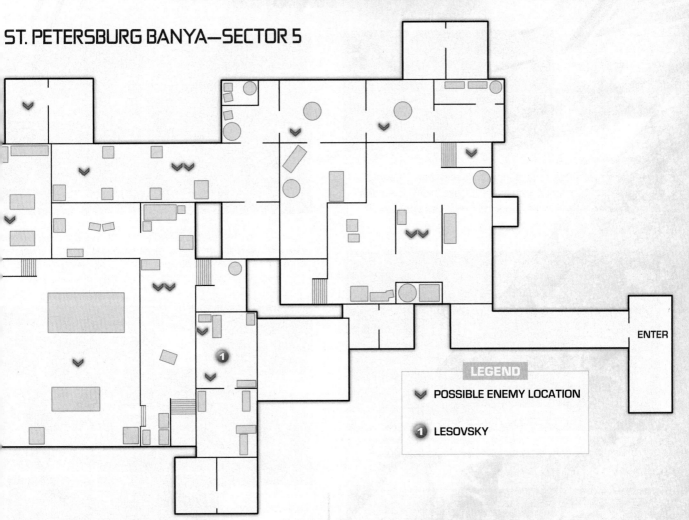

ENTER

LEGEND

⌄ POSSIBLE ENEMY LOCATION

① LESOVSKY

ECTOR 5 STRATEGY

ter securing the contact list, you must find Lesovsky
nd escape the banya. You must first clear out the human
afficking den just inside the sector entrance. Slip into the first
om and look for a guard on the stairs opposite the door and
least one more to the left, near some cowering girls.

ⓣ TIP

Use the fuel drums in the red-lit rooms as makeshift bombs.

*Keep moving through the red rooms on the opposite side of
the first area, looking out for hostiles with shotguns at every
corner.*

Lesovsky is locked in a room on the far side of the sector. To reach him, you must clear out a long hallway. Split apart—one on the floor, one on the ceiling. Blast the thugs in the hall and then peer into the room to the left for any stragglers. Take them down and then converge on the locked door that requires two players to breach.

Breach the door and eliminate Lesovsky's bodyguard.

One of you must grab Lesovsky and interrogate him, forcing him to make a phone call that sets up the deal.

Lesovsky turns the tables on you, grabbing the player that was interrogating him. You must work together to break his chokehold. The seized player must dodge, giving the other a clear shot at Lesovsky.

Killing Lesovsky doesn't end the mission in St. Petersburg. The Russian police breaches the garage, searching for you. Now, you must sneak back to the elevator in the room with the human trafficking, near the start of the sector. If you are spotted, your cover is blown and an international incident ensues. So, work together to circumvent the police as they swarm through the garage. Use EMP blasts to knock out lights and stun the police so you can slip by without detection. Use pipes whenever possible to sneak over the police. As soon as both of you enter the elevator, the mission ends.

RUSSIAN EMBASSY

RUSSIAN EMBASSY

elligence pulled from the contact list reveals that the front man for the cabal
at wants the EMPs is Leonid Bykhov, a former colonel in the Russian army.
anks to his connections, you can be sure that he has access to top secret
es and military-grade weaponry. Bykhov is at
e grand opening of a new Russian embassy
Azerbaijan to sell the EMPs. You must
ate and recover the stolen warheads.

ECTOR 1 STRATEGY

ur mission at the embassy is still
remely secret. You are advised to enter
e embassy with as little fanfare as possible.
ere are many guards moving around the
erior of the embassy. Killing one of them
plain sight will end the mission in failure.
ou do eliminate one of the guards, make
re you do it in the shadows. Otherwise,
ay in the dark and circumvent the guards
creeping along walls.

*Use the planters along the left of the
courtyard as cover while moving on the
ntrance of the embassy, which is at the
top of the multi-tiered stairs.*

You must not only
avoid detection in this
leg of the mission, but
you must also never
kill any of the guards.
If you kill a single
guard, the mission
immediately ends.

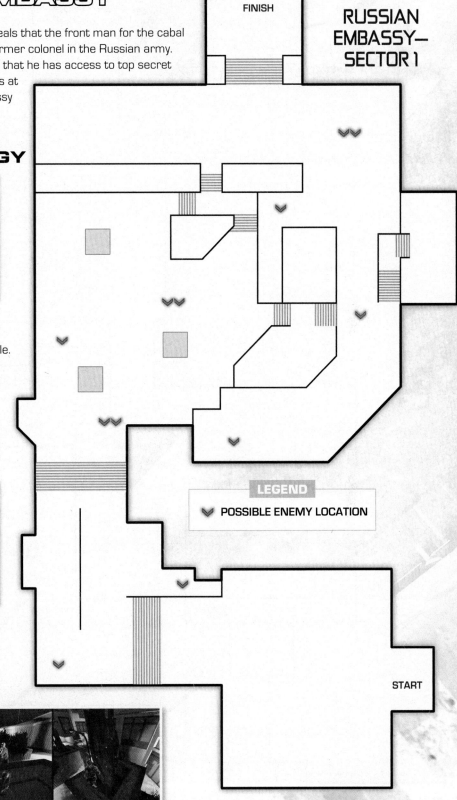

RUSSIAN
EMBASSY—
SECTOR 1

FINISH

LEGEND

∨ POSSIBLE ENEMY LOCATION

START

Stay close to each other and move cautiously through
the planters or hang by the ledges. If you do come
across a guard, either pull him from a ledge or pop an EMP to stun the target. In addition to stunning
the guard, the EMP blast also puts out all nearby lights, creating even more cover for reaching the
embassy entrance.

RUSSIAN EMBASSY—SECTOR 2

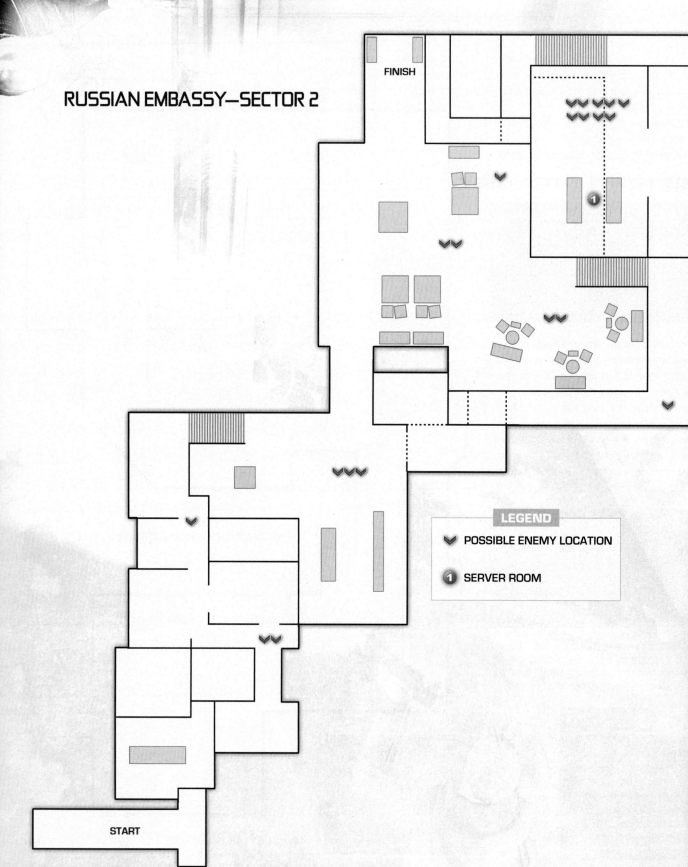

FINISH

START

LEGEND

POSSIBLE ENEMY LOCATION

1 SERVER ROOM

RUSSIAN EMBASSY

ECTOR 2 STRATEGY

*Even after breaching the embassy, you must still exercise
straint in dealing with threats. You cannot cause an incident,
lethal force is absolutely forbidden.*

wly approach the reception area inside the embassy.
e arms deal is taking place—and it goes bad. You are now
thorized to use deadly force and treat all of Bykhov's men as
eats to national security.

*'tart taking out the hostiles by dropping the chandelier on the
remaining thugs following the sour arms deal.*

The situation
inside the
embassy is
deteriorating. You
must fight through
the next wave of
hostiles to reach
the security room
and establish an

uplink to send all data about the situation to Third Echelon. The
security room is illuminated by blue lights.

*Before hacking the computer, which takes time, set up a
perimeter. Shoot out all lights. If you have proximity mines,
place them just outside the security room in the hallway.*

As soon as you start the hack, guards begin their assault.
Hunker down behind cover and repel the attack. You do not
want to let anybody into the room, but if you are overwhelmed,
swing over the ledge and use it as last-ditch cover. EMP blasts
are good for stunning the incoming guards, giving you a few
seconds to push back against the assault.

RUSSIAN EMBASSY— SECTOR 3

SECTOR 3 STRATEGY

After exiting the embassy, you must cross another courtyard to continue making y[...]
escape. First, you must disable the laser tripwires on the door leading outside. Use
the control panel upstairs from the door to switch off the lasers, then pass throug[...]
the door.

Outside, you must cross the courtyard.
There are two paths—the main floor and
the catwalks above. Take out the first
patrol together and then split up. Use
the railings on the upper level for cover,
secretly moving into range to score kills.

FINISH

LEGEND

⌄ **POSSIBLE ENEMY LOCATIO[N]**

STAR[T]

*You must commu-
nicate to take out
the teams. If you
spot a guard, tell
the other player.
They may be
able to move into
a more advan-
tageous position.*

Continue sweeping
through the
courtyard, using
sonar goggles to
spot guards in
advance. Shoot
out lights to keep
making shadows,

*You must inspect the crate at the finish area of this missio[n]
It is an American smart bomb guidance package that Kestr[el]
"acquired" some time ago, and now it's turned up in Russia. [The]
two spies have no time to argue over the stolen tech right n[ow]
The package must be secured and destroyed before moving
to the next area and closing in on Bykhov.*

and rely on railings to slip up on hostiles unnoticed. You need to
reach a door leading back into the embassy on the other side
of the courtyard.

RUSSIAN EMBASSY

RUSSIAN EMBASSY— SECTOR 4

START

FINISH

LEGEND

⌄ POSSIBLE ENEMY LOCATION   ① INTERROGATION

SECTOR 4 STRATEGY

...ack inside the ...mbassy, you ...ust breach a ...llery to continue ...ur pursuit of ...khov. Slip up to ...e door and use ...ur snake cam to ...npoint any guards near the door. Once you mark targets or ...e satisfied you can enter undetected, enter the gallery.

...here are several guards inside ...he gallery. Clear ...he guards from the office area that overlooks the gallery.

...ork together to ...ear the gallery. ...se the walls as ...ver. Scramble ...o the walls, hang ...om them, and ...immy above ...e patrols. Shoot ...em from above. You must empty the gallery and then move ...to the bar adjacent to the gallery.

...After eliminating the guards at the top of the ...allery, work with your partner to ...ove through the ...emainder of the ...oom. Use sonar goggles to spot ...the security lasers and avoid them, lest you sound the alarm and bring forth reinforcements.

ⓣ TIP

While hanging from the gallery walls, use Death from Above on guards walking below.

Mark targets under the door to the bar and then perform a Co-op Execute as you burst through. You need to kill everybody but Bykhov.

Interrogate Bykhov to get intel on the next stage of your operation: Yastreb Complex.

After you finish "chatting" with Bykhov, another patrol bursts into the bar. Immediately seek cover to repel the attack. Use the couches and the bar for cover. Grab one guard for a hand-to-hand kill so you have another execution to use on the guards. Once the room is clear, exfil through the door in the rear.

There may be one or two last guards at the bar exit.

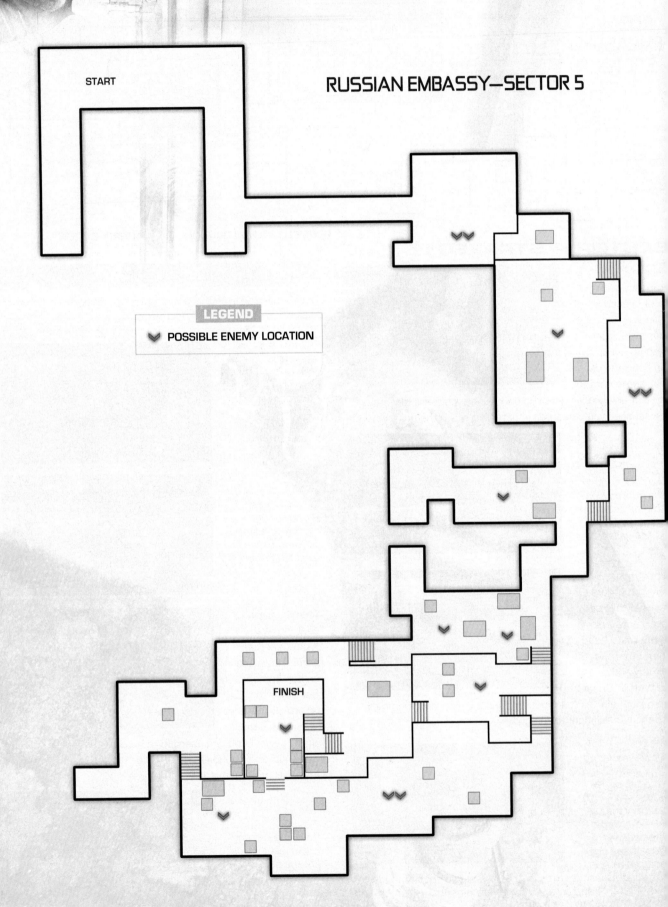

START

RUSSIAN EMBASSY—SECTOR 5

LEGEND

POSSIBLE ENEMY LOCATION

FINISH

RUSSIAN EMBASSY

ECTOR 5 STRATEGY

k outside the embassy, you must fight across the rooftop to
ch the exfil site. Start by shooting the first guard patrol just
side the bar. Stay back so as not to alarm the rest of the
rds on the roof.

Communicate as you cross the rooftop. Use the fuel drums
as bombs to take out large groups of hostiles. Stay down
behind the air conditioning units and use those as cover. Work
together and advance foot by foot. There is no reason to rush.
Rushing leads to mistakes.

*Use the ledges to creep across the walkways over the
courtyard. This is the best way to creep up on the guards.*

When you reach the marked exfil site on the roof, place
infrared strobes on the ground (as directed) to call in your
extraction. Now, the guards make one final push to stop you.
You must hold your ground until the chopper arrives. Duck
down and call out incoming enemies to each other. Use every
gadget you have to repel the attack for several seconds.

*careful when crossing the actual rooftop. Not only are there
several guards on patrol, but laser tripwires sound alarms.*

YASTREB COMPLEX

The intelligence gathered at the embassy has led to the discovery of the Yastreb Network, a terrorist cell operating within Russia. Its headquarters is a repurposed bunker deep below Red Square. You are to infiltrate the bunker and locate the weapons that have just been sold to Iranians. Stop this shipment by any means necessary.

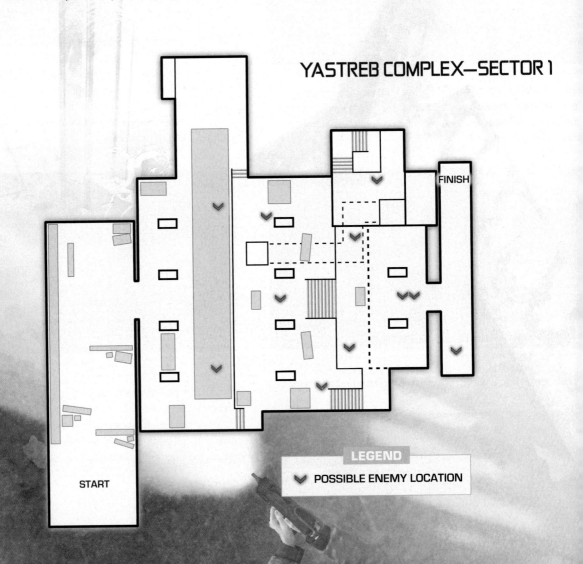

YASTREB COMPLEX—SECTOR 1

FINISH

START

LEGEND

⌄ POSSIBLE ENEMY LOCATION

YASTREB COMPLEX

ECTOR 1 STRATEGY

Sweep through the station together, each player taking one side of the sector. You must advance up the stairs to reach the exit in the back of the platform. Watch for enemies coming down the steps from the upper level of the sector. Use EMP blasts to turn off the lights and stun enemies so you can exit the sector and continue pursuing the weapons.

e first action inside the complex is to breach the tunnel wall t connects you to the interior of the Yastreb Complex. The r of you must approach the marked wall and set charges to trate. The blast makes considerable noise. A small group guards approaches the hole. Take them down with silenced apons so you don't bring everybody down on your position.

nside, move into the stopped train car and use it as cover to take down the remainder of the patrol in the station.

 TIP

hoot down the red star hanging from the ceiling to crush nemies below.

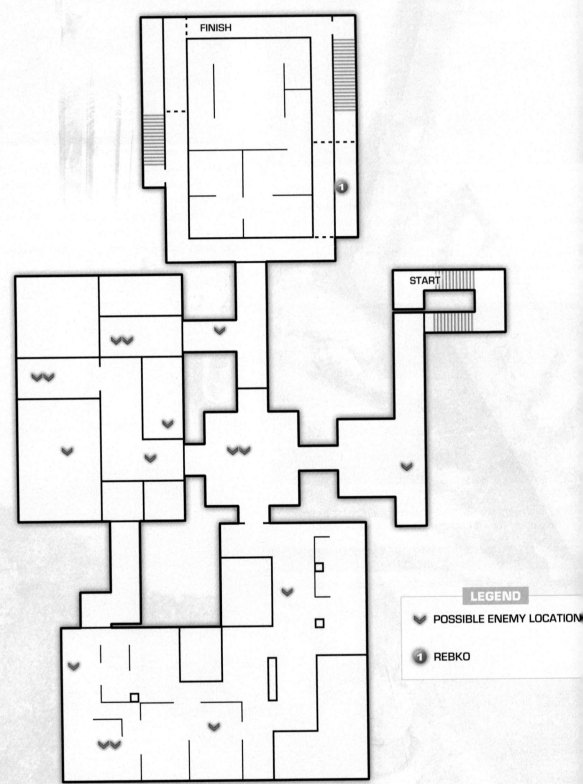

FINISH

START

LEGEND

POSSIBLE ENEMY LOCATION

1 REBKO

YASTREB COMPLEX

ECTOR 2 STRATEGY

de the bunker, you access an office area. There is a patrol
r the entrance to the office. Silently take out the guard
t inside the sector and then infiltrate the security station.
sure to vault over the desk and not pass through the metal
ectors. Hit another EMP to stun the guards at the station
l take them down.

ontinue pushing through the office entrance, relaying guard
locations to each other.

e interior of
office area is
ubicle farm.
ere are several
all offices with
er walls. Hang
m those walls
survey the
ards inside the

ce. Follow their progress by observing their flashlight beams.
g above them and take them down with headshots.

Move deeper
into the less
glamorous
ffice area. Pull
rselves into the
wl space above
the ceiling.

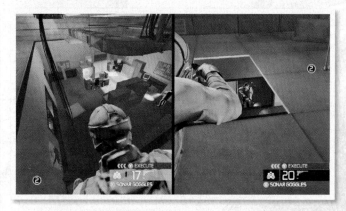

*Target the guards from the holes in the ceiling tiles. If your
location is ever made, pop an EMP and disappear.*

After clearing out the offices, breach the locked door together
and then zero in on Rebko, the next person in Yastreb's chain
of command. Interrogate Rebko to convince him to give you
access to the Yastreb servers where you can download
additional intelligence on the weapons.

Force Rebko's face into the biometric security system on the
lower floor of the office to gain access to the archives where
you will find the servers. However, as soon as you unlock the
doors, Rebko turns on the player who held him. The other
must hurry to take Rebko down. Coordinate your ducking and
shooting so the bullet meets the right mark.

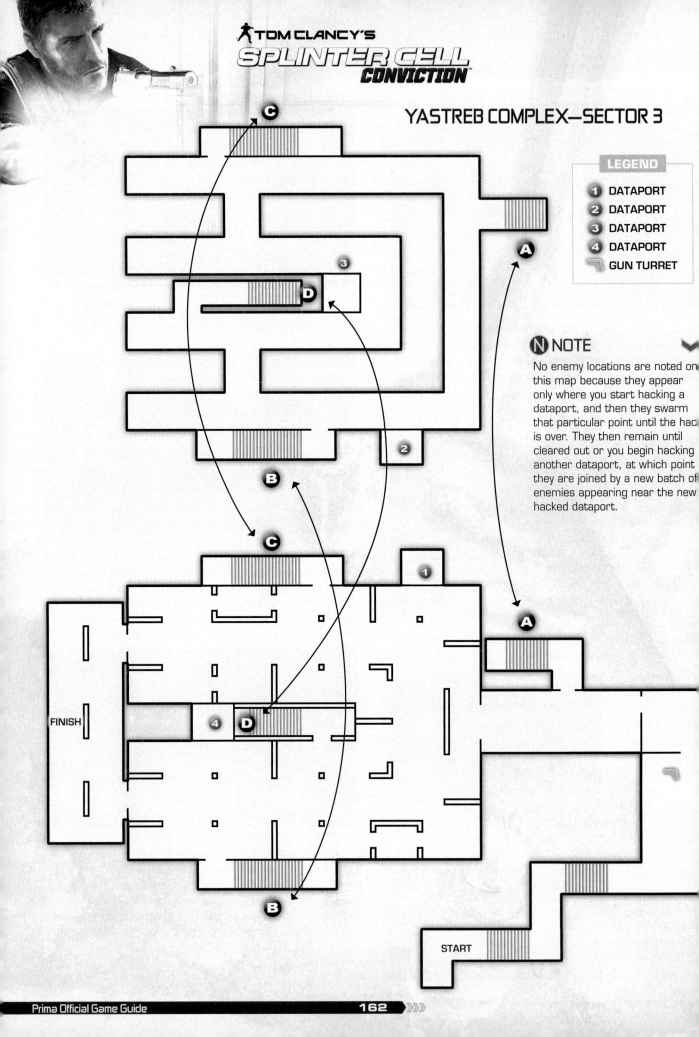

YASTREB COMPLEX—SECTOR 3

LEGEND

1 DATAPORT
2 DATAPORT
3 DATAPORT
4 DATAPORT
GUN TURRET

NOTE

No enemy locations are noted on this map because they appear only where you start hacking a dataport, and then they swarm that particular point until the hack is over. They then remain until cleared out or you begin hacking another dataport, at which point they are joined by a new batch of enemies appearing near the new hacked dataport.

FINISH

START

INTRODUCTION   THE FISHER FILES   TRAINING   P.E.C. CHALLENGES   WALKTHROUGH   **CO-OP STORY**   DENIABLE OPS   ACHIEVEMENTS

YASTREB COMPLEX

~ECTOR 3 STRATEGY

Work together to keep guards back from the dataports. Hang from ledges and target enemies as they attempt to swarm the dataports.

~access the archives, you must first slip through a field of ~ving laser tripwires. If one of you breaks the beams, the ~-turret hanging from the ceiling swings into action and ~rts shooting. Fortunately, there are pillars in the room ~e enough for one person to take cover. Use those until the ~oting stops.

TIP

Shoot the chandeliers hanging from the ceilings to crush the guards below.

CAUTION

Don't get greedy. Do not access two dataports at once. It's hard to hold off enemies from two locations while split apart.

~de the archive, you must access four dataports to download ~ necessary intelligence. It takes a few moments to download ~ data from the blue terminals. But as soon as you start that ~ download, hostiles breach the archives. While it's active, ~ must prevent enemies from retaking the port before the ~nload completes. You have seven minutes to access all four ~aports and complete the downloads.

After hacking all four data terminals, escape the archive through the rear of the library.

TIP

~ke control of ~e turret by ~ccessing the ~ntrol panel ~ the office ~st beyond it ~d eliminate ~y of the ~arby guards. ~e sure to ~ap over the desk to avoid the metal detector. If you step ~rough the metal detector, the alarms sound and guards rush ~e office.

«« 163   www.primagames.com

YASTREB COMPLEX—SECTOR 4

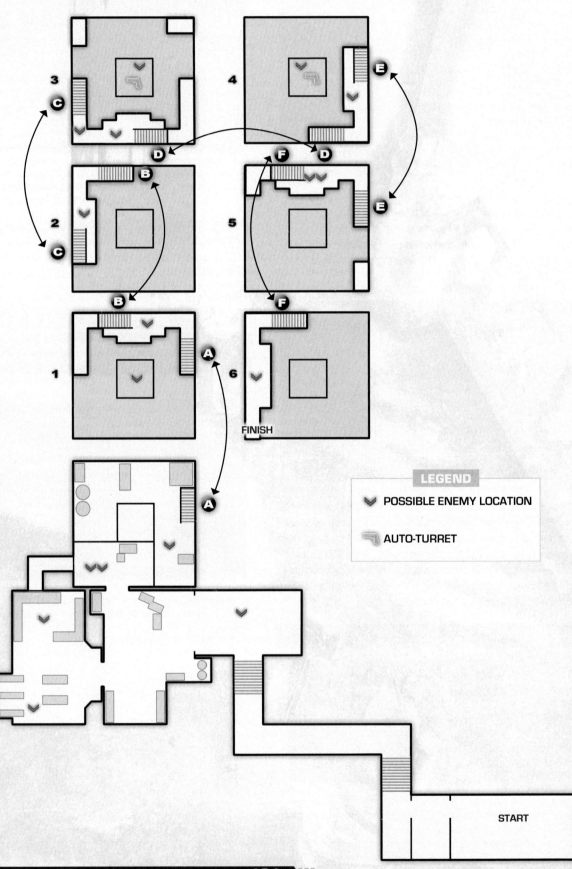

LEGEND

∨ POSSIBLE ENEMY LOCATION

⌐ AUTO-TURRET

YASTREB COMPLEX

ECTOR 4 STRATEGY

ou descend the steps to the bottom of the bunker, slow
look for guards. One typically lurks near some crates to
left. After taking him out, swiftly move through the corridor,
ing for additional targets. A vault off to the left contains at
t two guards. Duck down and take them out.

*Activate the dual EMP blast inside the vault to sabotage
security systems.*

r performing
dual EMP
t, exit the
t and move to
right. There
nother blast
r with guards
sing through it.
ot them down.

can ascend the tower in the center of the tall chamber
egin your escape from the bunker, or climb the stairs on
outer edge of the circular chamber. Use the pipe to start
bing. As you climb together, look for the sweeping flashlight
ms from guards on the stairs surrounding the tower. The
er itself has two auto-turrets. Use the ledges to climb
und the tower and avoid the turrets. Shoot the guards who
rate the control panels and then use the panels to disable
guns.

*Communicate guard positions to each other, both on the tower
and the stairs that circle it. And shoot out lights to create
shadowy areas on the tower whenever available.*

The sector exit is at the top of the chamber. Move away from
the tower via the pipe at the tower's top. The exit is at the top
of the stairs. However, before crossing to the outer stairs of
the chamber, make sure you either shoot all guards or pop an
EMP to stun them into temporary submission.

YASTREB COMPLEX—SECTOR 5

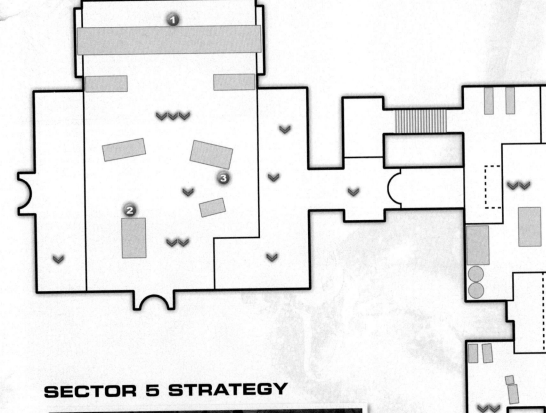

SECTOR 5 STRATEGY

The only escape from the complex is via a rail tunnel. However, every surviving Yastreb guard in the bunker is now on high alert and hunting for you. As soon as you enter the sector, raise your weapons and start shooting. Use the fuel drums as bombs to blow up patrols.

START

LEGEND

⌄ POSSIBLE ENEMY LOCATION

1 MASSIVE GUN
2 CRANE SWITCH
3 CRANE CONTROLS

YASTREB COMPLEX

...alk your assault through, relaying enemy positions to each ...er. Mark targets so you both can follow hostile movements. And always stay in cover.

To raise the crane above the gun, press the giant red button on the wall. The other player must provide cover while you do this.

... multitude
...uards
...major
...lem, but
... greatest
...at thus far
...giant gun

...tioned in the rail tunnel that serves as your exit. You cannot ...ape without destroying the gun. To do so, you must push ...on the patrols. Use mines and frags to eliminate enemy ...tions. And if enemies do get too close, stun them with ...blasts.

...gun can only be destroyed by activating a crane. The crane ...s a heavy cargo container. The crane moves the container ...e the gun. Once it is in place, you can move to disable ...gun.

You must wait for the crane to move the giant cargo container over the gun at the far end of the room. As soon as the container is over the gun, blast the mechanism holding it up. The container falls on the gun, ending the threat. Now leave through the tunnel to the left of the destroyed gun.

...fore using the ...ane controls ...destroy the ...n, you must ...power up the ...ane with the ...ow switch on ...this pillar.

You must perform an assisted jump to escape Yastreb. One player must duck down and then vault the other up to the pipe to initiate the escape.

MOZDOK GROUNDS

The warheads have been traced to the Mozdok Proving Grounds, where Yastreb is planning to fly them to a new buyer within 24 hours. Third Echelon has placed asset Andre Kobin on-site to secure the plane Yastreb was going to use to deliver the warheads to the waiting buyer. You must take Mozdok off the grid so local air defenses do not blow that plane out of the sky once Kobin has lift-off.

MOZDOK AIRBASE—SECTOR 1

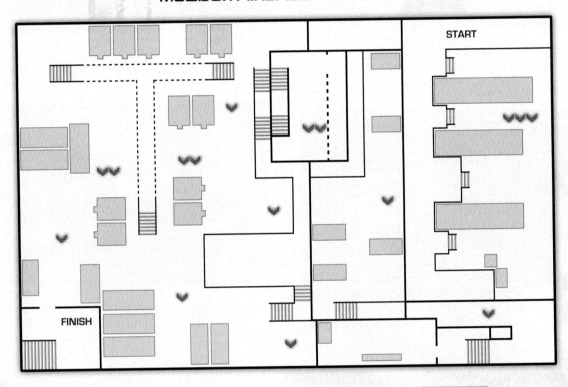

START

FINISH

LEGEND

⌄ POSSIBLE ENEMY LOCATION

SECTOR 1 STRATEGY

To infiltrate Mozdok, you must first push through the loading dock. You must use total stealth to enter the testing grounds. If the men guarding the docks detect you and report the intrusion, the mission ends. So climb on top of the trucks and split up the targets. Once the men by the trucks are down, creep through the rest of the dock and finish off any stragglers. There is usually one near the back wall of the docks. In addition, there is one in the small office overlooking the docks. Take him by climbing up to the window and popping off a headshot.

MOZDOK GROUNDS

...ow the same
... in the next
...a. You must
...hain hidden
... you sweep
...ough the
...m on your
... to the communications center of Mozdok. Stay in cover to
...ve up through the room. Don't hesitate to use an EMP blast
...stun any incoming threats. The communications room is at
... top of the stairs.

...erform a dual EMP in the communications room. However,
...make sure nobody is around. There is an outside chance a
...uard will pop through the door to the left of the EMP panel.

...w that
...mmunications
... down, you can
...a little more
...eral with your
...ack tactics.
...ve into a giant
...ngar where
... Russian
...my keeps a fleet of tanks. Several guards patrol the hangar.
...ng from the ledges over the tanks to eliminate the guards,
...pping grenades and using EMPs to stun.

TIP

Have banked executions? Perform a Co-op Execution to double
their effectiveness and take out several guards in one fell
swoop.

As you move through the remainder of the garage, a panicked
Kobin comes over the air. There are only three EMPs at his
pick-up site. He is supposed to deliver four to Third Echelon.
This changes the mission. You must now locate the fourth
device. It is in the test lab below. You must locate it and move it
to Kobin's position in the hangar at the edge of Mozdok.

*Exit the sector via the stairs in the back left corner of
the hangar.*

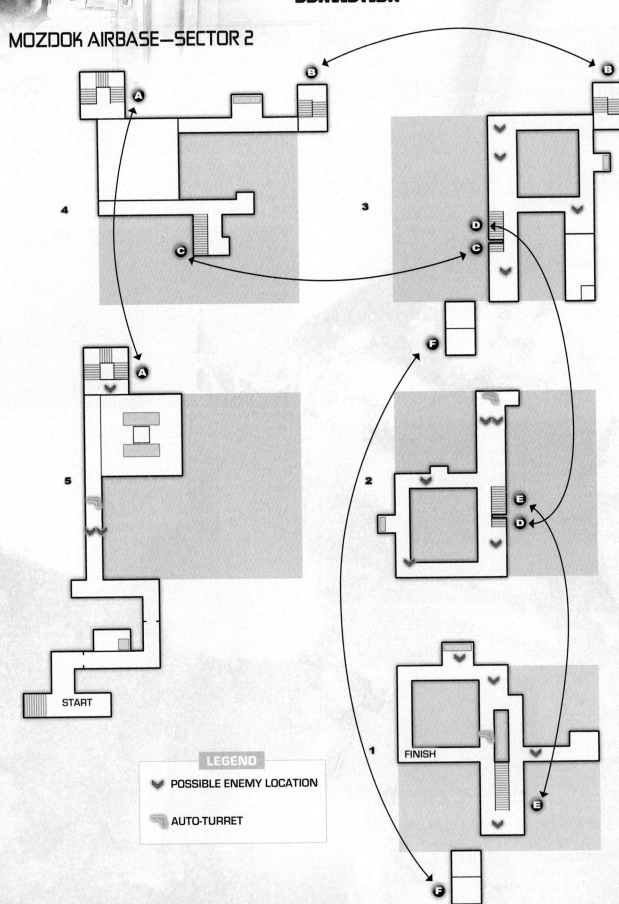

LEGEND

⌄ POSSIBLE ENEMY LOCATION

🔫 AUTO-TURRET

START

FINISH

MOZDOK GROUNDS

ECTOR 2 STRATEGY

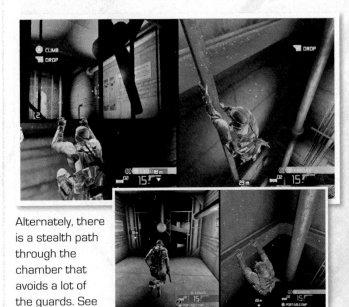

 next sector is a tall chamber. You must reach the bottom
 he chamber to move into the next sector. To start moving
 ough the sector, clear out the first pair of guards on the
 g bridge spanning the middle of the room. But after shooting
 m, hold back. There is an auto-turret on the bridge. So
 mmy along the outside of the railing to pass the camera and
 rt your descent.

Alternately, there
is a stealth path
through the
chamber that
avoids a lot of
the guards. See
the four fans
on the walls? They are marked with green lights. The fans are
connected. Shimmy along the ledge out to one of the upper
fans and slip through the slow-moving blades. Then, use the
pipes behind the fans to slide down to the lower level of the
chamber. You are now a straight shot to the exit. Be sure to
use the back side of the catwalk to slide undetected below the
security camera and turret.

🛈 TIP

 plit up in this room and climb down opposite sides to double
 ur coverage area. However, keep each other abreast of your
 cations in case one of you is incapacitated or grabbed into a
 noke hold.

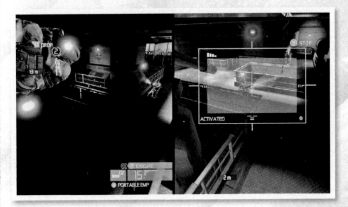

*Use the control panel near the exit to take control of the turret
and clear a path for your partner.*

 st guards in this chamber patrol the giant stairwell in the
 ad center. Watch out for two auto-turrets located on the
 irs, too. Use the railings to pass the watchful camera eyes
 the turrets and hijack them via the nearby control panels to
 her disable the turrets or use them against the guards.

 caught by one
 of the auto-
 rrets, dive over
 the railing to
 take cover.

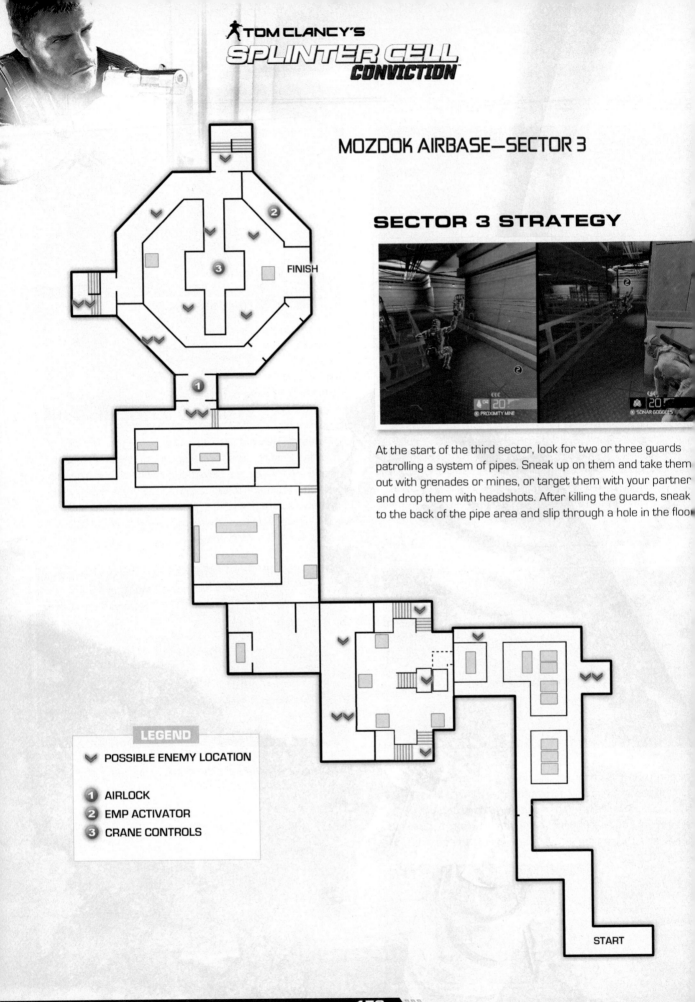

MOZDOK AIRBASE—SECTOR 3

FINISH

SECTOR 3 STRATEGY

PROXIMITY MINE   SONAR GOGGLES

At the start of the third sector, look for two or three guards patrolling a system of pipes. Sneak up on them and take them out with grenades or mines, or target them with your partner and drop them with headshots. After killing the guards, sneak to the back of the pipe area and slip through a hole in the floor

LEGEND

⌄ POSSIBLE ENEMY LOCATION

① AIRLOCK
② EMP ACTIVATOR
③ CRANE CONTROLS

START

MOZDOK GROUNDS

Crawl through the service tunnel beneath the sector and then ascend via a pipe into a test room. Slow up at the top of the pipe, because several guards patrol the test area.

An EMP blast stuns the guards in the room, giving you a small break to climb up to the surface and take cover. Look for at least one or two guards at each side of the room as well as directly in front of the hole in the floor. Then, move up to the office above the room. Lob a frag through the window and then enter to clear up any survivors.

Move through the blue test facility, keeping watch for one or two guards patrolling the hallways. Use sonar goggles to track them.

To move into the next testing room, you must pair up and open the airlock together.

The testing room is another tall chamber. There are three levels to the room. The ground level

has a handful of guards and enemy scientists who you can take out with headshots. The mid-level balcony is connected to the main floor via stairs, where you may encounter an enemy or two. However, to escape, you must climb up the trellis in the middle. You must fire the EMP in the lab in order to get it on to the crane system and out to the hangar where Kobin is waiting. To do this quickly, you need to split up. One player must enter the office on the mid-level balcony, neutralize the scientists and activate the EMP. The blast temporary turns off all power in the area.

Now, the other player should be climbing the pipes in the center of the room to reach the top of the trellis. As soon as

the system comes back online, access the open floor panel to hotwire the crane system and get that EMP moving. However, expect massive resistance. All three levels of the chamber fill with guards. You must fight your way to the exit on the lower level to escape the lab and move to the crane system, escorting the EMP to the hangar.

CAUTION

EMP blasts will not put out the lights in this test room—they are chemical lights. But the blast will stun hostiles.

MOZDOK AIRBASE—SECTOR 4

START

FINISH

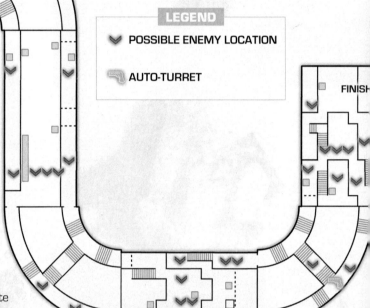

SECTOR 4 STRATEGY

You finally have one of the EMP warheads in sight. You must escort it through the service tunnel to a hangar at the edge of the testing grounds where you can get it off-site. There are seven segments to this tunnel: four blue-tinged areas where you must draw down on Mozdok guards and three orange rooms where you must keep moving alongside the EMP. Each segment is unlocked by holding a pair of buttons on opposite sides of the tunnel together.

Keep in contact so one player doesn't get too far ahead and hold a button while the other is still contending with hostiles.

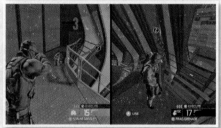

The orange areas usually just have one or two guards in them.

As you near the end of the sector, watch out for an auto-turret and a swarm of guards in the final orange segment. Use the narrow passage between the tunnels to gang up on the guards and slip around the turret's camera.

The guards in the blue areas grow more aggressive as you get closer to the end of the sector. However, you should still split up and clear out each side of

the room. Just talk about any hostiles spotted and alert each other when you are about to deploy a gadget, such as an EMP blast, that will stun enemies in the immediate area.

ⓣ TIP

Stock up on explosives at the weapons stash before entering the fifth sector.

MOZDOK GROUNDS

MOZDOK AIRBASE—SECTOR 5

SECTOR 5 STRATEGY

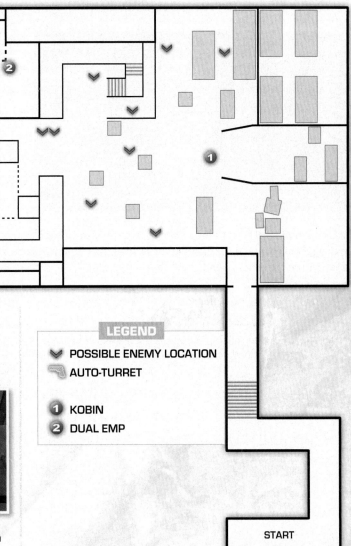

The final sector in Mozdok is the hangar where Kobin is waiting for you to help him escape with the stolen warheads. Meet Kobin at the crates in front of the plane. As soon as you reach Kobin, multiple agents storm the hangar to intercept you. You must push back hard and fast. Use explosives to stop the advancing patrols attempting to surround Kobin and the plane.

LEGEND

▼ POSSIBLE ENEMY LOCATION

⬚ AUTO-TURRET

① KOBIN

② DUAL EMP

Before the plane can leave, you must disable a turret at the back of the hangar. Without taking it out, you cannot leave. The only way to disable the turret is a dual EMP blast in the communications room, which is just above the turret. You must shoot or sneak your way to the communications room in the corner and perform a dual EMP blast to knock out the turret.

Creep into the office above the turret and perform a Co-op EMP blast to disable the rest of Mozdok's defenses.

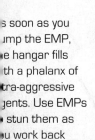

As soon as you pump the EMP, the hangar fills with a phalanx of ultra-aggressive agents. Use EMPs to stun them as you work back across the hangar to the plane. Try to nab one or two into hand-to-hand kills so you can use Co-op Executions to wipe out the advancing patrol.

Finally, you and your partner must board the plane and get those warheads out of Mozdok. Quickly split up and grab a crank on each side of the ramp. Spin the cranks to close the cargo hold of the plane so you can take off and get these warheads out of Russia.

THE AIRPLANE RIDE HOME...

Archer and Kestrel have formed an unlikely partnership over the course of the mission, but the fragility of it is about to show. Each agent is ordered by his handler to kill the other. The hunt is then on. Inside the cargo hold, use crates and boxes as cover to take down the other agent. This battle is over fast. A well-placed frag or mine is enough to shatter the other agent, as is a pinpoint headshot.

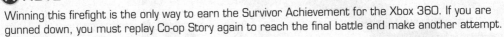

N NOTE

Winning this firefight is the only way to earn the Survivor Achievement for the Xbox 360. If you are gunned down, you must replay Co-op Story again to reach the final battle and make another attempt.

DENIABLE OPS

DENIABLE OPS

...niable Ops are a series of side missions separate from the ...op Story, detailed in the previous chapter. These missions ... split across several game types and can be played either ...gle-player or multiplayer with a friend over the Internet. You ... also play with a friend locally on the same Xbox 360 via ...t-screen play. You assume the roles of Archer and Kestrel ...m Co-op Story, but instead of following a set of mission ...ectives, you are assigned specific objectives as per the ...sen game mode. All maps for Deniable Ops are pulled from ...op Story, plus two additional maps that are only available in ...niable Ops: Printing Press and Lumber Mill.

NOTE

...ven though these missions are not related to the single-player ...ame, you still earn points from completing P.E.C. Challenges ...hile playing Deniable Ops.

...ETTING UP

...ce you choose either Deniable Ops or Multiplayer, you drop ... a set-up menu. From this menu, you select the desired ...me mode appropriate for the number of players as well as ... map. After selecting mode and map, you can also choose ... difficulty for the game: Rookie, Normal, and Realistic. The ...rder the difficulty, the more aggressive the enemies.

...ere are four Deniable Ops missions: Hunter, Last Stand, ...ce Off, and Infiltration. Face Off is the only mode of the four ...t requires a second player. The remaining three can be ...yed by yourself.

NOTE

...Vhen playing Deniable Ops missions with a friend, you can still ...se co-op tactics such as Co-op Mark and Execute, Revival, ...d Choke-Hold escapes.

HUNTER

The goal in Hunter is to defeat all enemies on a map. You select a map from the Deniable Ops menu and then begin the mission in first sector of that map. After you eliminate all enemies in a sector, the next sector opens. Once you clear out all sectors, the mission ends in success.

Between sectors in Hunter, you access weapons stash crates to refill spent ammo and gadgets, just like Co-op Story.

The number of enemies per sector varies depending on whether you're playing solo or co-op. However, if you are spotted and do not neutralize the enemy before he can relay your position to the others, reinforcements arrive. These additional enemies spread out across the sector and must also be eliminated before moving on. If you have only one enemy left in a sector and the alarm goes out, you must then work your way back through the sector and flush the new arrivals before you may move on to the next sector.

NOTE

A counter in the screen's upper right tracks the number of hostiles still in the sector.

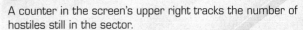

CAUTION

Enemies in Hunter are randomly placed each time you play, so each game is a new experience. However, our maps show the general areas in which you will encounter enemies.

The match settings for Hunter are:

Time Limit: Set the time limit to unlimited or select 2, 3, 4, or 5 minutes

Pistols Only: Limit weapons to only pistols for a greater challenge

No Gadgets: Toggle the use of gadgets on/off

LAST STAND

Last Stand tasks you with eliminating waves of enemies that are attempting to destroy an EMP generator, typically located in the center of the map. You must protect the generator from their incoming fire. The EMP generator has armor and can withstand quite a bit of abuse, but if the armor plating shatters, the EMP is disabled and the mission ends.

As long as you remain hidden, the enemies will concentrate on the generator. While the foes are targeting the generator, you can slip above, below, and behind them to deliver the killing blow. When an entire wave of enemies has been dispatched, the EMP will deploy its self-repair mechanism and recharge up to the last damage threshold passed (100%, 50%, 25%).

Enemies attack in waves. When you clear out one wave, you have several seconds to seek cover before the next wave arrives. During that time, you may wish to boobytrap the area with mines or just find a great hiding spot above the generator. Your enemies grow more aggressive with each wave. You can also adjust the fierceness of the thugs with a difficulty selector on the Deniable Ops main screen.

(T) TIP

Playing Last Stand with a friend? Assign roles. Have one of you run interference with the enemies while the other strictly guards the generator.

The match settings for Last Stand are:

Starting wave: Choose the starting wave of enemies from wave 1, 5, 10, or 15. The higher the wave, the tougher the enemies. In wave 1, you encounter only low level thugs. By the final wave (20), though, you face down elite soldiers and spies who are experts at running down Last Known Positions and other stealth tactics.

FACE OFF

Face Off is the only game mode that requires a second player. This is an adversarial mission that pits two spies against each other. However, there are multiple hostiles in the same area hunting both players without prejudice. Points are awarded for eliminating the AI-controlled enemies, but the big scores come from dropping your fellow spy. Do not treat the other enemies as unimportant. If you are spotted by an AI-controlled enemy, your Last Known Position is relayed to your opponent.

(N) NOTE

Face Off takes place on the same maps as Hunter, so use those maps as reference. AI-controlled enemies do not have set starting positions or follow set routes.

The match settings for Face Off are:

Time Limit: Choose 2, 3, 5, 7, or 10 minutes

Pistols Only: Limit weapons to only pistols for a greater challenge

No Gadgets: Toggle the use of gadgets on/off

Point Limit: Choose the number of points required to win (between 30 and 100) or turn points off so expired time determines the winner

Enemy Density: Set the number of AI-controlled enemies in the match between off, low, and normal

DENIABLE OPS

FILTRATION

ltration is similar to Hunter. You must eliminate a gauntlet
enemies in each sector of a map. However, you cannot be
otted—ever. It's game over if you trigger an alarm (either by
ng spotted, being noisy, tripping a camera, etc.). So, stick to
e shadows, hang off ledges, and remain unseen for the entire
ssion. Infiltration uses the same maps as Hunter, so refer to
m and the associated tactics for remaining hidden.

e match settings for Infiltration are:

Time Limit: Set the time limit to unlimited or select 2, 3, 4,
or 5 minutes

Pistols Only: Limit weapons to only pistols for a greater
challenge

No Gadgets: Toggle the use of gadgets on/off

Infiltration is not available when you first turn on the game. It

 NOTE

must be unlocked by accessing Uplay, Ubisoft's online service.
o access the mode, select Uplay from the main menu
nd follow the on-screen instructions to create an account
nd profile. After you've registered, Infiltration becomes
vailable within Deniable Ops and Multiplayer. All content and
egistration activity via Uplay is the responsibility of Ubisoft.

QUIPMENT

fore going out on a mission, you may adjust the weapons
d gadgets taken into the field. Choose equipment you feel
ost comfortable with or equipment that you think will be
rticularly useful for that specific map or game type. For
ample, in Infiltrator, you must never be seen by an enemy so
rag grenade is out of the question because it draws so much
ention. In Hunter, getting spotted draws reinforcements,
a silenced pistol that keeps things quiet is incredibly useful.
re are the equipment categories:

Gadget 1: Select a gadget to take into the field

Gadget 2: Select a second gadget to take into the field

Pistol: Select a personal default sidearm

Alternate Weapon: Select a secondary weapon from the
non-pistol categories such as shotgun and assault rifle

Uniform: Choose a uniform from the locker

UNIFORM LOCKER

In Deniable Ops and Co-op, each spy is given either the 3E Eclipse
uniform or the VR SV1 AKULA uniform (Kestrel). There are five
extra uniforms you may buy via points accrued by completing
P.E.C. Challenges, plus a sixth awarded for participating in Uplay:
Russian Soldier. Uniforms offer only cosmetic changes.

UNIFORMS

UNIFORM	COST
VR Vympel	200
VR Mozdok Telecom	200
3E Black Arrow	200
3E Urban Tracker	200
Classified	200
3E Eclipse	open

However, you may also buy up to a total of 3 upgrades for your
uniforms (either the maxed level of one, a mid level and a low
level, or a low level for each upgrade type). These upgrades
are split across three categories: armor, ammo, and gadgets.
Armor upgrades fill the armor bar in the upper-left corner,
which increases the number of bullets you can take before
falling. The ammo upgrade increases your ammo stocks for
carried weapons. The gadget upgrade increases the number
of each selected gadget you can carry. (You may still only carry
two different gadgets.) Each upgrade costs 250 points and is a
worthwhile investment.

No upgrade is necessarily better than another—it all depends
on your play style. If you prefer to stick to guns, you definitely
want to upgrade your ammo stocks. If you prefer to stick to
the shadows and go for close kills, upgraded armor for those
moments you get caught is beneficial. And if you find yourself
adept with some of your favorite gadgets and gear, such as
remote mines, then definitely upgrade gadget counts.

LAST STAND

Hostile forces are converging on fragile EMP technology. You are the last line of defense. You must repel multiple waves of enemy thugs and soldiers so they cannot destroy the EMP generator at the center of the map. Each shot chisels away a little of the generator's armor plating. However, the generator is equipped with a self-repair mechanism that undoes the damage done to it up to the last threshold passed (100%, 50%, 25%) between waves of attack.

Each wave of enemies is more aggressive than the last. At first, you must repel only basic criminal lowlifes and thugs. Soon, though, you must deal with guards and soldiers who have weapons training. And as the training and aggression of the soldiers increase, so does the quality of their weapons. Thugs with pistols don't do too much damage to the generator. But an elite agent with an assault rifle and deadly aim? You better figure out exactly who is targeting the generator and bring them down ASAP.

ST. PETERSBURG BANYA 1

The EMP generator is in the middle of a grand foyer, surrounded by alcoves. A balcony circles above it. Enemies approach from all four halls that stretch away from the EMP on the bottom floor as well as the rooms that line the upstairs balcony. With so many angles to cover, you better stay central and use your sonar goggles to keep track of incoming thugs and agents. Stray too far from the generator and you will lose it.

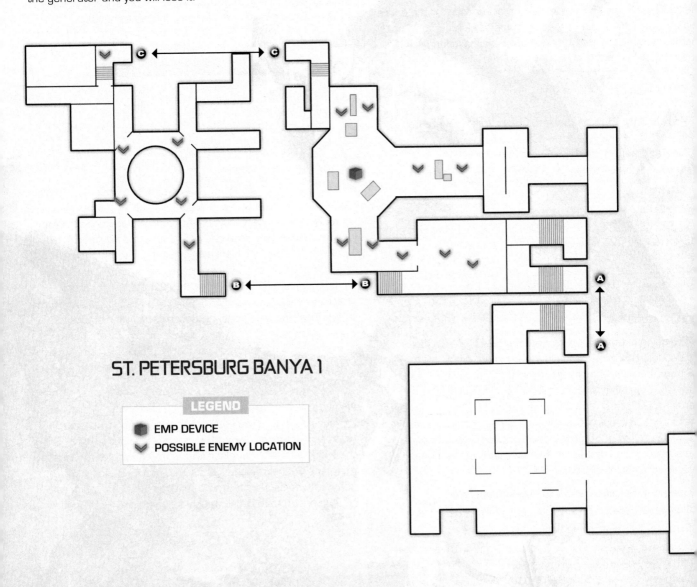

ST. PETERSBURG BANYA 1

LEGEND

▣ EMP DEVICE

∨ POSSIBLE ENEMY LOCATION

LAST STAND

STRATEGY

Dropping the chandelier not only crushes enemies below, but also cuts the amount of light in the foyer, increasing your shadow opportunities.

...ough there are many shadows to use in this map, the best ...ace to watch for incoming foes is the balcony overlooking the ...nerator. From up here, you can fire on the chandelier that ...ashes down on enemies in the middle of the foyer, and use ...ur sonar goggles to get a good look at every direction. One of ...e best places to hide is hanging off the balcony interior. You ...t clean shots at incoming foes and can slide left and right to ...ange your view if you need to move to target your prey.

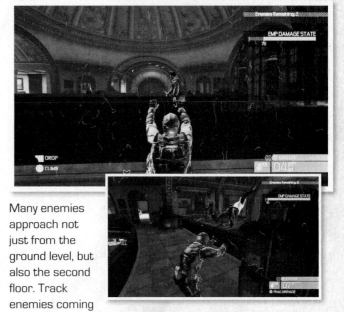

...e balcony ...w is great for ...ooting enemies ...empting to ...e the planters ...cover. You ...n also spy the ...coming enemies ...m the four ...llways and ...t them down ...th gadgets ...ch as frag ...enades. Prevent ...em from even ...aching the ...nter of the ...er!

Many enemies approach not just from the ground level, but also the second floor. Track enemies coming up from the stairs at the end of the four hallways on the ground floor. If multiple hostiles appear on the second floor, hang from a ledge and watch them circle the generator. When you have your shot, take it. This can reveal your LKP, so be prepared to either drop down and escape detection or slide away to avoid a flashlight beam. Some enemies come to the edge of the balcony and look down. Grab them and pull them to their deaths or jump up and take them down with an execution. If you see an enemy on the ground floor below, fling the body off the second story either to smash the foe below or at least cause a distraction and disrupt their firing.

 TIP

...Frags are always a great weapon to have in game modes that ...o not rely on stealth, such as Last Stand.

Do not ignore the rooms around the center of the foyer. Stairs at the end of each hallway lead to the second floor, and as you progress in the match, the

smarter hostiles will use these rooms to flank you or draw you away from the generator. Watch for groupings in the room. Don't stick your neck out for solo enemies. They will come to you (or the generator). But if you have a group in a room, roll a frag in there or stun them with a flashbang. As they recoil from the grenade, you can either shoot them up or systematically execute until they recover.

...Hear gunshots ...ut don't see the ...hooter? Activate ...e sonar goggles ...nd look around ...o spot the next target.

ST. PETERSBURG BANYA 2

The EMP generator in this map is in the center of the gazebo outside of the building. Most of the gazebo entrances are blocked by gates, although enemies can shoot through the bars. There are a few places to hide when approaching the gazebo, but the multiple lamps on the lawn leave few shadows. Watch out for the windows on both stories of the building next to the gazebo. Not every enemy is brave enough to breach the yard and run straight for the gazebo.

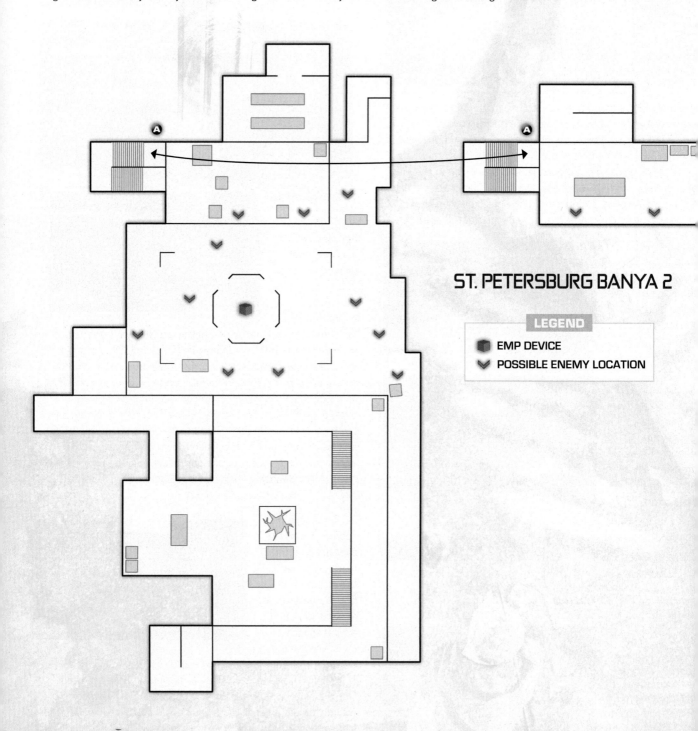

ST. PETERSBURG BANYA 2

LEGEND

⬛ EMP DEVICE

∨ POSSIBLE ENEMY LOCATION

LAST STAND

TRATEGY

The lights around the gazebo can really limit your movement options. Between rounds, shoot out the lamps to cast the yard in darkness. If you don't have time to take them all out, an EMP blast not only temporarily disables the lights, but also stuns any enemy nearby. Take advantage of stunned enemies for easy kills to protect the generator.

the beginning of a wave, either make sure you are close to
e gazebo or at least boobytrap it with mines so that others
nnot approach it while you are cleaning out the two-story
ilding or the alley directly across from it. This yard can really
up with enemies fast, so try to never get caught out in it.
r a quick escape, use shadows (or create them with an EMP
ast) to rush to the gazebo and clamber up to its roof.

om the gazebo
of, you can see
most the entire
ap. Plus, you are
mfortably in the
adows on top of
e gazebo. From
here, it is easy
target incoming
nemies. And the rooftop is wide enough that if you are spotted
ooting a hostile, you can retreat to the opposite side and
mp down without being spotted.

Watch the windows of the building next to the gazebo.

After a few waves, hostiles begin using the building's upper floor. This presents a real problem when your enemies start using advanced weapons that can really damage the generator from a distance. Getting an accurate shot at an enemy in the upper floor windows can be tricky, but lobbing a mine or

frag through a window works for quickly cutting down a threat if you cannot cross and ascend the interior.

se Death from Above on the gazebo roof to take out enemies that get too close to the generator.

⟨⟨⟨ **CAUTION**

Watch for enemies to "group" in the yard. If you pop a shot at one of them, they all look up at you.

TIP

The second story window also offers a clean view of the yard, but doesn't have the 360-degree accessibility of the gazebo roof.

RUSSIAN EMBASSY 1

The courtyard of the Russian Embassy provides a lot of shadows and ledges to use for cover when handling the advancing waves of thugs and soldiers. The generator rests on a small pedestal in the center of the courtyard, which gives enemies lots of angles for attack. However, with architecture that allows for lots of hanging and hiding, the embassy courtyard is one of the easier Last Stand locations to hold. Just make sure you shoot out the lamps above the generator to bathe the courtyard in darkness. The more shadows you create, the greater your chances for success.

RUSSIAN EMBASSY 1

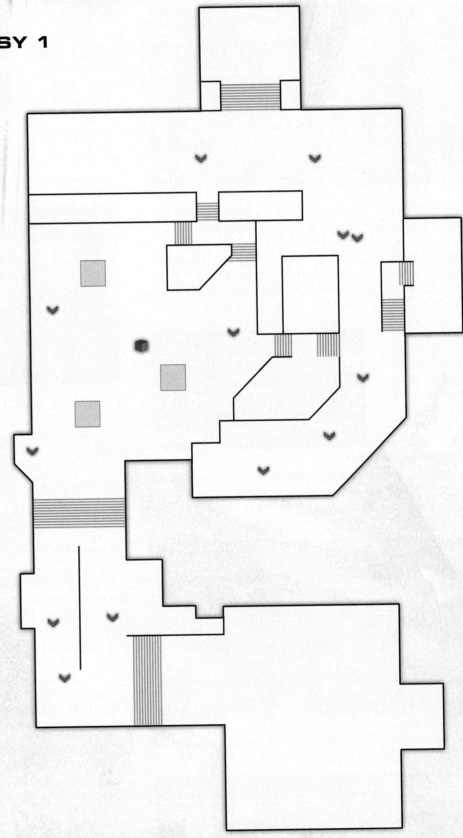

LEGEND

⬡ EMP DEVICE

∨ POSSIBLE ENEMY LOCATION

LAST STAND

TRATEGY

e lamps above the embassy offer a lot of light. In addition
the tall lamps that cast a gentle glow over the arena, the
aller lights throw harsh pools of light on the ground. Avoid
ese so as not to be easily detected.

ⓘ TIP

Many of the smaller lights cannot be shot out thanks to
rotective grills, but they can be disrupted with EMP pulses.

early waves,
platforms
und the
erators
the best
ces to hide—
pecially if you

st the surrounding lamps. From these platforms, you can
e a lot of the courtyard. Look for the telltale sign of arriving
ards—flashlight beams—around the stairs and planters.
w enemies to get within range and then blast them with
adshots so you eliminate them without drawing attention to
ur position.

*Whenever you have a chance in any Last Stand match, shoot
out a light. Use a silenced pistol so nobody notices you.*

The more
darkness you
create, the more
opportunities
you have to
slip through
the shadows
and attack.
Hand-to-hand kills

are great because not only are they pretty much silent, but they
also result in earning a Mark and Execute.

The architecture
around the
stairs is pretty
crazy. You have
multi-level planters
to grab onto and
hang from, which
are both great
hiding spots and
good vantage
points for taking
out enemies. Also,
you can slide from
the planters to
the railings on the
ledges overlooking
the courtyard. It's

easy to reach up and yank an enemy off his feet from these
ledges, especially in the dark.

*Use the archi-
tecture of the
stairs to flank
enemies as
they rush the
generator.*

RUSSIAN EMBASSY 2

The second Russian Embassy Last Stand map is inside the art gallery. There are many standalone walls in the gallery, each laden with paintings. The EMP generator is in the middle of the lower level. A small office on a landing overlooks the gallery. Use the ledges on those gallery walls as cover while hunting the waves of enemies filtering through the room. As long as you don't give away your location while hanging there, you can remain hidden for a very long time.

RUSSIAN EMBASSY 2

LEGEND

- ⬢ EMP DEVICE
- ⌄ POSSIBLE ENEMY LOCATION

LAST STAND

TRATEGY

Use EMP blasts not just to put out the lights in the gallery. The blasts also stun enemies that may be too far away to accurately target inside the gallery.

While the hostile doubles over or holds his ears, you can close the gap between the two of you. Just be mindful of the distance your blasts stretch. If you feel you always come up short, upgrade your devices with points earned by P.E.C. Challenges.

e gallery is
ed with light,
use the first
v moments
the match
put out as
ny bulbs as
ssible before scurrying up a gallery wall. While hanging, slip
ound the corners to seek out incoming enemies. (Use your
nar goggles to seek out unseen hostiles.) When enemies are
se, use a silenced pistol to take them down without being
otted. If enemies group together, drop a frag on them.

Watch out for enemies attempting to flank you via the landing above the gallery. These enemies have a stronger chance of seeing you hanging from the gallery walls. So, if you see flashlight beams on the landing or spot an outline via sonar goggles, zero in on the landing and take out the threat.

The sharp corners and winding walls in the gallery present a
t of opportunities to sneak up behind enemies and take them
down with hand-to-hand kills.

YASTREB COMPLEX 1

The map inside the Yastreb Complex is of the train station that connects the underground bunker with the rest of the Moscow Underground. The EMP generator is on a stack of crates near the abandoned train car. Enemies can take multiple routes in this map, coming down the tunnels where the train pulls through and pouring through the offices on the landing above the loading platform.

YASTREB COMPLEX 1

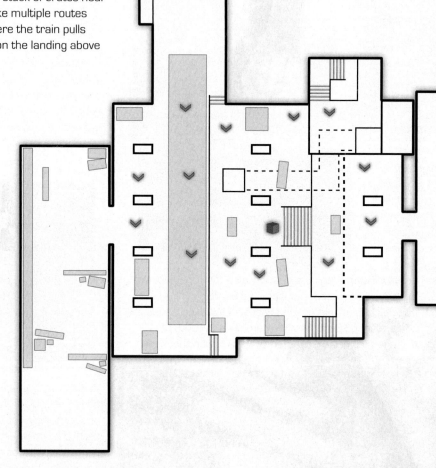

LEGEND

- EMP DEVICE
- POSSIBLE ENEMY LOCATION

STRATEGY

On the station's main floor, watch for enemies to come rushing through the doors in the train cars. You can gun them down from the windows or as they move through the doors. Enemies can fire upon the generator from the train and still enjoy cover. Watch for hostiles to use the crates on the loading platform as cover while taking aim at the generator.

TIP

Blast the chain holding up the huge red star and drop it on enemies that move too close to the EMP.

LAST STAND

The upstairs office offers a moderately good view of the platform, but you cannot see the generator itself from the window. However, if you jump through the window and hang from the ledge outside, you have a much better view of the floor. Use your sonar goggles to spot anybody hiding just out of view (such as behind a support column on the main floor).

...ving around the main floor of the station is dangerous. ...use the service tunnels below the station to silently sneak ...m one side to the other. The holes in the floor leading to the ...nel can be tough to spot at first. Look for the railing around ...holes as well as crates blocking them from easy view.

 **CAUTION**

You can give away your position in the tunnels if you make too much noise near an enemy on the floor above you.

Use LKP to get the better of your enemies. Find good hiding spots and then jump out for hand-to-hand kills to bank an execution.

Watch for enemies on the stairs leading up to the office overlooking the station.

The loading platform is well lit by the ceiling lamps. Between rounds, shoot out as many lights as possible. With the main floor of the station so bright, you need to create as many shadows as possible. The enemies can still see the generator and shoot at it, but you'll have an easier time hiding among the pillars and crates. The closer you get to enemies, the easier it is to take them down without drawing too much attention to your position.

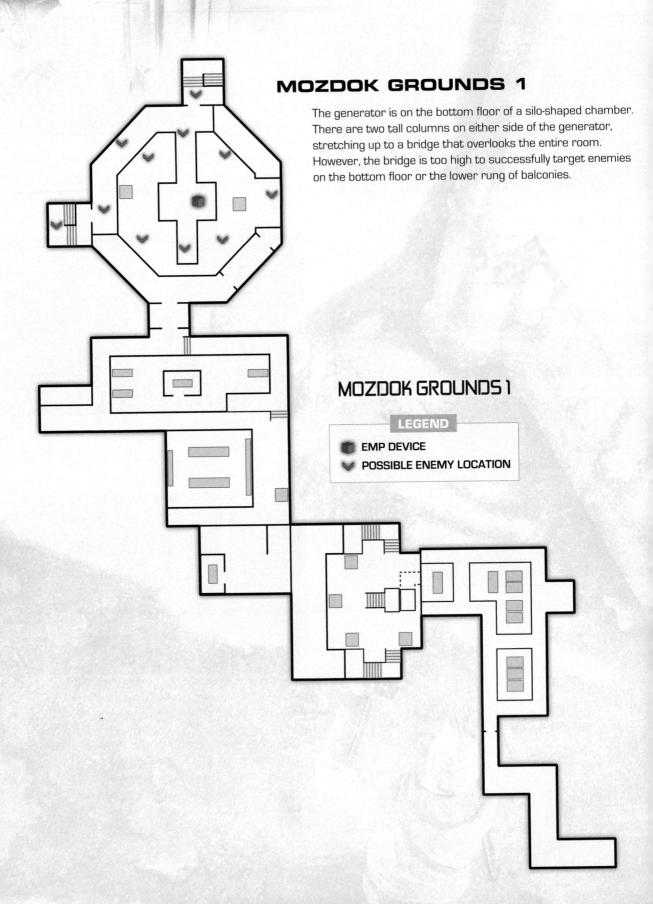

MOZDOK GROUNDS 1

The generator is on the bottom floor of a silo-shaped chamber. There are two tall columns on either side of the generator, stretching up to a bridge that overlooks the entire room. However, the bridge is too high to successfully target enemies on the bottom floor or the lower rung of balconies.

MOZDOK GROUNDS 1

LEGEND
⬛ EMP DEVICE
⌄ POSSIBLE ENEMY LOCATION

LAST STAND

RATEGY

ugh the bridge at the top of the room is too high to
cessfully get off accurate shots, the pipes that run up the
mns are perfect for quickly ascending from the bottom
to the mid-level balcony and drawing a bead on threats.
great thing about the pipes is that if you spot a menace
e bottom floor and cannot get a good shot off, it's easy to
down the pipe and be on the floor in mere seconds.

If you cannot
get a clean shot
at enemies on
upper levels
from the pipes,
you may need to
use the stairs.

Hit the sonar goggles before moving upstairs, though, so you
are not surprised by a hostile hiding between the floors on the
landing. An EMP pulse in the stairwell stuns any interlopers,
giving you a chance for a hand-to-hand kill before moving out to
the balcony and targeting enemies. Look for targets to gather
around the control room because it provides cover.

More hostiles fire upon the generator from the mid-level
lcony rather than the ground floor as the game continues.

*Many of the lights in the room cannot be extinguished with
bullets. A pulse will take them out, but otherwise, you must be
mindful of keeping out of direct lines of sight.*

LUMBER MILL 1

The first map in the Lumber Mill is the yard just outside the actual mill. You can climb multiple stacks of logs and hang from the railings around them. You can only pull yourself on top of about a quarter of them though, providing a good vantage point and a relatively secure position. The yard is illuminated by tall lampposts that can (and should) be shot out as early in the game as possible to cast most of the yard in darkness.

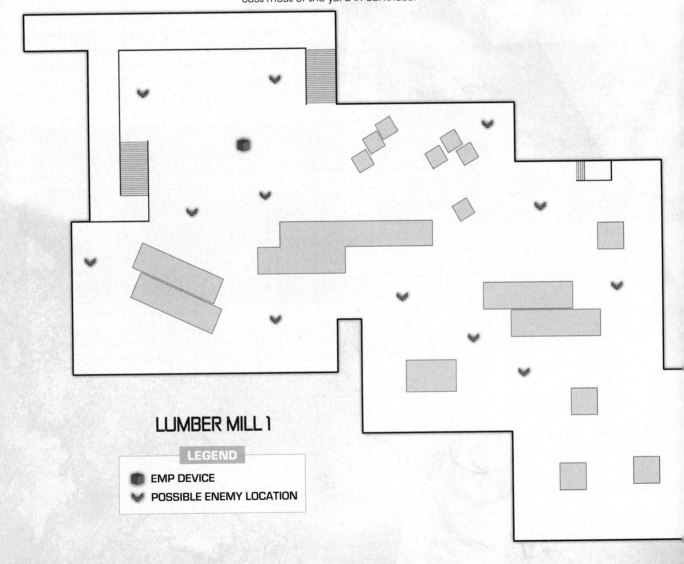

LUMBER MILL 1

LEGEND

⬢ EMP DEVICE

∨ POSSIBLE ENEMY LOCATION

LAST STAND

TRATEGY

ju can climb on top of some of the log piles and stand on
veral crates around the generator. If you blast most of the
nps, these crates are great shooting platforms for taking out
stiles surrounding the EMP.

Get spotted on the crates to create a distraction. While the
hostiles swarm the LKP, you can pick them off.

TIP

large container hangs by a crane near the generator. Wait
r an enemy to stand under it and then blast the chain.

LUMBER MILL 2

The second Lumber Mill map is the truck yard. Several large trucks are parked near the building. Fuel drums also litter the area, which can be used as makeshift bombs. (Because stealth is not a huge concern in Last Stand, setting off the drums does not threaten reinforcements.) The generator is on a small crate in the middle of the trucks, near a pool of light caused by a tall lamppost.

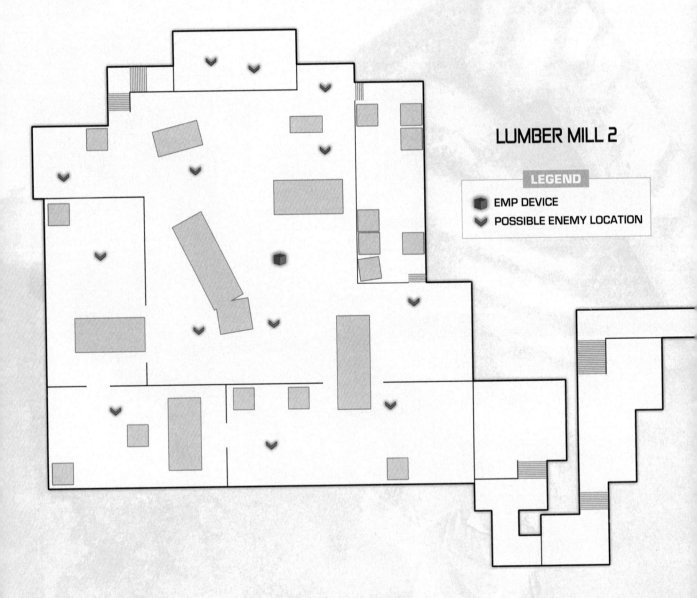

LUMBER MILL 2

LEGEND

⬢ EMP DEVICE

ᐯ POSSIBLE ENEMY LOCATION

LAST STAND

STRATEGY

...s map features several objects that you can ascend to get ...od view of the area. Pull yourself on top of stacks and trucks ...get a 360-degree look. From up here, it is easy to pick off ...ts. However, unless a hostile runs near the trucks or stack, ...u may not have an accurate shot.

...ook for fuel drums around the yard and use them as bombs. ...u may wish to save these for later waves, though, as you may ...eed the help with elite troopers when you are running low on gadgets and grenades.

...Jse Mark and ...xecute to take ...lown enemies ...ho have a bead ...the generator ...ut are too far ...away to get a ...ean headshot.

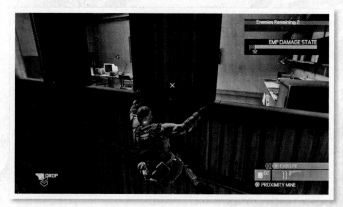

There is a dispatch office above the truck yard. At least two or three enemies per wave may come through the yard. The ledge outside the office is a great spot to view much of the yard and target enemies.

Leave LKPs around the yard to distract enemies and then flank them.

LUMBER MILL 3

The third Lumber map is in a courtyard outside the buildings. The generator hangs from a chain in the center of massive stacks of cut lumber. Most stacks can be climbed, although only a few stop short enough of the ceiling for you to stand on and target hostiles below. This area is largely dark, although several floodlights illuminate the paths between the stacks. Take out those floodlights and you cast most of the mill in darkness, making it your playground.

LUMBER MILL 3

LEGEND
- EMP DEVICE
- POSSIBLE ENEMY LOCATION

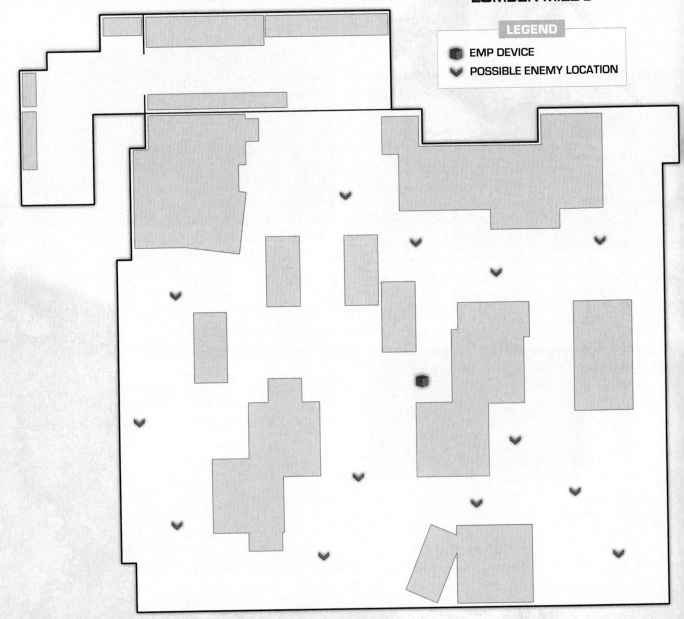

LAST STAND

STRATEGY

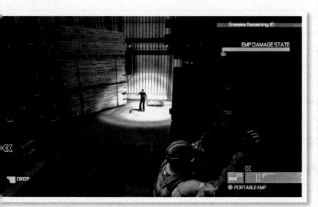

g from the giant stacks of cut lumber to stay well above the
and make your targets. None of the enemies will attempt
imb the stacks, leaving you plenty of real estate to control
out resistance. Leave a few of the floor lights active around
site for setting traps. Get spotted in the light and then run
into the shadows. When enemies investigate your LKP,
are right in the open and easy pickings.

The generator is obviously going to be the focal point of the
map. Fortunately, the area around the hanging EMP has
enough shadows and corners to use for cover. Use sonar
goggles to track the hostiles as they weave through the stacks
toward the generator and then crouch down to pick them off
as they look skyward. They will never see you coming through
the dark.

With so much darkness in the mill, sneaking up for hand-to-hand kills is easy.

Is an enemy getting too many shots off? Stun them with an EMP blast and the rush them. If they recover before you reach them, slide into their legs to knock them down.

...henever you have a spare moment with no enemies around or targeting the generator, pop the lights.

PRINTING PRESS 1

There is just one Printing Press map in Last Stand. It covers the actual presses where the newspaper runs are made. The EMP generator hangs from the ceiling above the presses. A platform next to it offers easy shots. Each level of the presses is flanked by several platforms and walkways you can hang from and monitor the generator as well as watch incoming enemies.

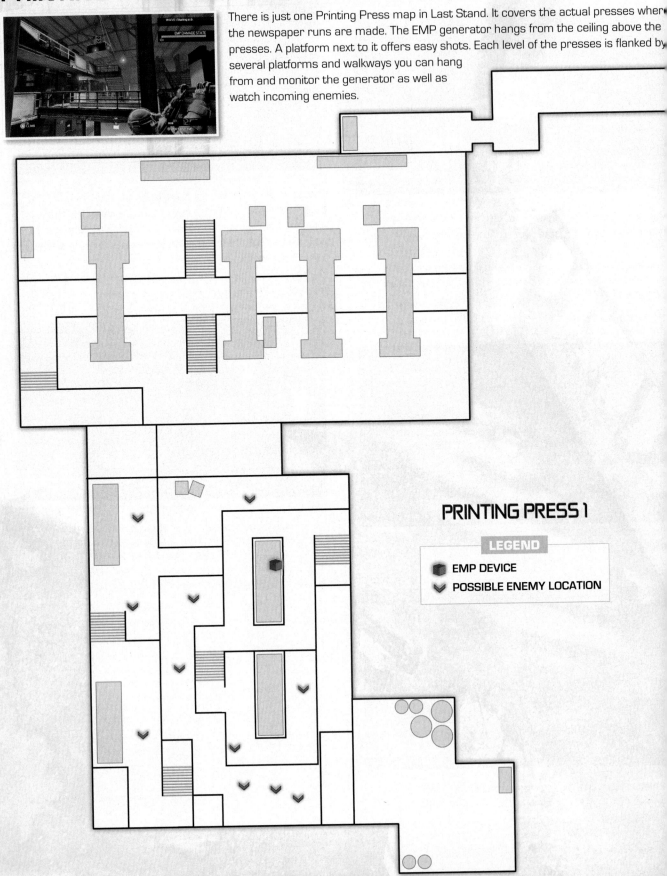

PRINTING PRESS 1

LEGEND
- EMP DEVICE
- POSSIBLE ENEMY LOCATION

LAST STAND

STRATEGY

The early waves of enemies are poorly armed, so they must close in on the generator to damage it. Use the walkways to monitor the generator and pick off the hostiles who attempt to swarm. As the waves progress, the enemies can attack from greater distances, such as lower floors. If you cannot quickly close the gap between you and hostiles, use the fuel drums as makeshift bombs or throw grenades.

Use the pipes that stretch over the presses to track enemies without getting spotted.

 CAUTION

There is a lot of light in the Printing Press. Between waves, take out bulbs and lamps to create shadows.

 TIP

Save the fuel drums as long as possible. They are useful to detonate in later waves against tougher enemies. Use LKP to draw enemies close to a drum and then scurry away to shoot it from a safe distance.

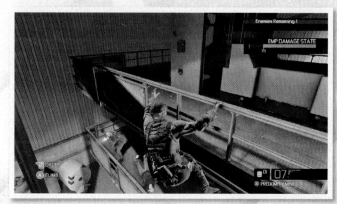

Targeting enemies from the floor above is tricky. However, if you are on the upper level of the press, you can drop to the lower level. Either make sure the hostile is not looking, or use an EMP blast so you drop without notice.

HUNTER

Hunter is a Deniable Ops game mode that runs through the same maps and stages of Co-op Story, but also adds the Lumber Mill and Printing Press maps to the rotation. In Hunter, you are charged with clearing out every enemy in a sector (all maps have five sectors) to unlock the doors to the next area. At first, there are just 10 enemies in each sector. However, if you are spotted and do not immediately take down the hostile who saw you, an additional 10 reinforcements arrive and spread out across the sector. At this point, no additional reinforcements are added to the sector, even if you are seen and your location again relayed to other enemies. The maximum number of enemies you will ever encounter in a single sector is 20.

TIP

Because stealth is in order, always bring at least one silenced weapon. An EMP device is also useful for causing silent distractions. Loud noises from frags just alert the guards of your presence and typically result in immediate reinforcements.

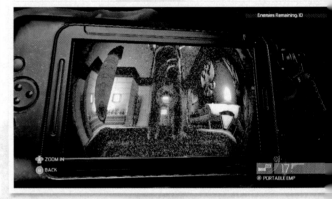

Between each sector, you may replenish ammo and gadget stocks at a weapons stash, as well as make any desired loadout changes.

You always have your snake cam, so use it to peek under doo before just wildly walking into a new room.

NOTE

Use the maps in this section for Face Off and Infiltration as well.

NOTE

Enemies spread across the map in different patterns every time you play Hunter, Face Off, or Infiltration so they always offer a new challenge every time you play. Plus, if you are spotted, reinforcements move in from different angles. So, there are no enemies on these maps.

HUNTER

ST. PETERSBURG BANYA

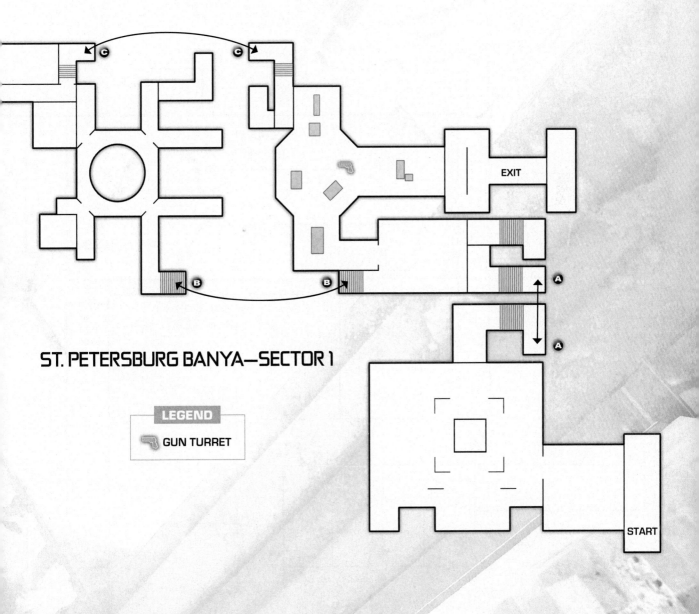

EXIT

ST. PETERSBURG BANYA—SECTOR 1

LEGEND

🔫 GUN TURRET

START

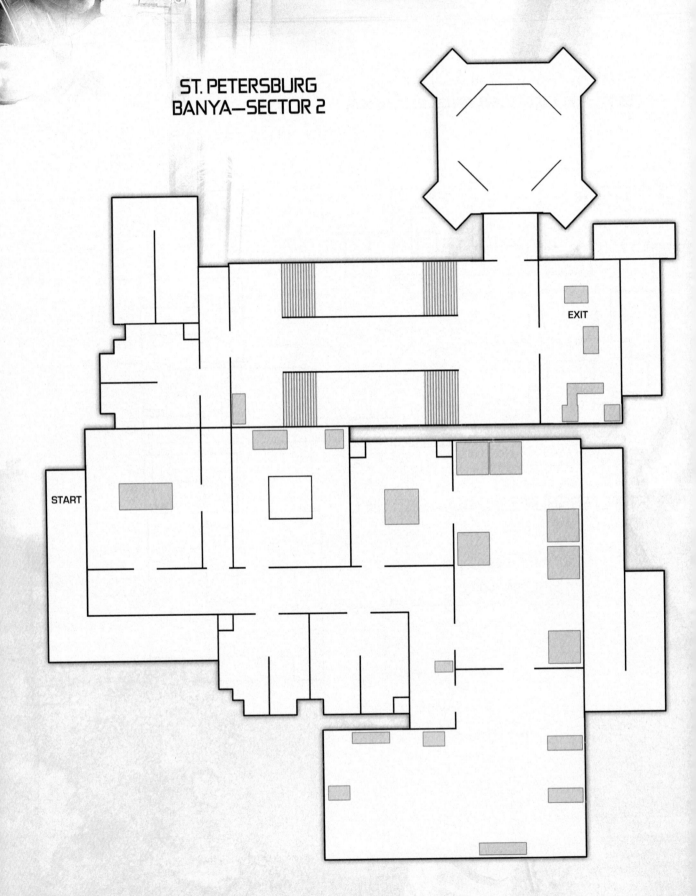

EXIT

START

HUNTER

ST. PETERSBURG
BANYA—SECTOR 3

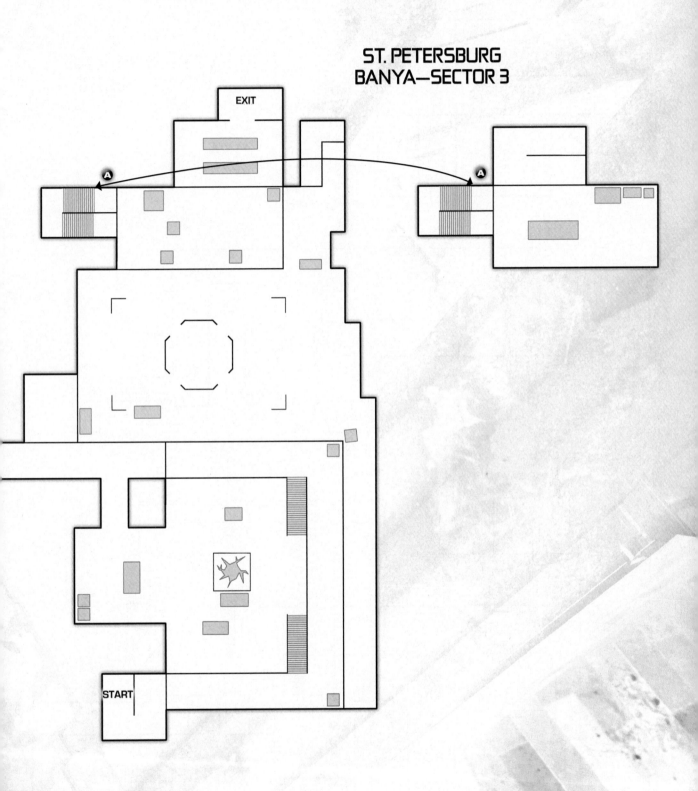

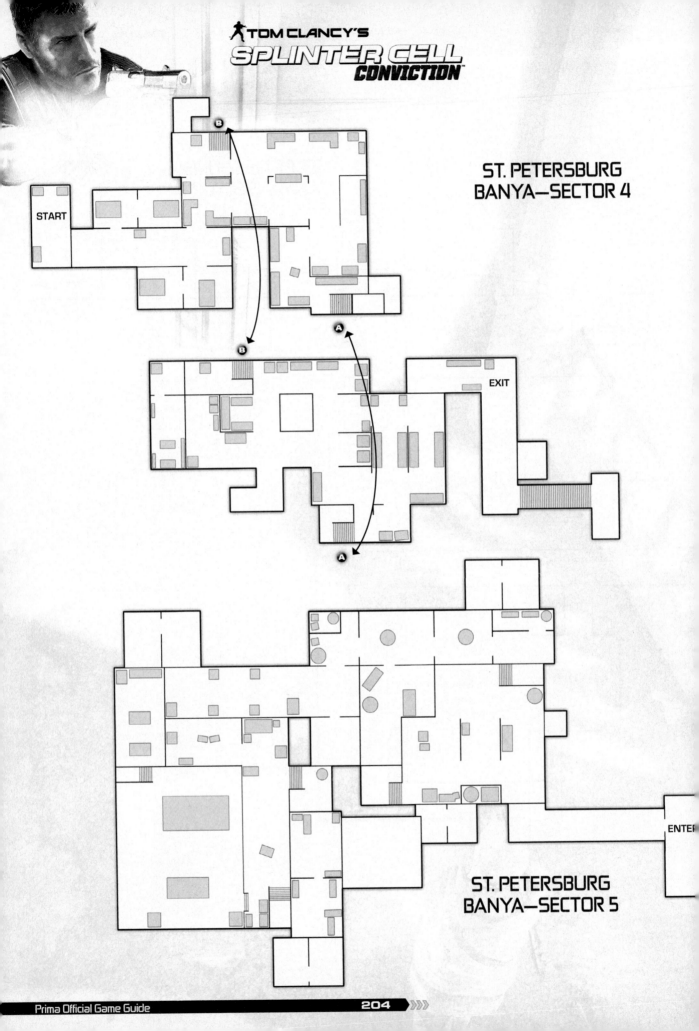

TOM CLANCY'S
SPLINTER CELL
CONVICTION

START

B

B

A

A

EXIT

ST. PETERSBURG
BANYA—SECTOR 4

ENTER

ST. PETERSBURG
BANYA—SECTOR 5

HUNTER

SECTOR 1

e first sector of the banya starts outside the grounds. You
ust move through the exterior fence and target the hostiles
the courtyard without being spotted. Move up to the fence
d pop them as they split apart. Then, enter the building either
the ground level door or the second story window.

he window gives
u a great view of
e interior, which
s crawling with
hugs. An EMP
ast stuns them
f there are too
many to target
without giving
vay your position.

ce inside, move
ward the grand
ver. Clear the
llway on the
ttom floor
ding into the
er and then
nk up the stairs
d target the
ugs on the circular balcony. If there are any hostiles in the
nter of the foyer, drop the chandelier on them by shooting
e chain holding it up.

n auto-turret on
the balcony will
shoot you if you
tep into its field
vision. However,
ou can hack the
turret via the
console on the
upper floor and
use it to attack
your enemies. Just watch your flank. It's easy to get spotted
while using the turret.

SECTOR 2

As you move into the bathhouse, use the pipes along the
ceilings as cover to sneak over enemy positions. With all of the
smaller chambers in the bathhouse, it is easy to miss enemies
in the dark, so rely on your sonar goggles to spot targets in
advance and then move to strike. Although enemy movement is
never the same in each game, the guards in the bathhouse do
tend to patrol the halls quite often, so unless you are pressed
for time, be patient and let them come to you.

Typically,
the largest
congregation of
guards is located
in the large
chamber near
the back door of
the bathhouse.
Slink along the

pipe in the ceiling to zero in on this large chamber and peer
through the door. Guards are on the bridge, probing with their
flashlights. They will occasionally sweep the ceiling, so watch
out. If one starts to look up, hit an EMP blast to disable the
beam.

*Use the large, ornate wall with the windows in the large
chamber for cover when seeking the last few guards. You can
hang from the upper windows or duck behind the low ones to
finish off your targets.*

SECTOR 3

In the next sector, you enter another massive foyer. The sector is divided into two pieces: foyer and yard. The foyer inside has two stories. In addition to the main floor, a square-shaped balcony lines the room. Guards patrol both floors, often moving up and down the stairs. Blast the lights in the alcoves to create shadows while hunting the guards.

Slip through the window on the second story to crawl out on the fire escape and get a good view of the yard with the gazebo. There are always many guards out here.

Remaining undetected with several guards in a small area is very difficult. Hand-to-hand kills maintain silence, but they are slow enough to leave you vulnerable to exposure. If you are confident you can take out guards before they report your position, at least use a human shield to protect yourself from gunfire.

CAUTION

Watch out for guards in the windows on the building opposite of the gazebo. They have great views up there and will easily spot you moving through the well-lit yard.

SECTOR 4

After clearing out the yard around the gazebo, you move into the underground club. Be careful down here. Not only are the hallways very well lit, but guards already seem on high alert. With so many corners, you can easily be caught by surprise. Use sonar goggles to track guards in the rows of barrels above the dance floor and use only a silenced weapon to bring them down.

Oops. You just got spotted. Pump an EMP to stun the group and take them out before they recover. They may still call for reinforcements, but at least you can take down part of the patrol before the cavalry arrives.

TIP

Key to survival in the club: shoot out lights.

HUNTER

e bar next to the downstairs dance floor is a good staging
sition for clearing out the rest of the guards in the club. Stay
 and watch their patrol patterns. Then sneak out and flank
m for silent kills so they cannot report your presence.

*Use the pipe that runs the length of the main hallway to target
unsuspecting guards.*

ECTOR 5

CAUTION

The fuel drums are tempting bombs, but do not use them
unless you have already been spotted and reinforcements
have arrived. The exploding barrels are dead giveaways that
you are on the prowl.

 final St. Petersburg sector is the old warehouse next
 the club. The warehouse is dangerous, because the best
ards patrol this area, each armed with an assault rifle and a
shlight. Carefully sneak into the first room and assassinate
 closest guard, slowly working your way through the
ge chamber before moving into the halls that are easier
manage.

*ABSK: Always Be Silently Killing. Wait next to doors and then
pop out for hand-to-hand kills that attract no attention.*

TOM CLANCY'S SPLINTER CELL CONVICTION

RUSSIAN EMBASSY

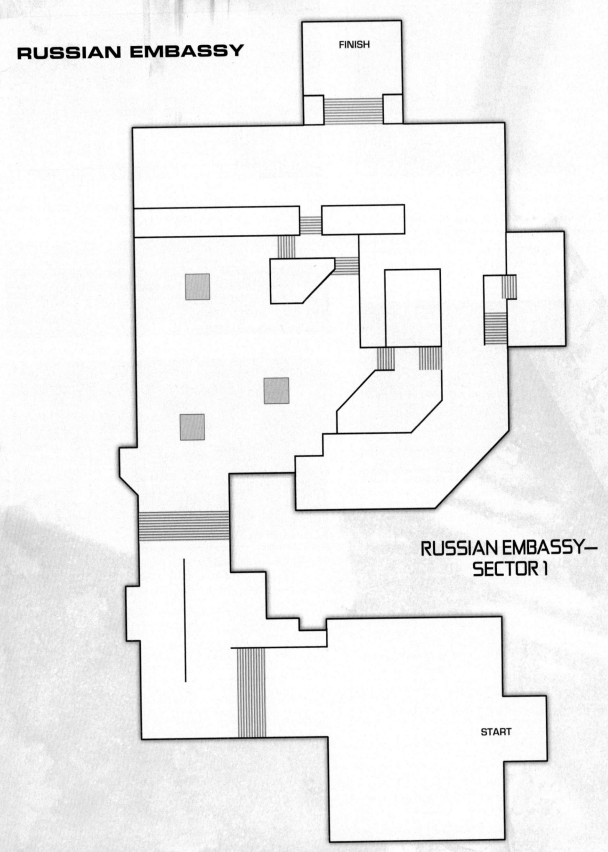

FINISH

RUSSIAN EMBASSY—
SECTOR 1

START

HUNTER

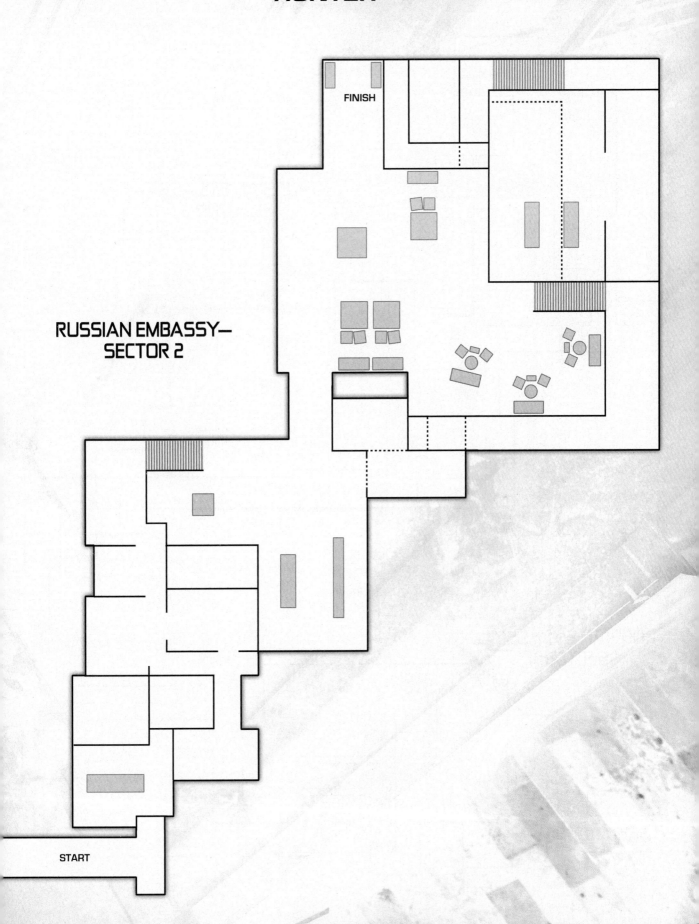

FINISH

RUSSIAN EMBASSY—
SECTOR 2

START

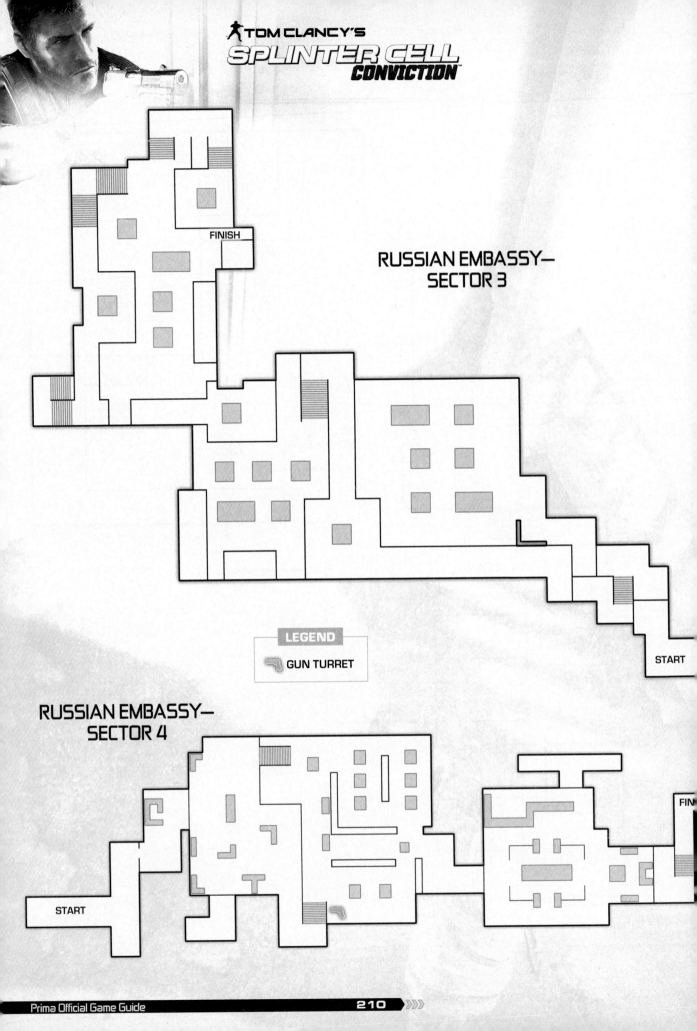

RUSSIAN EMBASSY—
SECTOR 3

FINISH

START

LEGEND

GUN TURRET

RUSSIAN EMBASSY—
SECTOR 4

START

FIN

HUNTER

START

LEGEND

GUN TURRET

RUSSIAN EMBASSY—
SECTOR 5

FINISH

SECTOR 1

The exterior of the Russian Embassy is a large courtyard full of dark corners and funky architecture for you to use as hiding spots. When the mission starts, look for the first set of guards at the outer edge of the courtyard, either on patrol or standing in the pool of light near the stairs.

The main courtyard is where the remainder of the guards are milling about. Any guard on the main level of the courtyard and not patrolling the

huge, multi-tiered planters to the right is within earshot of his comrades and will cry for help if you are spotted. This is the easiest place to accidentally trigger reinforcements, so do not go in with guns blazing. Instead, use the perimeter of the courtyard, either moving through planters or hanging from ledges, to drop the guards one by one.

TIP

Shoot out the tall lampposts above the courtyard to bathe it in darkness.

N NOTE

Climb on the sculpture in the courtyard to hide just out of view.

Mark and execute guards to take them down quietly, but make sure you eliminate anybody around or you raise a slight ruckus.

The guards never look into the planters. They mainly stick to the stairs and corridors. Use the planters to stage attacks and shoot the guards in the back so they never see you coming.

The cool, multi-tiered architecture near the entrance is perfe for hiding. Unfortunately, it's not just perfect for you. The guards use it as cover while stalking a potential intruder. Use sonar goggles to spot the guards among the planters and tiered landings to finish off the sector and move inside the embassy.

SECTOR 2

Once inside, carefully sweep the halls as you move toward th two large reception areas. You typically find at least one or t guards in the corridors leading to the reception areas. Use corners for cover and then slowly move up on the guards to take them silently.

HUNTER

The chandeliers over the reception halls are great traps for killing guards below. Just make sure you shoot down the chandeliers with a silenced weapon to not draw attention.

Hang from the ledges and railings on the walkways to avoid detection and target the guards on the lower level.

...ing on the ...dges of the ...fices overlooking ...e two reception ...lls not only to ...t good views of ...e main lobbies, ...t also to peek ...side the smaller ...oms and pick out targets. The guards occasionally walk to ...e edge of the windows. Make sure nobody is below you and ...en grab the guards.

You must eventually move down to the lower level to reach the far side of the courtyard. Pop as many lights as possible to create some shadows

before heading down the stairs and moving through hostile territory. These guards have flashlights, so if you think you are in immediate danger, pop an EMP to put out all lights and then seek cover or go for a hand-to-hand kill to thin the herd.

...oo many guards ...n one room to ...ill without giving ...yourself away? ...tun them with an EMP first.

SECTOR 4

...ECTOR 3

The gallery is a tricky place to clean out. Guards move through the walls in the gallery below the office landing, and an auto-turret provides extra support. Stay against the left wall of the gallery to avoid the turret.

If you don't mind the reinforcements and can cover your flank (easier to do with two players), use the turret to clean the gallery.

...ck outside, push through another exterior courtyard to ...ach the gallery on the far side of the embassy. Guards patrol ...e walkways above the courtyard and on the main floor below. ...e entire sector is well-lit, so be mindful of the globes and ...oot them out with a silenced weapon when nobody is looking.

The bar/reception room on the far side of the gallery is positively brimming with guards. When you enter the room, use a gadget to kill the lights and slip behind the bar so you can take out the remainder of the force without exposing your position. The bar area is extremely well lit, so repeat EMP pulses may be necessary.

Watch the guard patrols on the rooftop before scaling the chain link fence. When you see that their backs are turned, h[...] the fence and immediately seek cover at an air circulator.

TIP

You refill your gadgets every time you access the weapons stash, so don't be too stingy with them. Plus, you can always backtrack to the weapons stash at the start of a sector if you run low on supplies.

SECTOR 5

Use the railings around the rooftop to remain out of sight. T[...] rooftop lights may be bright, but guards just do not look to t[...] ledges for you.

The final sector of the embassy is the rooftop. The first resistance on the rooftop may be a guard, but commonly, you encounter an auto-turret right away. Watch that roving camera eye (stay out of the pool of light to avoid detection) and then swing around to make a push across the rooftop and exit the sector.

Continue slinking across the rooftop, moving from vent unit to vent unit. Do not hurry (unless you set a time limit). Wait in th[...] shadows and watch the guards move around the vents and along the stairs until you can get the perfect shot. There's no reason to risk reinforcements with just a few enemies left on the map.

HUNTER

ASTREB COMPLEX

YASTREB COMPLEX— SECTOR 1

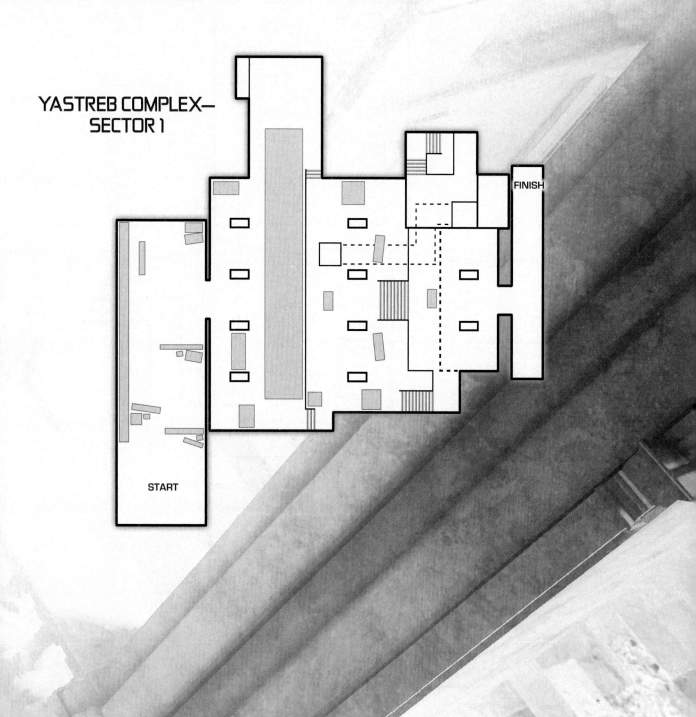

START

FINISH

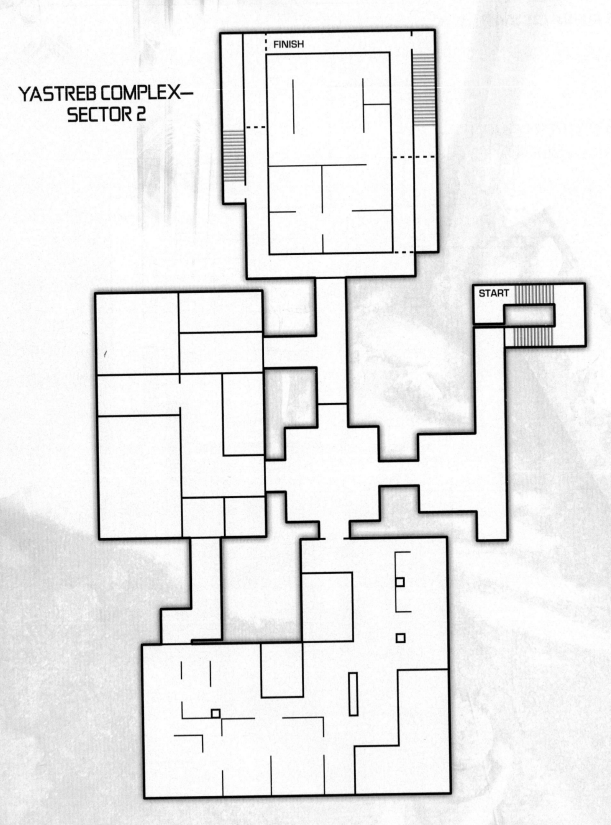

YASTREB COMPLEX—
SECTOR 2

FINISH

START

HUNTER

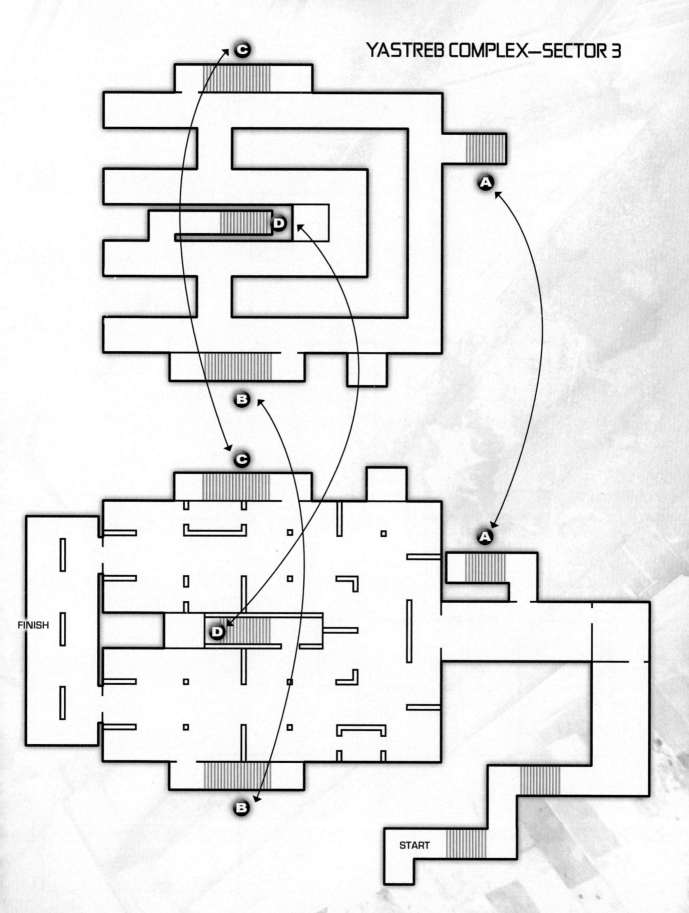

YASTREB COMPLEX—SECTOR 3

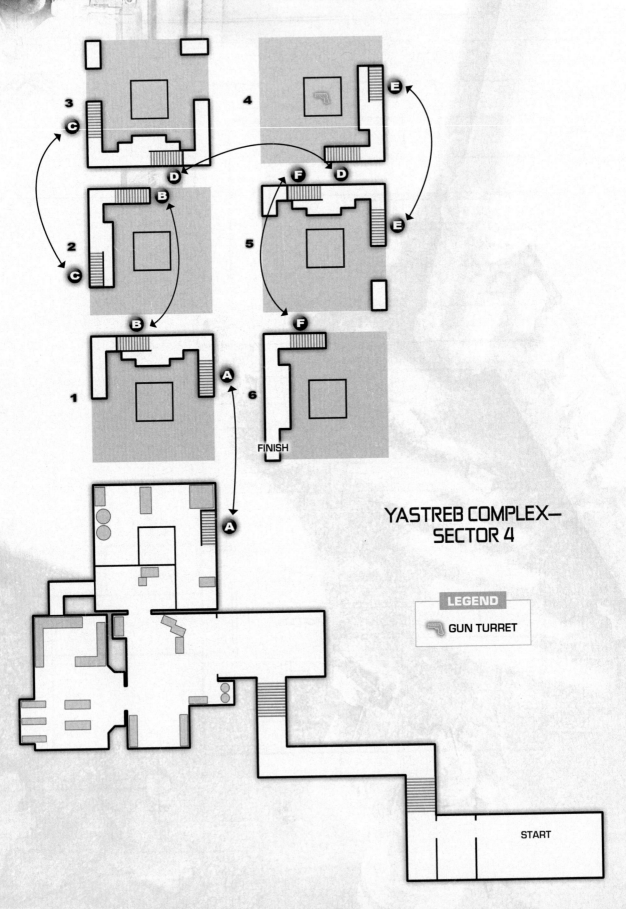

YASTREB COMPLEX—
SECTOR 4

LEGEND

GUN TURRET

FINISH

START

3

4

2

5

1

6

HUNTER

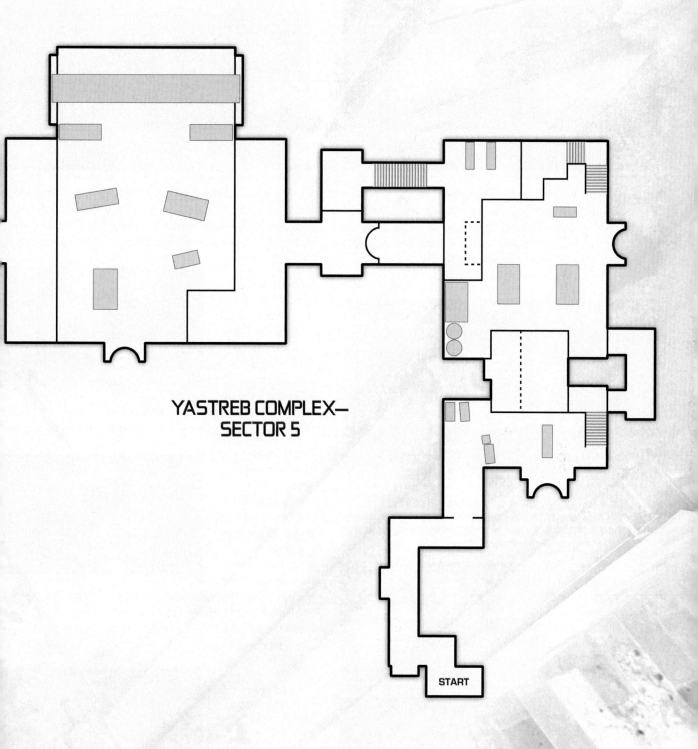

YASTREB COMPLEX—
SECTOR 5

START

SECTOR 1

The first area in Yastreb is the train platform. As you approach the hole in the tunnel that leads to the station, duck down and observe the movement patterns of the guards inside. Wait until you spot one by himself and then open fire. If you are spotted at the hole, 10 more guards appear and they all swarm that opening. It's overwhelming.

Pop the fire extinguishers on the platform to kill guards standing next to them. If the guard is more than a few steps away, though, they are merely stunned. If they get to their feet before you eliminate them, they call for help.

Watch out for guards on the landing above the train. There may be one or two guards in the small offices or hiding around the support pillars. If you stumble into a patrol, punch your EMP and stun them. Rush in and clean up your mess before the guards recover and call in reinforcements.

SECTOR 2

The first area in the sector is the entrance to an office. Metal detectors go off if you walk through them. Instead, leap the desk next to the detectors to avoid sounding the alarm, and then clear out the guards on patrol around the checkpoint.

The office just beyond the checkpoint is a maze of cubicles. Guards hide among the cubicles, but if you scale the walls and hang by ledges, you can sweep through the office complex and bring down the remainder of the patrol without being spotted.

As you close in on the next sector, watch out for guards just beyond the doors leading into the larger office area. Peek under the doors with a snake cam. If you have nearby hostiles, open the doors and immediately hit an EMP to stun them. Take them down and then leap over the ledge to vanish before any other guards in the sector spot you.

Most of the guards in this sector mill around the bottom floor of the office. This looks like a perfect frag situation, but avoid the temptation unless you don't mind another 10 guards taking their place.

HUNTER

к to the upper
ony in this
or as long as
can. Several of
guards move
he stairs and
stigate the
ony. If you
e the time, stay
e corners and just take them down with hand-to-hand kills.
en you have an execution ready, you can then flush out the
of the hostiles.

tch flashlight beams in the cubicles below and then zero in
on your prey. Stun them first!

CTOR 3

fourth sector
arge library.
entrance
e library is
rded by one
wo hostiles.
the pillars as
er and slowly
nce through
shadows to clear out the guards and then enter the library.

main floor
e library is
l with reading
ns that make
t places to
. The guards
v this, too,
ch is why they
rch them
larly. Watch the patrol patterns and then move in for
к, close kills among the reading alcoves.

T TIP

Scramble up one of the support pillars and hang from the
railing to see both floors of the library at the same time.

The chandeliers hanging over the library are small, but still
deadly if dropped on a foe.

Shoot out the lights in the alcove to create cover.

After safely
clearing the
bottom floor
of hostiles, pull
yourself over a
railing onto the
balcony (if you use
the stairs, just
hit sonar goggles

before going into the stairwell to make sure there are no
surprises). Hunt the last of the guards in the sector by sticking
to cover at corners and pillars.

SECTOR 4

The only way out of the complex is to keep going deeper. Exit
the library and then carefully descend the steps into the bottom
of the bunker. There is almost always one guard at the bottom
on patrol. Take him out from the stairs and then move to the
left to seek out any remaining trouble on the ground floor.

TOM CLANCY'S SPLINTER CELL CONVICTION

Check out the vault interior for one or two more guards before ascending the tower of turrets to the right.

Start up the central tower in the tall chamber via the pipe. Creep around the tower, taking out guards while hanging from the railings. There are auto-turrets on the tower, but if you just access their control panels (located below them), they are disabled. Don't use the turrets on the hostiles. You just cannot hit them all and the turret only alerts them to your presence, guaranteeing reinforcements.

SECTOR 5

The final sector is composed of a handful of rooms connected by narrow corridors. There are offices overlooking the rooms, so watch for guards with a better view of the room than you. Fuel drums make useful bombs, but detonate them only if you can kill every guard in room with the explosion. Otherwise, you just invite 10 more guns into the sector.

Use flashlight beams to track your targets. If you need a li breathing room, hit the EMP for a quick stun and then rush close kills.

The ceiling pipes are good staging areas for clean up duty. S along the ceilings and monitor traffic patterns. Single out th guards whenever possible to not arouse suspicion. Once yo have just one or two guards left, try to get them near a fuel drum for an explosive finish.

HUNTER

OZDOK GROUNDS

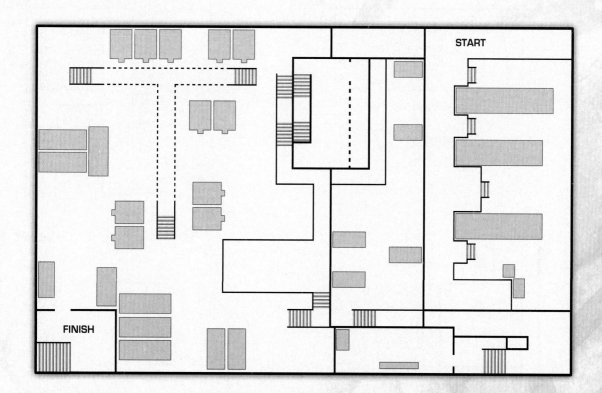

MOZDOK GROUNDS—
SECTOR 1

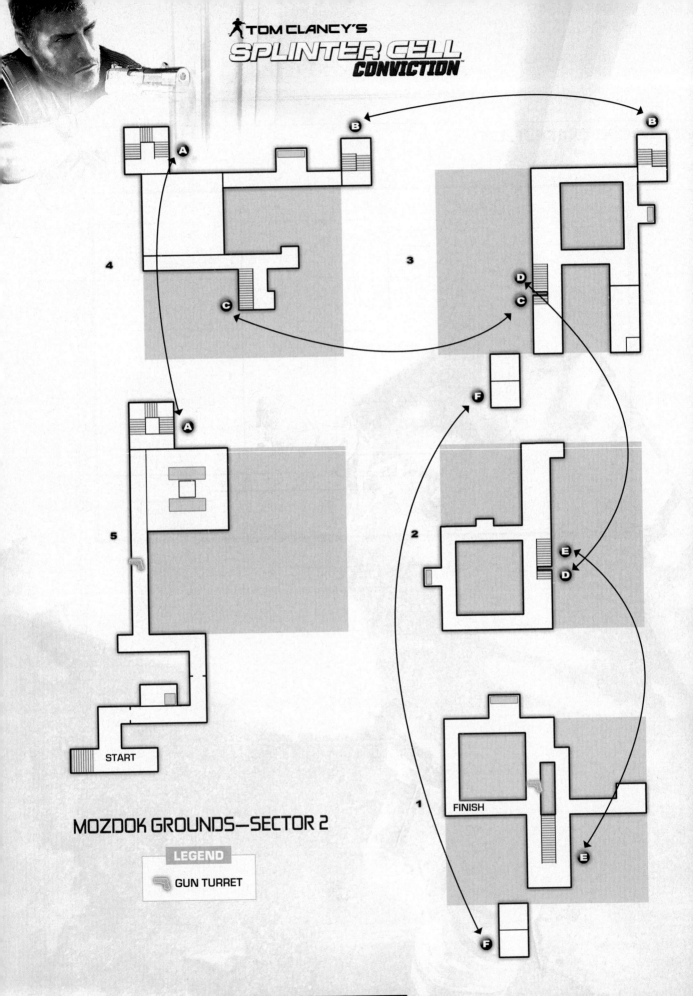

B

B

A

4

3

D

C

C

A

F

D

E

5

2

D

E

MOZDOK GROUNDS—SECTOR 2

1

FINISH

LEGEND

GUN TURRET

START

E

F

HUNTER

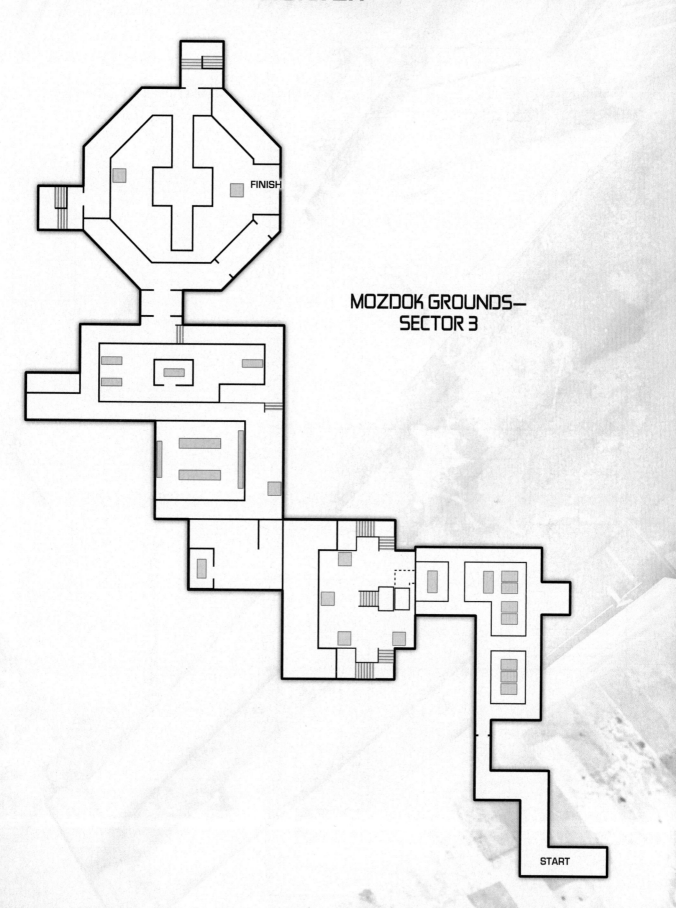

FINISH

MOZDOK GROUNDS—
SECTOR 3

START

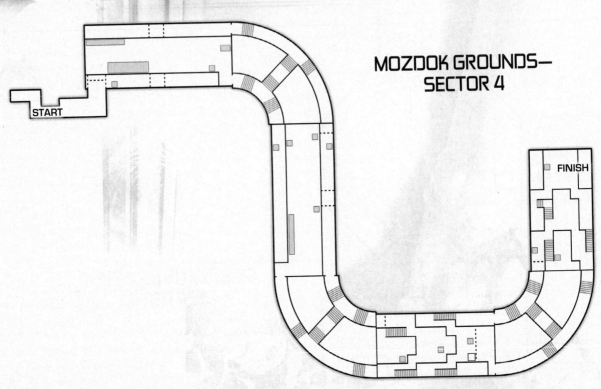

TOM CLANCY'S SPLINTER CELL CONVICTION

MOZDOK GROUNDS—SECTOR 4

START

FINISH

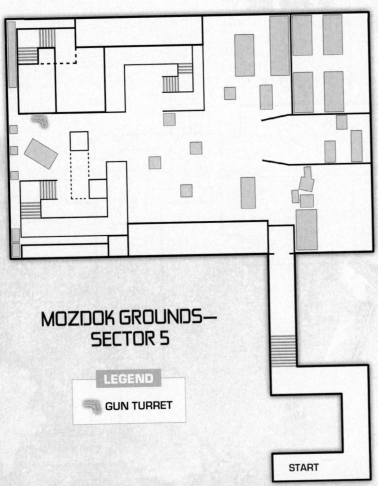

MOZDOK GROUNDS—SECTOR 5

START

LEGEND
GUN TURRET

START

HUNTER

SECTOR 1

...you start infiltrating the Mozdok Grounds, you must first ...sh through a loading dock. There is usually a single guard ...ong the trucks with a second in the office upstairs watching ...scene. Silently kill the guard in the trucks and then ...amble up the wall to neutralize the guard in the office. Pull ...through the window for another quiet kill.

...ect a few ...rds in the ...pping area ...ind the truck ...k. Drop the ...t cargo ...tainer on the ...gs for a few ...ck kills—just ...ke sure you get them all. Any survivor will sound the alarm.

...re is a giant warehouse behind the shipping area where ...Russians store tanks. Slip along the railing of the platforms ...ve the tanks to watch patrol patterns. Single out guards ...quick kills. Do not pop the fuel drums unless you can kill all ...aining guards with a single blast.

CAUTION

...'s very difficult to put out all of the lights among the tanks, ...o just stick to the natural shadows.

SECTOR 2

Beyond the tanks is a tall chamber with multiple stories, all connected by stairs. Creep up on the door that leads to the room, looking out

for at least a single guard patrolling the area. Take him quietly because this is a bad place to suddenly have 19 guards looking for you.

Auto-turrets are positioned around the central stairs. Watch for the pools of light in their camera paths. Clamber up on the ledges and containers

overlooking the stairs in the room and monitor patterns.

Take your time and just observe. Look for opportunities to get the guards alone.

TIP

Don't forget to disable auto-turrets by accessing their nearby control panels.

Linger on railings and pull guards to their deaths as they walk by or shoot them in the back of the head.

SECTOR 3

Beyond the tall chamber is the main testing area for EMP tech at Mozdok. Slip into the maintenance area and watch for at least one guard on patrol. Slip around the railings in a crouch and take the guard, then access the test area by diving into the narrow tunnel and following it until it pops up in a large white room.

Before pulling yourself all the way up, look around for guards and track their movements.

The huge test chamber is a tall, silo-shaped area. There will be at least one guard on the main floor (likely two or three, depending on how many guards are left) and one more on the mid-level balcony that surrounds the silo. The balcony is accessed via stairs. You cannot reach it via the pipes that shoot up alongside the trellis that occupies the center of the chamber.

Looking for that last, pesky guard? Be careful—they may be at the top level of the test room. If you ascend via the pipe, stop occasionally and use sonar goggles to make sure you don't pop up into a surprise and inadvertently call reinforcements.

SECTOR 4

This sector is different. You do not encounter 10 guards in a single area. Instead, you must pass through four smaller zones, each with eight guards. If you are spotted, they call in six reinforcements. An area within the sector is split into two parts: a large room and a tunnel. To open the door to the ne zone, you must press a green button at the end of the tunne segment.

Use railings for cover in the non-tunnel areas. These guar are aggressive and you will not last on the floor or the balc for long.

CAUTION

EMP blasts are not as effective in this sector because ma lights are chemical, not electronic.

HUNTER

You must push through four zones to clear out this sector.

...deeper you get, the more antsy the guards. Because 14 is ...more manageable then 20, you can risk using grenades to ...out large swaths of guards. Double your detonation power ...bbing a frag next to a fuel drum and you can slay six or ...n guards with a single attack.

Watch for guards in the tunnels that connect the zones.

SECTOR 5

The final sector of Mozdok is an airplane cargo hangar. A giant plane is parked in the hangar and guards patrol the stacks of crates and cargo on the main floor. There are multiple fuel drums in the area to use as bombs, but before turning this joint into the Fourth of July, watch movement patterns so you can pull stragglers into close kills.

Spotted a few guards near a drum? If you can shoot it from halfway across the hangar, you may get away with not being seen.

There is an auto-turret near the office in the back corner of the hangar. Avoid the camera's eye as you hunt the last of the guards around the office. A good stun will keep them busy while you hop the fence and take them in hand-to-hand kills.

LUMBER MILL

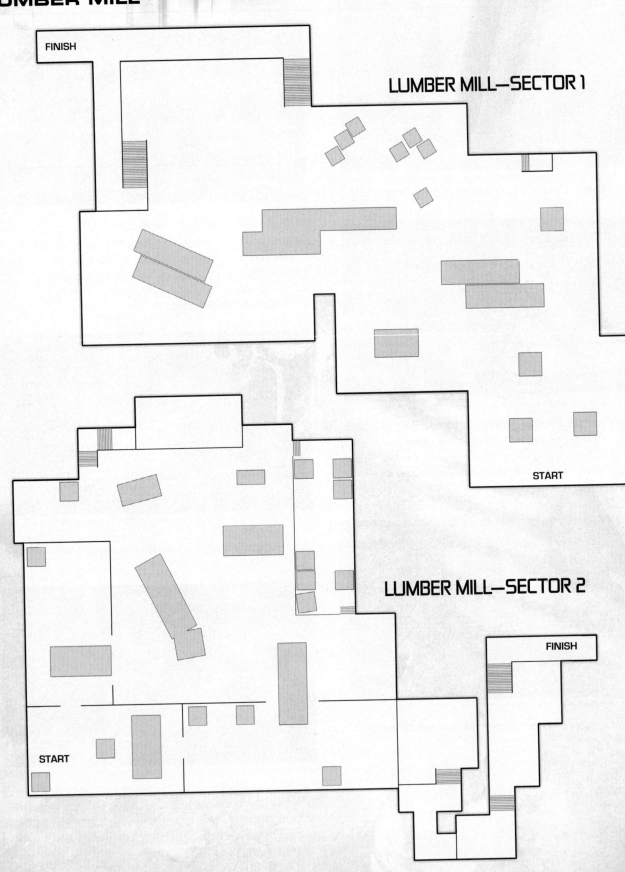

TOM CLANCY'S

SPLINTER CELL
CONVICTION

FINISH

LUMBER MILL—SECTOR 1

START

LUMBER MILL—SECTOR 2

FINISH

START

HUNTER

LUMBER MILL—SECTOR 3

START

FINISH

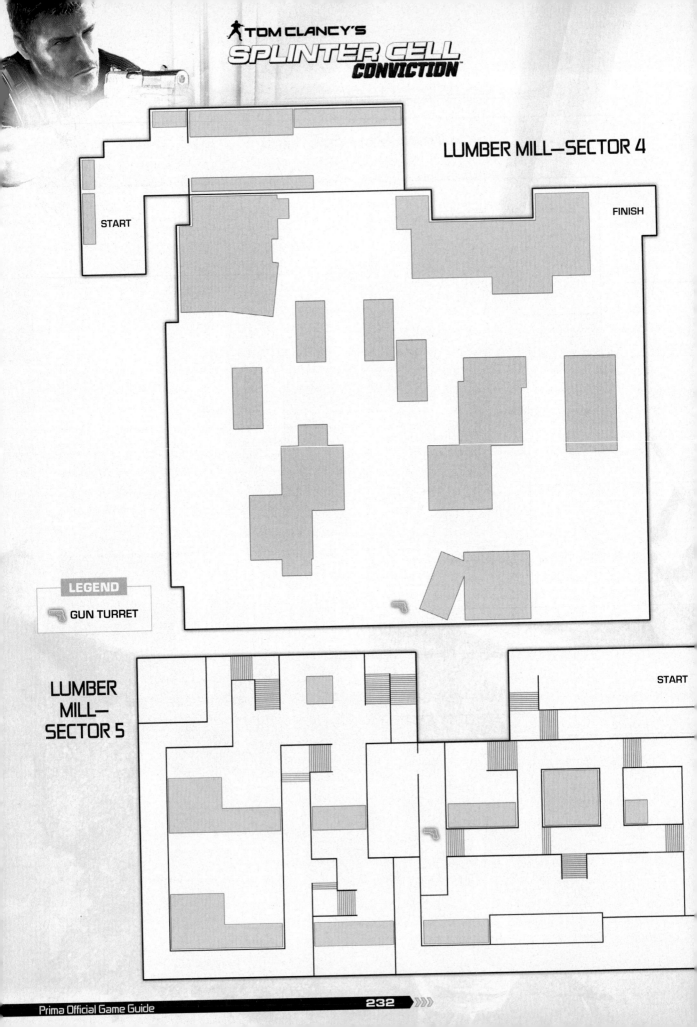

TOM CLANCY'S SPLINTER CELL CONVICTION

LUMBER MILL—SECTOR 4

START

FINISH

LEGEND

GUN TURRET

LUMBER MILL— SECTOR 5

START

HUNTER

ECTOR 1

first sector of the Lumber Mill is outside. You can climb up
ral huge stacks of logs and hang from them while hunting
ds. However, when the mission begins, hang back and
h the first push of guards. They spread out from a small
along the fence.

*those guards
before they
t too far into
the yard.*

the log stacks
onitor the
ds as they
around
ard. Watch
as they
, using
goggles to
movement.

good thing about Hunter is that guards do not call for
forcements when they spot dead bodies. So you can take
hostiles anywhere in the Lumber Mill.

CTOR 2

ou move into
terior of the
ber Mill, look
least one
d in the small
between
ard and the
king area.
tly sneak up
e guard and kill him. Then, use your snake cam to peek
r the door and look at guards in the trucking area before
ng deeper.

*Jump up to the lumber stacks to avoid detection in the
shipping area.*

NOTE

Most guards in this sector are moving around the trucks and
stacks of cut lumber.

*Another guard
is in the small
shipping office
overlooking
the yard.*

SECTOR 3

Beyond the office is series of storage areas with cut and
stacked lumber. As you creep down into the sector, take out
lights to create shadows and just watch the guards move
around. Two or three guards are usually near the entrance
of this sector all within blast distance of a fuel drum. You use
this drum at your own risk, though, because if even one guard
survives, 10 more rush in.

Hang from the windows of the offices above the lumber stacks to track hostiles.

As you weave around the stacks, beware of getting caught. (Regularly using sonar goggles reveals guard positions, though.) If you are spotted, hit an EMP before the white arc turns red, meaning the alarm has gone out. While the target is stunned, hammer him with a close kill or a headshot.

SECTOR 4

Carefully approach the entrance to the next sector and peer inside to watch guard movement. Most of these lumber stacks stretch to the ceiling, but you

can climb up and stand on a few to remain totally hidden. Clear a path to the stacks as you enter the sector and then climb to avoid immediate detection.

Stay on the lumber stacks for the majority of this sector. You can take almost all of the guards from the stacks.

Not many guards left? Then go ahead and pop a fuel drum to finish off the patrol and move on to the next sector.

SECTOR 5

The saw area of the Lumber Mill is the most dangerous. It looks like you have the advantage with many railings and corners to hide around, but these

guards are highly trained and will empty a full clip in you if the even sense your presence. You must stay low and methodic move through the area to take them out. Taking risks does r pay off as consistently as being patient.

Move to the back half of the sector via the catwalks. There is auto-turret on the main floor.

The back of the saw area is particularly dangerous. The equipment looks like it offers cover, but there are too many cracks and crevices the

guards can see through. Only the lumber stacks are solid. Watch for those flashlight beams because they can peer through the spaces between the equipment and spot you, which results in an immediate 10 reinforcements.

There is a lot of light in the mill. Popping bulbs may draw attention to your area, so be judicious with shooting out lights and just try to flank.

HUNTER

RINTING PRESS

FINISH

PRINTING PRESS—SECTOR 1

START

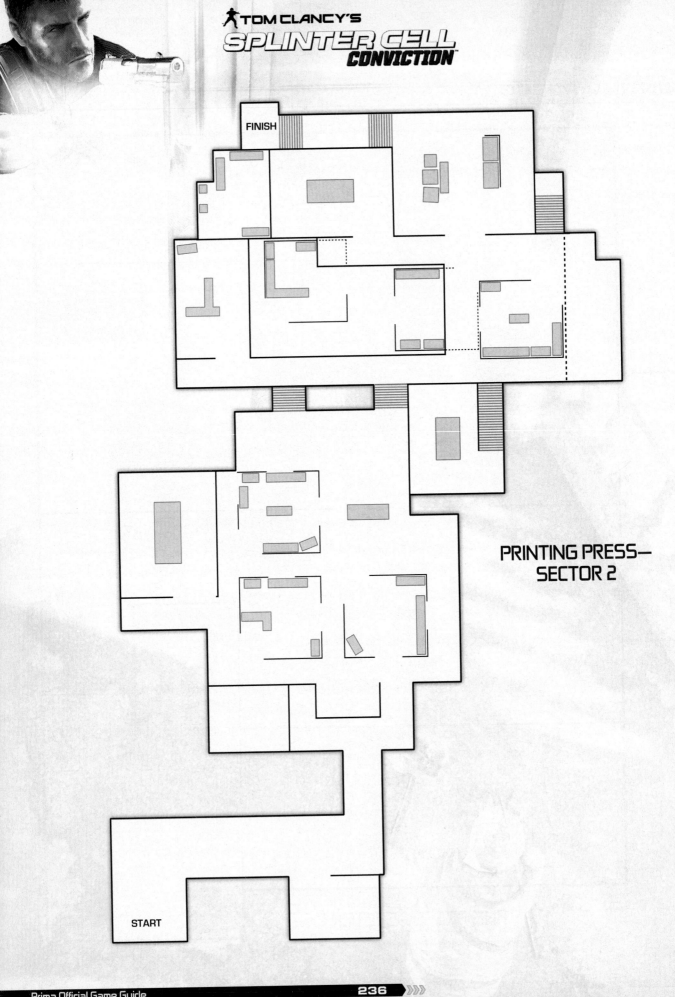

TOM CLANCY'S
SPLINTER CELL
CONVICTION

FINISH

PRINTING PRESS—
SECTOR 2

START

HUNTER

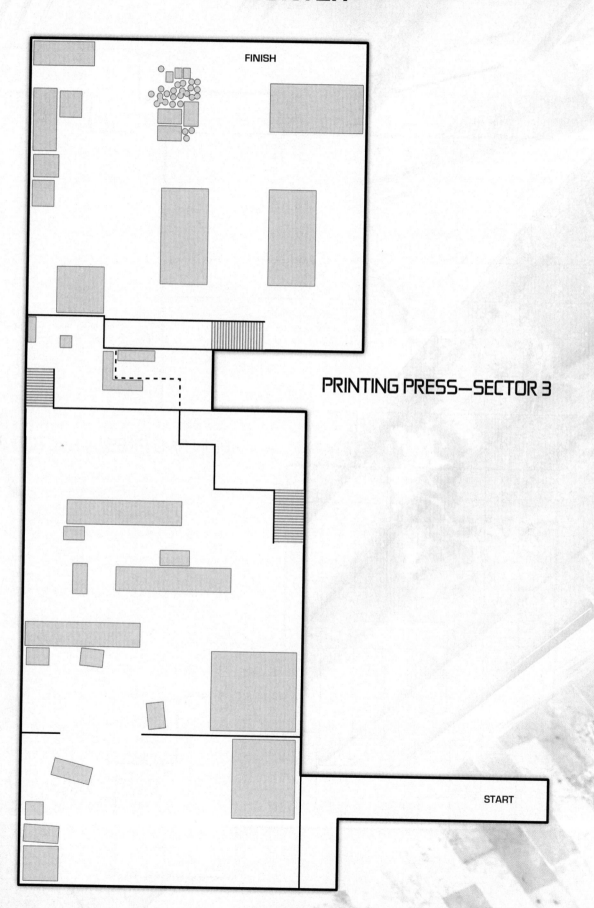

FINISH

PRINTING PRESS—SECTOR 3

START

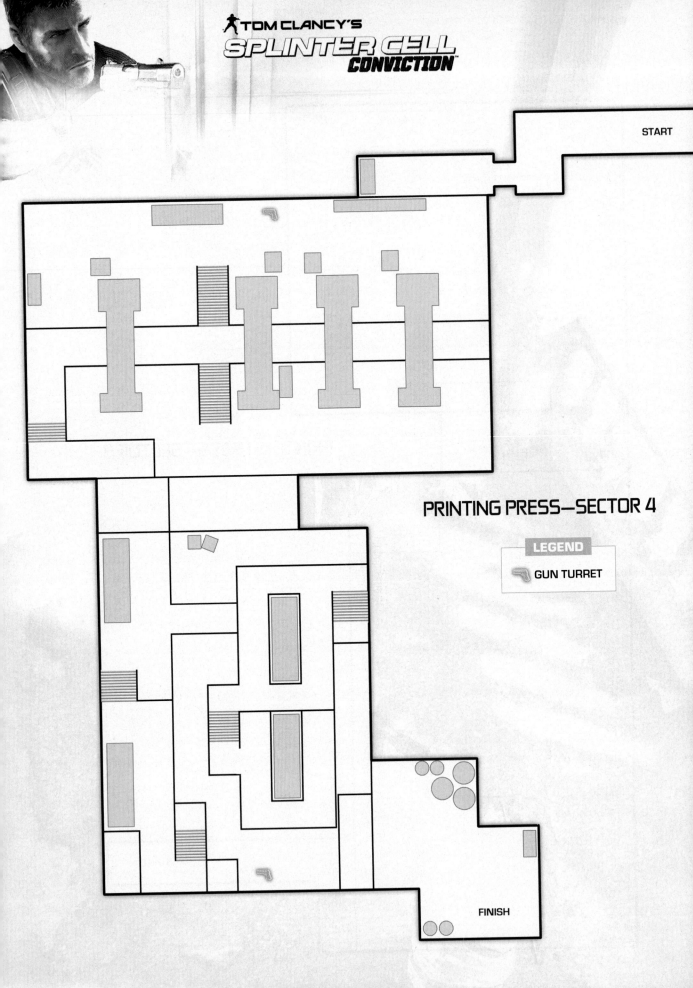

TOM CLANCY'S SPLINTER CELL CONVICTION

START

PRINTING PRESS—SECTOR 4

LEGEND

GUN TURRET

FINISH

HUNTER

PRINTING PRESS— SECTOR 5

LEGEND

GUN TURRET

START

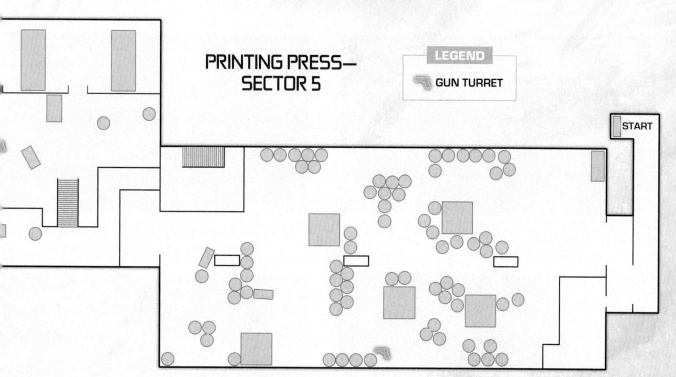

SECTOR 1

On entering the outer perimeter of the Printing Press, stay and look for an early guard patrol. There is a lot of open space inside the first sector, so stick to corners and doors for cover and pull enemies into close kills to minimize exposure.

...el drums tempt, ...ut pop them ...nly if you can ...l everybody in ...e room with a single blast.

You always have an advantage when you are high. Seek out crates, presses, paper rolls, and more to get a bird's eye view of the sector and hunt your targets from above. Rarely do these low-level thugs look up. Punish them for thinking you'd be so common as to work the floor.

SECTOR 2

The next sector is inside a small office area. Ten guards mill around the cubicle farm, looking for any traces of your presence. Find a good hiding spot at a major intersection and hold your ground. (But do keep an eye on your flank or use sonar goggles to peer through cubicle walls.) When an enemy walks by, go for the close kill so you bank an execution.

The guards in the office have flashlights. Turn them off with an EMP blast.

Use the small tunnel under the storage room to pop up and target enemies when they aren't looking.

After sweeping through the cubicles, ascend the stairs in the back to look for any stragglers in the small editor's office. Watch for those flashlight beams to pick your target out of the darkness and then wait for them to look away. Rush for the kill.

SECTOR 3

Finished newspapers are stacked in this sector. High-level guards swarm the sector, each armed with flashlights and shotguns. If you are caught in a close-quarters situation, hit the EMP to frazzle them. You cannot recover from a shotgun blast to the chest. Take the guards apart one by one, being cautious of them in groups.

The tunnel is excellent for flanking. Just monitor movement with sonar goggles and then rush behind enemies.

SECTOR 4

As you enter the fourth sector, look out for the auto-turret scanning the room for hostiles— namely, you. A control panel to the right of the turret lets you either take control of it or deactivate it. Be mindful of the camera on the turret as you make your way to the presses, which is where most of the guards patrol.

HUNTER

...ang from the railings along the presses to target guards as they watch for enemy activity.

Climb on top of the paper roll stacks and target the guards below. Be careful detonating the fuel drums (as tempting as they are) because they can result in reinforcements.

...e guards that
...rol the presses
...e merciless. You
...st take them
...n headshots or
...se kills. If you
...oot and miss,
...y radio for help
...ore you can

..."oops." You can shoot out several lights along the presses
...create darkness, but you are better off just lying in wait in
...already shadowy spot and going for kills as they become
...ilable. Mark and Execute works quite well here, too.

...ECTOR 5

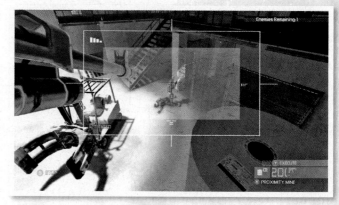

Take control of the auto-turret in the sector to wipe out the last of the enemies. Do not use it if there are five or more left. But just one or two? Happy hunting!

...final sector in Printing Press is where they store the giant
...s of paper. The guards in this area are aggressive, so keep
...r distance when you spot them in groups and only go for
...o guards. The only exception to this is if you can stun a duo
...n an EMP blast. Then rush in and take them down with
...d-to-hand kills to bank an execution.

TOM CLANCY'S
SPLINTER CELL
CONVICTION

ACHIEVEMENTS

ACHIEVEMENT LIST

Playing *Splinter Cell: Conviction* on an Xbox 360? Then there are a potential 1,000 Gamerscore points out there with your name them. We have the complete list of *Conviction* achievements and their point values. Use this table and our tips and tricks to score all 1,000 points and prove to the world you are not to be trifled with when it comes to strapping on sonar goggles and hunting mercenaries from the shadows.

ACHIEVEMENTS – FISHER

ACHIEVEMENT	DESCRIPTION	GAMERSCORE POINTS
*Merchant's Street Market	Complete "Merchant's Street Market" on any difficulty	20
*Kobin's Mansion	Complete "Kobin's Mansion" on any difficulty	20
*Price Airfield	Complete "Price Airfield" on any difficulty	20
*Diwaniya, Iraq	Complete "Diwaniya, Iraq" on any difficulty	20
*Washington Monument	Complete "Washington Monument" on any difficulty	20
*White Box Technologies	Complete "White Box Technologies" on any difficulty	20
*Lincoln Memorial	Complete "Lincoln Memorial" on any difficulty	20
*Third Echelon HQ	Complete "Third Echelon HQ" on any difficulty	20
*Michigan Ave. Reservoir	Complete "Michigan Ave. Reservoir" on any difficulty	20
*Downtown District	Complete "Downtown District" on any difficulty	20
*White House	Complete "White House" on any difficulty	20
Realistic Difficulty	Complete story on "Realistic" difficulty	50

Designates a secret achievement

FISHER'S MISSIONS

The most straightforward achievements are awarded for completing all 11 of the chapters in Fisher's mission, which stretches from Malta to Washington DC. There is an achievement for finishing each mission, plus a larger Realistic Difficulty Achievement if you finish all 11 chapters on Realistic difficulty, which is the hardest setting.

Realistic difficulty is pretty brutal. Your enemies are much more aggressive than on Normal difficulty (and even then, they are pretty crafty). If you hope to make it through the game on Realistic, you must use every stealth trick in the book to avoid getting blasted by these trigger-happy guards and mercs.

But sticking to the shadows isn't enough to survive. You must make the most out of the Mark and Execute tactic, which lets you get the drop on enemies with minimal resistance. So, while playin seek out hand-to-hand kill opportunities whenever possible. Tr to always have an execution "banked" so that you can quickly mark and execute if you ever sense the odds wavering away from your favor.

On Realistic difficulty, enemies are much faster about relaying information, such as your Last Known Position.

 TIP

Rely on headshots more than ever to swiftly take down enemies on Realistic difficulty.

O-OP & DENIABLE OPS

ACHIEVEMENTS – CO-OP

ACHIEVEMENT	DESCRIPTION	GAMERSCORE POINTS
*St. Petersburg Banya	Complete co-op "St. Petersburg Banya" on any difficulty	20
*Russian Embassy	Complete co-op "Russian Embassy" on any difficulty	20
*Yastreb Complex	Complete co-op "Yastreb Complex" on any difficulty	20
*Mozdok Proving Grounds	Complete co-op "Mozdok Proving Grounds" on any difficulty	20
Co-op Realistic Difficulty	Complete the co-op story on Realistic difficulty	50
Quality Time	Invite a friend to join and participate in a co-op story or game mode session	20
Hunter	Complete any 1 map in "Hunter" game mode in co-op	10
Last Stand	Complete any 1 map in "Last Stand" game mode in co-op	10
Face Off	Win one match in "Face Off" game mode on any difficulty in co-op	10
Survivor	Battle your co-op teammate and survive	10
Hunter Completionist	Complete all maps in "Hunter" game mode on Rookie or Normal difficulty	20
Hunter Master	Complete all maps in "Hunter" game mode on Realistic difficulty	50
Last Stand Completionist	Complete all maps in "Last Stand" game mode on Rookie or Normal difficulty	20
Last Stand Master	Complete all maps in "Last Stand" game mode on Realistic difficulty	50
Face Off Completionist	Complete all maps in "Face Off" game mode using any connection type	20
Perfect Hunter	Complete any map in "Hunter" without ever having been detected on Realistic difficulty	20
Last Man Standing	In "Last Stand," survive all enemy waves of any map in one session without failing on any difficulty	50

*Designates a secret achievement

In addition to Co-op Story, there are four additional online or split-screen co-op games to play: Hunter, Last Stand, Face Off, and Infiltration (which can be unlocked with Uplay). If you play and complete a single map in each of these game modes, you earn an achievement for doing so. Some maps are easier than others, just because of their architecture. If you are gunning for the co-op achievements outside of Story mode, try these maps:

Hunter: Russian Embassy
Last Stand: St. Petersburg Banya 2
Face Off: Lumber Mill

ere are four full missions in Co-op Story mode, plus one fight
he very end of the mission set. One achievement is awarded
mission. However, if you want all of the achievements in
op Story mode, you must win the battle in the cargo hold
he escaping airplane. Only one player will earn the Survivor
ievement, so if you fall to the hands of your so-called
rade, you need to play through co-op again in order to take
a friend in the cargo hold and make a new run at this elusive
ievement.

DENIABLE OPS

The Deniable Ops achievements are awarded for playing through all maps in the Deniable Ops game modes Hunter and Last Stand.

The Perfect Hunter Achievement is pretty difficult to earn, but if you stick to the shadows, you can do it. You have a greater chance of earning it on one of the earlier

maps pulled from Co-op Story mode, such as St. Petersburg or the Russian Embassy. Stay in the shadows, use ledges and windows to your advantage at all times, and always be careful about leaning out of cover. You may think you are hidden, but guards are very adept at picking out your head if there is even a little bit of light in the area.

P.E.C. CHALLENGES

ACHIEVEMENTS – P.E.C.

ACHIEVEMENT	DESCRIPTION	GAMERSCORE POINTS
Preparation Master	Complete all Prepare & Execute challenges	30
Stealth Master	Complete all Vanish challenges	30
Best of the Best	Complete all Splinter Cell challenges	30
Well-Rounded	Complete all challenges	50
Weapon Upgraded	Purchase all 3 upgrades for any 1 weapon	10
Gadget Upgraded	Purchase both upgrades for any 1 gadget	10
Weapons Expert	Purchase all 3 upgrades for all weapons	20
Gadgets Expert	Purchase both upgrades for all gadgets	20
Weapons Collector	Unlock all weapons in the weapon vault	20
Variety	Purchase any 1 uniform	10
Accessorizing	Purchase any 1 accessory for any 1 uniform	10
Ready for Anything	Purchase all 9 accessories for all uniforms	20
Fashionable	Purchase all 6 texture variants for all uniforms	20

Though the P.E.C. Challenges have their own rewards in the game, there is a series of achievements tied to the objectives. If you complete all P.E.C. Challenges in each of the three categories—Prepare & Execute, Vanish, and Splinter Cell—you earn the Well-Rounded Achievement, which is worth a solid 50 points. However, the 30 point reward earned for completing all challenges within a specific category is nothing to turn your nose up at. Just use our tips in the P.E.C. chapter to identify P.E.C. Challenge opportunities, such as Stealth Headshot and 10x Predator.

TIP

You are likely to finish up the majority of the Prepare & Execute P.E.C. Challenges just by playing through the single-player game once or twice.

NOTE

You must play at least a few multiplayer games to finish up the Vanish and Splinter Cell P.E.C. Challenges. For example, the Full Recovery challenge requires you to sit up and kill five enemies before your friend heals you.

few achievements are attached to the upgrades you buy
th P.E.C. Challenge points. Upgrade Sam's default silenced
stol, the 23, with all three attachments as soon as possible
earn the Weapon Upgraded Achievement. Not only do you
t 10 Gamerscore points, but you also have the benefits of
very lethal pistol. Fully upgrade one of the gadgets, such as
e EMP grenade or frag grenade to get the Gadget Upgraded
hievement.

NOTE

Use the weapon table in the Merchant's Street Market
chapter to see how all weapons are unlocked so you can earn
the Weapons Collector Achievement. Play through the whole
single-player game and co-op story, and also check out Uplay.

Don't forget the uniform closet! Use P.E.C. Challenge points
to buy uniforms and textures in the set-up screen for multi-
layer to earn the Variety, Accessorizing, Ready for Anything,
and Fashionable Achievements.

ADDITIONAL SECRETS

Shhh! There are three more super-secret achievements to unlock by
playing through the single-player campaign with Fisher. The Revelations
Achievement is unlocked when Grim reveals that she has been lying
to you for years about your daughter. The other two are assigned to a
specific action at the very end of the game. If you don't mind spoiling
the finale, read on...

ADDITIONAL ACHIEVEMENTS – SECRETS

ACHIEVEMENT	DESCRIPTION	GAMERSCORE POINTS
Revelations	Discover Anna Grimsdottir's dark secret	10
Judge, Jury, and Executioner	Take down Tom Reed	10
Man of Conviction	Allow Tom Reed to live	10

...alright, we warned you. You have a choice to kill or spare Tom Reed
in the White House at the end of Mission 11. The easiest choice is just
to kill him after the president leaves the room. After all, it's not like he
doesn't deserve to die after everything he's done not just to you, but to
your country.

But are you
really willing to
be Judge, Jury,
and Executioner?
If you think that
would make you
as bad as Reed,
then hold off on
pulling the trigger to earn the Man of Conviction Achievement. If you
want both, then play the White House mission twice and enjoy a taste
of vengeance and a touch of mercy.

The Art of
SPLINTER CELL
CONVICTION

SPLINTER CELL
CONVICTION

CHARACTER RENDERS

FISHER

GRIM

COSTE

KOBIN

The Art of
SPLINTER CELL CONVICTION

GAILLARD

REED

THE PRESIDENT

ARCHER

KESTREL

CONCEPT ENVIRONMENT ART

3RD ECHELON

MALTA

AIRPORT BASE

WASHINGTON MONUMENT

COSTE

WHITEHOUSE

LINCOLN MEMORIAL

HOLLOW WINDOW

The Art of
SPLINTER CELL CONVICTION

SCREENSHOTS

TOM CLANCY'S SPLINTER CELL CONVICTION

CONCEPT CHARACTER ART

SARAH FISHER

The Art of
SPLINTER CELL CONVICTION

ORIGINAL COSTE CONCEPT

TOM CLANCY'S SPLINTER CELL CONVICTION

MISC.

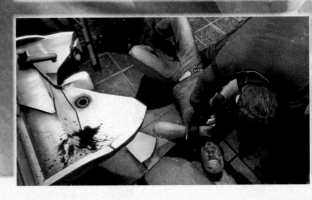

camera

HAND TO HAND TAKE DOWN